CONVERSING WITH GOD:

PRAYER IN ERASMUS' PASTORAL WRITINGS

In *Conversing with God* Hilmar M. Pabel examines Erasmus' understanding of prayer and how he taught western Christendom to pray in the Reformation era of the sixteenth century. To this end, Pabel adopts Erasmus' own rhetorical analysis of prayer, understood as a colloquy or conversation with God, and considers: Who is God, the audience of prayer? What sort of person should one be in order to pray? What is the proper object of prayer? With which words should one pray? Underlying this analysis is a principle both rhetorical and pastoral: accommodation. Pabel explains that in teaching his contemporaries how to accommodate their prayer to God, Erasmus engaged in a 'literary cure of souls,' or a pastoral ministry executed through the printing press.

Pabel follows his outline of Erasmus' principles of prayer with an investigation of his defence of the invocation of the saints at a time when Protestants were rejecting this form of devotion. He completes his study with an examination of Erasmus' interpretation of the Lord's Prayer, and an analysis of the prayer-book *Precationes aliquot novae*, published at the end of his life.

Conversing with God opens up for scholarly attention a much neglected aspect of Erasmus' *philosophia Christi*, building a lucid and cogent argument for the important theological aspect of Erasmus' prayers, which has often been discounted or denied by more traditional scholarship.

HILMAR M. PABEL is Assistant Professor of History at Simon Fraser University, and editor of *Erasmus' Vision of the Church*.

Domine doce nos orare. Luc. xi.

'Lord, teach us to pray' (Luke 11: 1).
From Erasmus' *Precatio Dominica* (Basel: Froben [1523]), A3.
Courtesy of the Beinecke Rare Book and Manuscript Library,
Yale University.

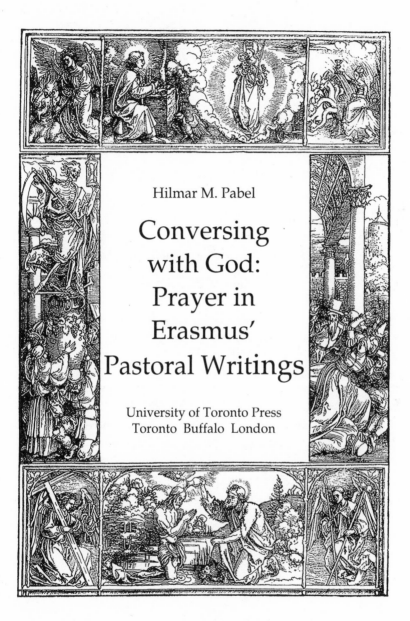

Hilmar M. Pabel

Conversing with God: Prayer in Erasmus' Pastoral Writings

University of Toronto Press
Toronto Buffalo London

© University of Toronto Press Incorporated 1997
Toronto Buffalo London
Printed in Canada

ISBN 0-8020-4101-9

Printed on acid-free paper

Canadian Cataloguing in Publication Data

Pabel, Hilmar M. (Hilmar Matthias)
Conversing with God

(Erasmus studies, ISSN 0318-3319 ; 13)
Includes bibliographical references and index.
ISBN 0-8020-4101-9

1. Erasmus, Desiderius, d. 1536 – Contributions in the
understanding of prayer.   2. Prayer – Christianity – History
– 16th century.   I. Title.   II. Series.

BV207.P32 1997   248.3'2'092   C96-932546-0

University of Toronto Press acknowledges the financial
assistance to its publishing program of the Canada Council
and the Ontario Arts Council.

This book has been published with the help of a grant from
the Canadian Federation for the Humanities, using funds
provided by the Social Sciences and Humanities Research
Council of Canada.

aviae benignae
matri carae
atque
in piam patris memoriam

Contents

꙰

Acknowledgments / ix

Introduction / 3

1
The Principal Elements of Erasmus' Teaching on Prayer / 21

2
Critique, Reform, and Defence of Prayers to the Saints / 69

3
Interpreting the Lord's Prayer / 109

4
Erasmus' Prayer-Book: The *Precationes aliquot novae* / 155

Conclusion / 191

Notes / 203

Bibliography / 241

Index / 255

Acknowledgments

I wish to thank Jaroslav Pelikan, John O'Malley, John Boswell of fond memory, J. Trapman, Joseph Goering, and Robert Barringer for reading and commenting on my doctoral dissertation upon which this book is based. James McConica, Virginia Reinburg, and Roy Hammerling provided valuable advice on revising specific chapters. Mechtilde O'Mara patiently responded to all my queries about my translations from Latin into English. I also wish to acknowledge the assistance of Clarence Miller, John van Engen, Jane Phillips, Ron Schoeffel, and Darlene Money, as well as the support of my colleagues in the Department of History at Simon Fraser University.

I gratefully acknowledge the Andrew W. Mellon Foundation and the Social Sciences and Humanities Research Council of Canada for their generous financial support. A senior fellowship from the Centre for Reformation and Renaissance Studies at Victoria University in the University of Toronto provided me with access to the Centre's excellent collection of Erasmiana as I began revising the manuscript for publication.

I thank the many friends who sustained me during my research and writing. Three people in particular deserve my gratitude. Without John Lawson this book might never have come to be. With her love and encouragement my wife, Lynda Robitaille, eased the book's completion. Our son, Adrian Benedict Pabel, arrived in time to keep me company as I made the final revisions.

It is to my maternal grandmother, Marianne Lork; my mother, Ingrid Pabel; and to the memory of my father and first teacher, Max Pabel, that I dedicate this book.

CONVERSING WITH GOD:

PRAYER IN ERASMUS' PASTORAL WRITINGS

Introduction

꙯

In this book, I examine how Erasmus of Rotterdam understood prayer and how he taught western Christendom to pray. With the exception of three articles, the theme 'Erasmus and prayer' has been neglected by modern scholarship.[1] This neglect lacks justification given Erasmus' contribution to early modern European devotion. His exposition of the Lord's Prayer, the *Precatio Dominica* (1523); his treatise on prayer, the *Modus orandi Deum* (1524); and his prayer-book, the *Precationes aliquot novae* (1535), have not received the study and treatment that they deserve.

Erasmus' place in the publication of devotional literature in the age of the Reformation has received scant attention from scholars partly because of a centuries-old prejudice against the most famous of the northern Christian humanists. Erasmus once assured William Blount, Lord Mountjoy, an English friend and patron: 'Neither piety nor religion, neither public morality nor the public peace will suffer from anything I write.'[2] From the sixteenth to the present century, however, most of Erasmus' interpreters have disagreed with all or part of his statement.[3] His commitment to the Christian religion and to the Roman church has been subjected to some four hundred years of doubt. Martin Luther rejected Erasmus as an enemy of Christianity, an impious sceptic who valued human affairs above divine affairs, peace above the cross.[4] Towards the end of his life, Erasmus complained: 'Luther now publishes nothing without berating Erasmus as a papist and an adversary of Christ.'[5] Yet to the throng of Catholic critics, the papists, Erasmus paved the way for Luther's heresy and schism with Rome and thereby disturbed the peace of Christendom.

Modern interpreters, such as Johan Huizinga, Augustin Renaudet, and Joseph Lortz, have developed the sixteenth-century Protestant and Catholic bias against Erasmus,[6] seeing him as a sceptic, indifferent or hostile to dogma, a rationalist, and a precursor of the Enlightenment. His humanism, his love of philology and of pagan letters and wisdom threatened Christian theology, while his 'adogmatism' led to a 'moralism' in which Christianity became confined to a life of moral purity.[7] Erasmus' religion was a Christianity reduced to a simple system of moral precepts. Eschewing creed, cult, and ceremony, the religion Erasmus promoted was also a 'spiritualized' one, a 'religion d'un pur esprit' in Renaudet's estimation.[8] Therefore Renaudet accuses Erasmus of 'modernism,' which reminds one of the heresy condemned by Pope Pius X in 1907, and passes this harsh judgment: 'the spirituality of Erasmus is nothing other than deception and hypocrisy. Erasmian modernism is neither a form of Christianity nor a religion.'[9]

Alfons Auer, in his study of Erasmus' famous manual of Christian piety, the *Enchiridion militis christiani*, refrains from discussing prayer, which according to Erasmus is the first weapon of Christian piety. Erasmus, according to Auer, cannot be counted among the great practitioners of prayer, and furthermore, 'it would surely not be unjust to say that he did not pray very much.'[10] Joseph Jungmann, in his historical survey of Christian prayer, concedes that the prayers that Erasmus wrote 'attained to a certain vogue.' Yet, while considering the context of the influence of Renaissance humanism on prayer, Jungmann declares: 'Erasmus' bitter criticisms of the externals of traditional piety, of certain forms of life in the cloister, of contemporary theology as well as his outlook on the world which was more pagan than Christian, hindered the salutary effect which his humanism was calculated to produce.'[11]

Similar notions linger on. For all his sympathetic treatment of Erasmus as a religious thinker, Roland Bainton writes in his popular biography that Erasmus 'spiritualized' all the external trappings of religion 'to such a degree that he was accused of reducing Christianity to an attitude.' In Erasmus' view, 'no rite of the Church, no external framework of the Church was necessary for salvation, which depends rather on a heartfelt piety which can be cultivated apart from outward aids.'[12] Richard Marius would agree with Bainton up to a certain point, but Marius' assessment of Erasmian piety ultimately leads in the direction of equating it with 'secular religion.' Erasmus was 'a Christian philosopher who believed in living in the world without any great preoccupation with salvation in a life to come,' and he was 'not far from saying that the good Christian is the good citizen.'[13] Jacques Chomarat refuses to admit that Erasmus was fundamentally a theologian and, displaying shades of Renaudet, discusses the humanist's 'purely spiritual' religion, his 'completely spiritual piety.'[14] Erasmus supposedly looked forward to the disappearance of ceremonies, ritual, cult, and liturgy. He believed that the Mass and the Eucharist should be purified and spiritualized; yet he thought they should not be abolished so as to maintain public peace and to give the unwashed multitude of nominal Christians some outlet for piety.[15]

Over the past thirty years, however, the tide has been turning against the traditional interpretation of Erasmus. In 1969, Jean-Pierre Massaut announced that the renewal of Erasmian studies was in full swing.[16] He argues that Erasmus re-established a synthesis between theology and spirituality, a theology solidly rooted in Christian dogma and in the tradition of the church fathers and a spirituality innocent of rationalism and moralism.[17] No longer an enlightened rationalist before the Enlightenment, Erasmus has now emerged as a forerunner of the Second Vatican Council![18] If *Lumen gentium*, the dogmatic constitution of the Catholic church, 'reads at times like Erasmus himself,'[19] then it is also true that the insistence on world peace of *Gaudium et spes*, the church's pastoral charter, harmonizes well with the humanist's uncompromising Christian irenicism. As opposed to Cornelis Augustijn, who once wrote that 'the Church as such does not mean anything' to Erasmus,[20] Georg Gebhardt and Willi Hentze assess Erasmus' ecclesiology positively.[21] In his synthetic interpretation of Erasmus, James McConica denies that the *philosophia Christi* represents 'a rather rationalistic, moralizing attitude to Christianity.'[22] Erasmus finds his most prolific advocate in Léon Halkin, who has sympathetically explained Erasmus' views on clerical marriage and celibacy, justified his Mariology, confirmed his dedication to Catholic orthodoxy, and acclaimed him as a herald of Catholic Reform.[23] Halkin's assessment of Erasmus' attitude towards prayer is much more positive than those of Auer and Jungmann. Erasmus' prayers provide sufficient proof to recognize in him 'un grand spirituel,' a great spiritual writer. 'With his books,' Halkin imagines, 'Erasmus erected a cathedral whose keystone is prayer.' Against all doubters, Halkin, surveying Erasmus' devotional writings, establishes that the humanist was a 'man of prayer.'[24]

After almost three decades of renewed interest in Erasmus' religious thought, no major study has appeared on Erasmus' concept of prayer, which he described as 'a certain principal part of piety' (*praecipua quaedam pietatis pars*).[25] Historians and theologians have carefully read Erasmus' religious works to establish his theological positions and sometimes even to construct a theological system from a rather unsystematic thinker.[26] Although the study of Erasmus' theology is a laudable enterprise in its own right, it ought not to overlook the main purpose of his religious works, namely the promotion of piety. Erasmus was not interested in writing theological textbooks. He sought to arouse his contemporaries from their spiritual torpor and awaken in them a revitalized Christian spirit, a spirit devoted to loving God and neighbour through obedience to Christ's teaching. Theology and piety go hand in hand for Erasmus, but they need to be completed by pastoral ministry. The integration of piety, theology, and ministry constitute what John O'Malley has called 'the seamless robe' of Erasmus' *pietas*.[27]

O'Malley has argued: 'Erasmus' *pietas* was pastoral, and even many of his so-called "devotional" writings look silently but reproachfully to a reform of the pastoral practice of the church ... The pastoral works of Erasmus are pre-eminently instruments of piety and represent in their very being an important quality or mode of that *pietas*.'[28] Some scholars have recognized the pastoral dimension in Erasmus' writing, notably Rudolf Padberg, who has studied Erasmus as a catechist, and Massaut, who has closely analysed Erasmus' thinking on the sacrament of penance.[29] Nevertheless, O'Malley has rightly pointed out that scholars have by and large neglected those of Erasmus' works that are intimately connected with ministry and its reform, 'with the result that we have failed to recognize ministry as an absolutely central concern of Erasmus and that we are only beginning to grasp its profound implications for understanding him.'[30] Without a serious consideration of the pastoral dimension in Erasmus' thought, we lack an adequate context in which to interpret his religious writings. Perhaps it is in part because this pastoral dimension has not been sufficiently appreciated that Erasmus' prayers and his treatise on prayer have been neglected. To place these in their proper context we need to consider more closely Erasmus' contribution to pastoral care.

On 25 April 1492, Erasmus of Rotterdam was ordained a priest by David of Burgundy, the bishop of Utrecht. Some forty years later, when in 1535 he published his famous manual on preaching, the *Ecclesiastes sive de ratione concionandi*, Erasmus recalled with great respect the pastoral solicitude of the bishop to choose only worthy men as candidates for ordination.[31] Would David of Burgundy have been proud of Erasmus? What sort of priest was this man, who is thought of more in terms of his scholarship and humanism than in terms of his priestly office? Opinions range from discounting Erasmus' priesthood altogether to asserting, albeit in a rather vague way, Erasmus' dedication to his ordained status. Accordingly, he was either 'a laicized monk,'[32] or he 'never renounced nor forgot his priesthood, even though he gradually broke with the conventual life,' and he 'became the priest he wanted to be, faithful to the duties of his priesthood, but disengaged from the demands of the monastery.'[33] Scholars may wish to make judgments about Erasmus' priestly vocation, but Erasmus seems never to have reflected in writing on how he saw his life as a priest. What we do know is that he entered the Windesheim Congregation of Augustinian canons at Steyn in 1483, was ordained in 1492, and spent the rest of his life outside of the monastery, although he never repudiated his status as an Augustinian canon or as a priest.

Erasmus was a priest without a cure of souls; that is, he never exercised a pastoral ministry within the church. For a few brief months in 1512, he held the post of rector of the parish of Aldington in Kent, having received this preferment from his good friend, William Warham, the archbishop of Canterbury. He never resided in the parish and eventually resigned his benefice, but, through the generosity of Warham, continued to draw a pension from the living. Apart from a few sermons that he delivered while a student at the University of Paris in the 1490s, he did not preach. Indeed, still at work on the *Ecclesiastes* in 1528, he anticipated that his critics would demand why they should learn how to preach from him, since he did not preach himself.[34]

Erasmus was 'a man of texts.'[35] His scholarship was his life's work. He is rightly remembered for his five printed editions of the Greek New Testament (1516–35), complete with a fresh Latin translation and annotations, a scholarly enterprise that merits him the title of the father of modern biblical criticism. His writings fill ten large folio volumes in Jean Leclerc's 1703 edition, and they will take up many more volumes of the critical edition under way in the Netherlands. The English translation of his works being prepared by the University of Toronto Press will run to 86 volumes.

There is, of course, no necessary connection between Erasmus' priesthood and his literary output, and yet I wish to establish as the necessary context for this study that much of Erasmus' scholarship constituted a pastoral ministry to all western Christendom, a ministry exercised through the printing press. The chief object of his scholarship was, as he would certainly say, the promotion of piety. Thus he describes his *Annotations on the New Testament* as 'a work of piety' and as a 'Christian work.' He asks his readers to attend to the *Annotations* with 'pious ears and a Christian heart.' Erasmus explains: 'It is with simple and pure zeal that I lay this before my Christian readers, in hope that hereafter this most sacred philosophy may find more men to follow it and with more enjoyment, in a word, that their labours may be less and their profit more.'[36] The 'most sacred philosophy' to which he refers is none other than his much championed *philosophia Christi*. By embracing this philosophy of Christ, by imitating Christ's life and following his teachings, Christians of the early sixteenth century, Erasmus' contemporaries, would be able to refashion their church and society, both in great need of moral and spiritual reform. The propagation of the philosophy of Christ and the promotion of piety lay at the heart of Erasmus' pastoral ministry through the printing press.

Erasmus self-consciously understood his religious writings to possess a definite pastoral character. Late in 1519, he dedicated to Philip of Burgundy, David's brother and bishop of Utrecht since 1517, his *Paraphrases on 1 and 2 Timothy, Titus, and Philemon*. Even in the winter, Erasmus assures Philip, 'the cornfield of literature never ceases to bring forth some kind of crop.' He thinks it fitting that some portion of this crop be given over to a bishop 'as a prince of this type of agriculture.' 'For whenever we promote to the best of our ability the business of the Gospel,' Erasmus continues, 'to some extent we take up the office of your solicitude.' Erasmus is referring to Philip's pastoral office as a bishop. He believes that preaching, 'the spreading of the teaching of the Gospel,' is the 'principal and peculiar office of a bishop.'[37]

One of Erasmus' sermons explicitly conveys the pastoral solicitude that he took upon himself. In 1523, Erasmus composed a Mass for the Virgin Mary honoured at her shrine in Loreto, entitled *Virginis Matris apud Lauretum cultae liturgia*. Two years later he published an expanded second edition, which included a sermon. Addressing his 'most beloved brothers and sisters in Christ,' he expresses the wish that

> I, who am [your] father and moreover [your] pastor, might from the most sumptuous pantry of the Scriptures produce for you, my children and flock in the Lord, food which does not perish but feeds and furthermore strengthens souls for eternal life, [and] the wine of the Spirit which gladdens your hearts with a sober inebriation so that even in the midst of the evils of this world you might sing with spiritual hymns and psalms to the Lord, who, although he is glorious in all his saints, has nevertheless made known the abundance of his glory in his mother.[38]

Erasmus, of course, intended these words to be spoken by the priests who celebrated his liturgy. They, in the most direct and immediate sense, were the fathers and pastors of the Christian faithful. Yet behind these priests stood Erasmus. He spoke through them, ministering to Christians by applying to their lives and for their benefit the teaching of Scripture. An overview of Erasmus' religious works shows that he took upon himself a sizable part of the pastoral office of bishops and priests to instruct the faithful.

I have already mentioned the culmination of Erasmus' pastoral writing: the *Ecclesiastes*. With this book, James Michael Weiss observes, 'he cast the whole wealth of humanist rhetoric in terms of Christian learning and pastoral service.'[39] Since the beginnings of Christianity, preaching, ultimately the responsibility of the bishops of the church, was the most important form of ministry. Erasmus still thought so. He duly acknowledged the other duties of the clergy, such as prayer and the administering of the sacraments, but his primary interest remained preaching and its reform. God has provided many charisms for attaining eternal life, he explains at the outset of the *Ecclesiastes*, but none is more noble or more efficacious than preaching. Erasmus exalts the office of preacher in the church: 'In the entire hierarchy of the church, no ministry (*munus*) is more distinguished in dignity, more difficult in its exercise, or more widespread in its application than to act among the people as the herald of the divine will and the steward of the heavenly philosophy.'[40] The *Ecclesiastes*, which O'Malley has described as 'the great watershed in the history of sacred rhetoric,'[41] is Erasmus' longest single publication, spanning 332 folio columns in Leclerc's edition. It consists of four books. The first, a sort of *speculum pastoris*, tells of the dignity of pastors or preachers, terms more or less equivalent in Erasmus' vocabulary. In the second and third books, the heart of the treatise, Erasmus concentrates on the rhetorical principles, objectives, and strategies with which a preacher should be familiar. The fourth and final book presents a survey of appropriate topoi for sermons.

Certainly his scriptural scholarship contributed to preaching in its own way, since Erasmus endeavoured to provide theologians with the most accurate text of the New Testament, which should be the foundation of all theological enquiry and of all preaching. The theologian's main task, Erasmus wrote in the *Ratio verae theologiae*, first published in 1518, is to expound the Scriptures with wisdom, to give an account of the faith, to discuss piety earnestly and effectively, and to move his listeners to tears.[42] The *Ratio* served as a preface to the 1519 edition of the New Testament. It was an introduction to the study of theology consisting for the most part of advice on how to interpret Scripture. Erasmus provides the aspiring theologian with several topoi around which he can organize his reading of the New Testament. The *Ratio* helped pave the way for the *Ecclesiastes*, since the practical application of theological study was preaching. A 'remarkable continuity' exists between the *Ratio* and the *Ecclesiastes*, André Godin affirms. 'In a certain sense,' he continues, 'the *Ecclesiastes* is nothing but a development, amplified a thousand times, of themes present in the *Ratio*.' It is evident from the *Ratio* that 'the exegete-theologian that Erasmus wants to form must also be above all a preacher according to the Gospel.'[43]

Erasmus was not happy with the state of preaching in his own day.[44] Well-known are his satires and criticisms of the moral shortcomings and the meagre intellectual capacity of priests, abbots, and bishops, who are more interested in material gain or political advancement than in ministering to the faithful. In the colloquy *Funus* (1526), he sympathizes with parish priests who disliked the intrusion into their jurisdiction of the mendicant friars, but at the same time he censures parochial clergy for scarcely being able to read the Gospel.[45] As he writes in the *Modus orandi Deum*, he knows that it is hard to believe that impious priests can be the vicars of Christ's power and teaching.[46] He complains of pluralism among bishops in the *Ratio*, and in the *Ecclesiastes* he protests that pastors sin when they fail to preach and that they dilute God's Word with human doctrines when they do preach.[47]

Those who have acquired some theological training and who do preach are not an asset to the ministry of the Word. They have imbibed too much scholastic theology and show off their knowledge of the great scholastic doctors to impress their audience with their intellectual prowess. These preachers burden their listeners with a host of intricate philosophical and theological problems or prattle on about ridiculous subjects from which one can attain little or no spiritual profit. The *Ratio* insisted on a departure from 'the scholastic wrestling arena.' 'We are not training a boxer,' Erasmus asserted, 'but a theologian, and the type of theologian who prefers to express what is profitable with his life rather than with syllogisms.'[48] In other words, theologians must teach the faithful as much by the example of a pious life as by their ability to reason and to speak.

Despite the many examples of inadequate pastors, Erasmus retains a high regard for the pastoral office. According to Emile Telle, Erasmus primarily viewed a priest as a celibate and not as a minister of God,[49] but in his essay on the adage *Sileni Alcibiadis* Erasmus claims: 'There is something heavenly about a priest, something more than human; nothing is worthy of his exalted position except what is heavenly ... This is the man chosen out of the heavenly body, which is the Church, by that heavenly Spirit for appointment to the highest place.' Erasmus severely criticizes the abandonment of pastoral service for the pursuit of wealth and secular power. Of a pope or a bishop he writes in *Sileni Alcibiadis*:

Why do you think the vicars of Christ should be ensnared in riches which Christ Himself called thorns? ... Why do you make the dispenser of the heavenly mysteries into a steward of all that is most worthless? The Christian world looks to him for its food of sacred learning, it looks for the counsel that leads to salvation, for fatherly consolation, for a pattern by which to live. Why thrust one destined and dedicated to such noble purposes into a prison-cell of vulgar cares, at one stroke robbing a bishop of his proper dignity and leaving the people fatherless without a bishop?[50]

Friedhelm Krüger has shown that in his *Paraphrases on the Gospels* Erasmus presents pastors with several lessons on how to be good ministers and particularly good preachers.[51] In a study of the *Paraphrase on John*, Jane Phillips argues that Erasmus' statements about appropriate clerical behaviour allow his lay readership 'to measure their own clergy by the gospel standards: by their own knowledge of the gospel message and specifically of what it has to say about clergy, they are equipped to recognize the good and the bad among their pastors.'[52] He, of course, recognized that not all was lost, that some of his contemporaries were faithful to their clerical vocation. William Warham of Canterbury and John Fisher of Rochester were exemplary bishops.

When he first published the *Ratio*, Erasmus had already begun work on another project that would help to reform preaching. The *Paraphrases on the New Testament*, written between 1517 and 1524, not only show how Erasmus interpreted Scripture but also could serve as guide and aid to preachers. Indeed, Cardinal Lorenzo Campeggi referred to Erasmus' 'sermon-paraphrase on the Pauline Epistles.'[53] In England, two royal injunctions of 1547 required every parish church to make available a copy of the *Paraphrases on the Gospels* and obliged clergymen 'under the degree of bachelor of divinity' to study the *Paraphrases on the New Testament*. We know from the report of a Swiss traveller that, in 1551, church services at Oxford included the reading of a section of the *Paraphrases* in English translation.[54]

Krüger believes 'everything indicates that in the *Paraphrases* Erasmus feels himself to be a preacher.' Through them he wanted to mediate the philosophy of Christ.[55] Augustijn associates the *Paraphrases* with Erasmus' eleven psalm commentaries in the humanist's contribution 'to the renewal of preaching and devotional literature.' He writes: 'In the commentaries on the Psalms he offered preachers an example of how to make fruitful use of them. In the *Paraphrases* he showed both cultivated and simple folk the way to Christ.'[56] Erasmus also published three sermons: one on the boy Jesus, written for the new school opened by his friend John Colet, the dean of Saint Paul's Cathedral in London; another on the mercy of God; and a third that appeared in the second edition of his liturgy in honour of the Virgin of Loreto.

For Erasmus, the foundation of all good preaching and indeed of all pastoral ministry was 'accommodation.' In the *Ecclesiastes*, he writes that a preacher must have a prudent and discerning heart so that he can determine what to say and what not to say and before whom and at what time. He must adjust his speech so that with Saint Paul he may know how to adapt his words and to become all things to all people, looking to bring about the salvation of his listeners in whatever way possible.[57] The accommodation or adaptation of an orator's words to the circumstances of a particular audience is an ancient rule of rhetoric. Quintilian wrote about how to speak appropriately, *apte dicere*, in book XI of the *Institutio oratoria*. *Omnia in omnibus* expressed the Christian concept of accommodation, formulated by Paul: 'I have become all things to all men, that I might by all means save some' (1 Corinthians 9: 22, RSV). According to Gregory the Great, author of the influential book *Pastoral Care*, the pastor must adapt his discourse to the characteristics of his listeners, meeting the needs of each individual while still edifying everyone together. He must touch the hearts of his audience with the same teaching but not in the same way.[58] Erasmus singles out Pope Gregory for special praise in the *Ecclesiastes*.[59]

In the *Ratio*, Erasmus maintains that, when interpreting a passage from Scripture, a theologian must consider not only what was said but also by whom and to whom it was said, with which words, at what time, on what occasion, and what preceded and followed it. As Manfred Hoffmann has pointed out, accommodation is 'the single most important concept in Erasmus' hermeneutic.'[60] In the *Ecclesiastes*, Erasmus writes that a preacher must know not only what to say, but when, before whom, how, with which words, order, figures of speech, facial expression, and gestures.[61] Accommodation is not merely a hermeneutical or rhetorical principle, however; it underlies all pastoral service. Jesus is the supreme pastor, and his life is a perfect example of being all things for all people. Christ, Erasmus writes in the *Ratio*, 'accommodated himself to those whom he eagerly wished to draw unto himself.' To save the human race he himself became human; to heal sinners he became their friend; to gain the favour of the Jews he was circumcised and purified, he observed the sabbath, he was baptized, and he fasted.[62] As Christ never disdained eating and drinking with tax collectors and sinners in order to promote the cause of the Gospel, 'so it is fitting,' Erasmus believes, 'for bishops and their vicars to accommodate themselves to everyone.' They should do so not for financial gain but for the improvement of those entrusted to their care.[63] The preacher, according to the *Ecclesiastes*, is obliged to minister to the wise and the foolish, to boys and girls, to youths, to men and matrons, to old men and old women, to magistrates and merchants, to sailors and shoemakers, to soldiers and farmers, even to pimps and prostitutes, for he must serve the high and the low. He must always be ready to help all. He must teach the ignorant, gently call back those who have gone astray, raise up the sick, console those who weep, help the afflicted, assist the oppressed, be at the side of the dying, bury the dead, support the needy, pray and offer Mass for the salvation of all. In short, he should extend his kindness to everyone whom he meets.[64]

Erasmus wanted preachers to accommodate themselves to their flocks in preaching and in every aspect of their ministry. In his pastoral writings, he acted as a steward of the philosophy of Christ; he himself exercised what might be called a literary cure of souls or a pastoral ministry through the printing press. *Omnia in omnibus* is a motto that seems to inspire these writings. We can see Erasmus' pastoral accommodation at work in the *Enchiridion militis christiani* (1503), his first major religious work. The title itself is an indication of how he tries to win the attention of a particular reader. The original impetus for writing the book came from a woman who asked Erasmus to help reform her unfaithful and abusive husband. This was Johann Poppenruyter, a well-to-do cannon founder who eventually owned several foundries in the Low Countries.[65] An *enchiridion* can mean a dagger or it can refer to a handbook. Erasmus' *Enchiridion* is the handbook of the Christian soldier. Its purpose, of course, is not to confirm Poppenruyter in his behaviour and in his business but to convert him and others into Christians engaged in a spiritual warfare against sin. Properly speaking, the book is not exclusively a manual of lay piety, for in it Erasmus addresses himself to laity and clergy alike. Indeed, some passages seem relevant only for priests.[66] The various rhetorical poses that Erasmus adopts also demonstrate his pastoral accommodation as he tries to effect a spiritual change within his readers. He reproaches them for their 'empty observances,' for not producing the fruit of a genuine Christian spirituality; but he also applies gentle persuasion when he urges them to give up grudges that they harbour against their neighbours.[67] Erasmus' pastoral advice was not lost on John Colet, who managed to overcome his passionate hostility towards his uncle after reading the *Enchiridion*'s remedy against anger.[68] Colet, of course, was a priest, and thus we can see that the *Enchiridion* did not benefit laypeople exclusively.

Erasmus attends to the various aspects of his contemporaries' spiritual lives, and his admirers assisted his literary efforts at accommodating himself to the needs of his readers by translating many of his pastoral works from Latin into the vernacular. He discusses how to make a good confession in the *Exomologesis sive modus confitendi* (1524) and how to prepare oneself for a holy death in the *De praeparatione ad mortem* (1534). He counsels married couples in the *Christiani matrimonii institutio* (1526) and consoles widows in the *Vidua christiana* (1529). Erasmus the pedagogue did not limit himself to teaching the young good Latin and polite manners. He also wanted them to have a firm grasp of the Christian faith. In 1514, Erasmus published the *Christiani hominis institutum*, a short catechism in verse written for Colet's school. In 1533, he produced a more substantial work, the *Explanatio symboli apostolorum sive catechismus*, in which he teaches the meaning of the Apostles' Creed, the Ten Commandments, the sacraments, and prayer. What he writes of the *Modus orandi Deum* can apply equally to the *Precatio Dominica* and to the *Precationes aliquot novae*: 'I will think that I have succeeded if, because of this effort of mine, I perceive as many people as possible either inspired or made more eager to pray often.'[69] Teaching western Christendom how to pray was another pastoral ministry that he took upon himself.

In the *Ecclesiastes*, Erasmus states that human beings resemble God most closely 'mente et oratione,' by virtue of their ability to think and speak.[70] *Oratio*, which here signifies speech or discourse, since the earliest beginnings of the Christian West acquired another meaning that pertained to a particular kind of discourse: prayer. Thus the North African church fathers, Tertullian (d. c.220) and his admirer, Cyprian of Carthage (d. 258), entitled their treatises on prayer and on the Lord's Prayer respectively *De oratione* and *De dominica oratione*. If for Erasmus *oratio* or speech is a sign that human beings are made in the image and likeness of God, then *oratio* as prayer is the means by which they communicate with God. Prayer is a conversation with God or a *colloquium cum Deo*, as Erasmus says.

The notion of prayer as communication with God is a commonplace. William James, the American psychologist and philosopher, considers prayer 'as meaning every kind of inward communion or conversation with the power recognized as divine.' In this sense of the word, prayer is 'the very soul and essence of religion.'[71] Friedrich Heiler in his classic study of the history and psychology of prayer writes: 'To pray means to speak and converse with God.' Heiler defines prayer as the 'living communication of the pious person with God, who is conceived of as personal and experienced as present.'[72] Like James, he calls prayer 'the central phenomenon of religion, the hearth of piety' and asserts: 'Not in dogmas and institutions, not in rituals and ethical ideals, but in prayer do we grasp the essential nature of religious life.'[73]

The 'central phenomenon of religion' merits the attention of historians, for by examining how people prayed and understood prayer, historians can learn much about the religious, cultural, and intellectual life of a given society. Prayer helps to shape religious belief – *lex orandi, lex credendi* – and is in turn shaped by belief. Religious ritual is principally the official and public way that human beings speak to God. Written prayers reveal the most important needs, aspirations, and fears of a religious culture and allow us to see how the people who recited them imagined or were supposed to imagine what their God or gods were like and how they interpreted the relationship between the human and the divine. Eamon Duffy has examined in great detail the private and public devotions of late medieval England and how this 'traditional religion' succumbed to 'reformed religion' in the sixteenth century. He enters the world of the prayers and devotions of the late medieval Books of Hours, 'in which religion was a single but multifaceted and resonant symbolic house, within which rich and poor, simple and sophisticate could kneel side by side, using the same prayers and sharing the same hopes.'[74]

In this study of Erasmus' conception of prayer, I concentrate on petitionary prayer, the prayer that asks for things, as distinct from contemplative or mystical prayer, the prayer that ascends to a spiritual union with God. Erasmus has much to say about the

former and little or nothing about the latter: 'De la vie mystique,
Erasme ne parle guère.'[75] I examine his concept of prayer according to the categories of analysis he follows in the *Modus orandi
Deum*. He asks his readers to consider to whom they pray, who
they are at prayer, for what they should pray, and how they
should pray: 'Mox ostendemus in orando quatuor potissimum
esse spectanda, quis sit quem oras, qui sis qui oras, quid ores et
quomodo sit orandum.'[76] This constitutes a sort of rhetorical analysis similar to the advice Erasmus gives to theologians as they
interpret Scripture or to preachers as they prepare their sermons.[77]
Prayer, as discourse, is a form of rhetoric, the spiritual rhetoric of
those who pray to God. When they converse with God, they must
speak appropriately. From Erasmus they learn how to adapt their
prayers in light of the divine recipient of their petitions, of their
own identity, of the proper object for requests made of God, and of
the manner in which they ought to make these requests. Thus the
principle of accommodation emerges again in Erasmus' efforts to
teach his fellow Christians how to pray.

For Erasmus, the God to whom Christians pray is a God of
power, wisdom, and goodness. The last of these qualities domi-
nates Erasmus' conception of God. God is good, kind, generous,
beneficent, and merciful, and the loving Father in heaven gladly
hears the prayers of his children. As sinners, they are quite unlike
God. In the state of exile from their heavenly homeland, they
fight as Christian soldiers against the world, the flesh, and the
devil, against everything that will ensnare them in sin. Yet Erasmus is more interested in what his readers should be than what
they are. In order to pray genuinely, they must possess certain
spiritual dispositions. Among these are humility, faith, and concord. Not surprisingly, concord ranks high on the list of the prerequisites for prayer demanded by Europe's leading advocate of
religious peace and most vociferous critic of war. His readers
should be good Christians in order to pray and become better
Christians as a result of speaking with their good God. Genuine
prayer therefore not only requires a spiritual transformation on
their part, a commitment to living piously, but also brings about
this transformation or makes them more pious. The *scopus* or
chief object of their petitions should be spiritual as well. All material needs are subordinate to the desire for the glorification of
God and for salvation.

My emphasis on spiritual transformation and on the spiritual *scopus* of prayer corrects the view that in religious matters Erasmus was nothing but a moralist. Yet I have not escaped the Scylla of moralism only to crash into the Charybdis of the spiritualization of piety. The spiritual transformation required for and effected by authentic prayer has nothing to do with the abandonment of ceremony. Erasmus, author of the *Virginis Matris apud Lauretum cultae liturgia*, takes liturgical prayer seriously; he desires the reform of the cult of the saints and not its abolition. Prayer, after all, is part of Christian cult.

To resume, prayer according to Erasmus is addressed to a good God by those who are under obligation to be pious and who become spiritually transformed as they ask God for whatever may contribute to the manifestation of his glory and the accomplishment of their salvation. In answer to the question of how one should pray, he teaches that Christians should pray in such a way that their prayers conform to the seven petitions of the Lord's Prayer, or take inspiration from Scripture, or pattern themselves on the ancient collects of the church.

Erasmus did not think and teach in a vacuum. Thus, at significant junctures, I put the Erasmian texts into the context of the religious thought and culture of the Church Fathers, the Middle Ages, and the Reformation. Erasmus' apology for the invocation of the saints in the *Modus orandi Deum*, for example, needs to be set against the background of the Protestant rejection of this form of devotion. A comparison of Erasmus' understanding of some of the seven petitions of the Lord's Prayer with that of Cyprian, Augustine, Thomas Aquinas, and of the Roman Catechism helps to place him within a long tradition of interpretation. His explanation of the second, fourth, and fifth petitions separates him from two of the great architects of Protestant theology, Luther and Calvin. A brief survey of the history of Christian prayerbooks prefaces the analysis of the *Precationes aliquot novae*, while references to Protestant and Catholic approaches to devotion in the 1520s and 1530s provide the intellectual milieu in which to understand more fully Erasmus' attitude towards praying for the dead and to the Virgin Mary.

Erasmus states in the *Modus orandi Deum* that Jesus would not have taught his disciples the Our Father with such diligence 'if prayer were not a certain principal part of piety.'[78] His understanding of prayer fits neatly into the Christocentric piety he espouses. Christocentrism is, as Halkin remarks, the 'golden rule' of Erasmian piety and theology.[79] Most of the prayers that Erasmus composed are addressed to Christ. In them his readers seek Christ's help, dedicate themselves to his glory, and acclaim their love for him. When it comes to prayer, Christ is 'princeps noster,'[80] the one who teaches Christians how to pray through word and example. In Erasmian piety, Christ stands out as teacher and exemplar for the life one must lead in order to imitate him. Yet Erasmus' philosophy of Christ does not forget that Christ is also Redeemer and Saviour. To preach about Christ means not only to preach about the virtues he wishes his followers to embrace but also to confess him as the Son of God, born of the Virgin Mary, who died so that the sins of all might be forgiven, rose from the dead, ascended into heaven, and sent the Holy Spirit upon the apostles.[81]

In the *Ecclesiastes*, Erasmus associates catechesis with preaching. A priest does not always administer the sacraments, 'but his teaching ministry never ends' (*docendi munus perpetuum est*). What benefit can adults derive from having been baptized if a catechist had not taught them what baptism means, what they should believe, and how they should lead a Christian life? Of what use to them is the Eucharist unless they learn how the sacrament was instituted, what effect it has on them, and with what sort of faith and purity they ought to take communion?[82] Erasmus' pastoral teaching ministry was also an ongoing enterprise. Through his books he was constantly engaged in teaching the elements of a sincere Christian piety. As with the preacher he wished to train in the *Ecclesiastes*, Erasmus assumed the duties of a steward of the heavenly philosophy in order to direct the hearts and minds of his readers to Christ, their 'prince.' Erasmus might well have asked: Of what use is Christian worship if no one has learned how to pray? He set out to teach western Christendom to pray so that his contemporaries would have a better understanding of an essential part of piety and thus pray more frequently and with greater devotion. His writings on prayer constitute a significant part of his pastoral ministry through the printing press.

ONE

The Principal Elements of Erasmus' Teaching on Prayer

꽃

A few months after receiving Holy Orders in 1492 Erasmus became a secretary of Hendrik of Bergen, the bishop of Cambrai. David of Burgundy, his ordaining bishop, may have recommended the young Augustinian canon to his episcopal colleague in Cambrai.[1] The year of his ordination signalled Erasmus' break with monastic life and his entry upon what eventually became for him a world of scholarly renown.

Working for Hendrik held out the bright prospect of a journey to Rome for Erasmus, since the bishop had ambitions of becoming a cardinal. By 1495, it was clear that the bishop's dream would not come true. The trip to Rome was off, and the bishop's secretary, robbed of an opportunity to visit Italy, 'the land of eminent scholars, the land of abundant manuscripts, the land of imperishable memories,'[2] was disappointed. Fortunately, Hendrik released Erasmus from his secretarial tasks and allowed him to take up studies at the University of Paris. With a small stipend from the bishop, Erasmus set out for Western Christendom's greatest centre for theological study. While in Paris, Erasmus sought to support himself financially by tutoring scions of wealthy families in Latin and by trying to secure the patronage of some late fifteenth-century Maecenas.

He first tried his luck with Lady Anna van Veere, the widow of Philip of Burgundy, the late admiral of Flanders and governor of Artois, and he counted on some inside help from his friend Jacob Batt. Batt, the former secretary of the town council of Bergen and the hero of Erasmus' *Antibarbari*, had entered Anna's service in 1496 as tutor to her young son, Adolph. The tutor suggested that his friend compose some prayers for the ten-year-old boy in order to ingratiate himself with the mother.

Erasmus complied. In 1499, he sent the lad a short exhortation to virtue, the *Oratio de virtute amplectenda*, along with three long prayers. Erasmus' highest hopes for the boy are that he grow up to be the rarest of men: 'someone who has combined a profoundly learned mind with a character utterly free of blemish.'[3] To virtue and learning Erasmus adds religious devotion at the very end of the *Oratio*. He tells Adolph: 'And so that you may begin to learn Christian doctrine along with your basic literary education, I am sending you some prayers.' If he makes regular use of the prayers, the boy will improve his style and come to 'scorn those rather warlike little prayers, marred by both a profound ignorance and an abysmal superstition, which generally give pleasure to the common sort of courtiers.'[4]

The three prayers, the first ones that Erasmus ever wrote, consist of two to the Virgin Mary, the *Paean Virgini Matri dicendus* and *Obsecratio ad Virginem Matrem Mariam in rebus adversis*, and one to Jesus, the *Precatio ad Virginis Filium Jesum*. The *Paean* opens the floodgates to a 'boundless ocean'[5] of praise for Mary, while the *Obsecratio* sends up to Mary urgent entreaties for help from the stormy seas of this life. The latter is interesting from a doctrinal point of view, for it affirms Mary's Immaculate Conception and Assumption and, in conformity with medieval tradition, asserts that Mary did not suffer labour pains when giving birth to Jesus, no doubt because of her sinless state.[6] Many of the titles that Erasmus bestows upon her are common to medieval prayers and hymns to the Virgin. She is, among other things, the Theotokos or God-bearer, the fleece of Gideon, the new Eve, another Judith or Esther, the holy city of Zion, Jerusalem, a safe harbour for sailors, the mother of mercy, one's only hope, the queen of heaven, star of the sea, one's refuge.[7] Erasmus allows himself a classical allusion when he hails Mary as 'the true Diana, both the source and example of perpetual virginity' in the *Paean* and as 'our Diana' in the *Obsecratio*.[8]

In 1523, Erasmus admitted that the two Marian prayers were written for the Lady van Veere 'in a childish style designed to suit her feelings rather than my judgment.' The prayer addressed to Jesus, however, 'was more to my liking,' he said.[9] The Marian prayers do not sound like the Erasmus of the *Enchiridion*, which he began to write at Lady Anna's castle at Tournehem in 1501.

The *Paean* and *Obsecratio*, which put Mary at the centre of the Christian devotional life, are a far cry from the rule that Erasmus lays down in the *Enchiridion*: 'place Christ before you as the only goal of your life, and direct to him alone all your pursuits, all your endeavors, all your leisure time and hours of occupation.'[10] Oddly enough, Erasmus included the prayers for young Adolph along with the *Enchiridion* in the *Lucubratiunculae* of 1503. Addressing Mary in the *Obsecratio* as 'my saviour, my salvation, my only and most certain refuge'[11] would certainly not suit the judgment of the Erasmus who disliked the hymn *Salve Regina* because it called the Virgin 'our life, our sweetness, and our hope,' and who insisted that Christ, and not his mother, was the 'anchor of our salvation.'[12]

For all its earnest invocations of Mary, the *Obsecratio*, as it concludes, shifts towards a warm devotion to Christ. The person who appeals to the Virgin expresses the wish 'that I may love or admire nothing besides your only Son, that I may be worthy to be transfigured into his image, so that it will even be sweet for me to bear the cross with him and in that cross to persevere happily through hope and patience to life's very end.'[13]

In this way, the prayer to Mary in time of distress sets the stage for the *Precatio ad Virginis Filium Jesum*. The first two words, 'adoro te,' announce that Jesus is the object of adoration and centre of devotion. He is the 'undying light,' the 'new sun of righteousness' that 'dispels the hellish darkness of our sins' and whose 'health-bringing rays make all things flourish and live.'[14] Jesus also is, as Erasmus describes him in the opening invocation, 'generis instaurator humani.'[15] As Redeemer, as Saviour, as the most spotless lamb,[16] he has restored the human race, and his work of restoration is ongoing. Again and again the *Precatio* implores Jesus to transform or to transfigure us. Lowly creatures that we are, we desire to be transfigured into God so that we can be one with Christ. We pray for the transfiguration of our spirits so that, united to Christ's spirit, nothing may disrupt 'our happy union.'[17] To be restored in purity to Christ is the goal of the prayers for transformation.

The *Precatio* therefore demonstrates for the first time an essential ingredient of Erasmus' conception of prayer: prayer brings about spiritual transformation. Erasmus will not let his contemporaries pray without planting within them the desire to undergo spiritual change. They must promise to forsake the world with its 'deadly allurements' and to find the 'delights of the flesh' increasingly repulsive.[18] This rejection of the world and of the flesh does not merely symbolize the repudiation of moral impurity; it serves as a means to union with Christ, enabling Christians to love nothing except in Christ or because of Christ.[19] Expressed differently, the prayer for union with Christ is also a prayer for the attainment of eternal life, a petition common to the two Marian prayers[20] and, as we shall see, the principal object for which Erasmus wants his readers to pray.

Besides adumbrating Erasmus' later insistence on spiritual transformation, the *Precatio* reveals for the first time Erasmus' conception of the essential nature of God. God is powerful, God is wise, and, above all, God is good. The Christ of the *Precatio* is good, kind, and merciful. Jesus is a 'most generous parent,' a 'most clement Creator,' a 'most forgiving Redeemer,' a 'most clement Saviour.'[21] He is the loving father who forgives and welcomes the prodigal son.[22] The *Precatio* accordingly lays down another fundamental Erasmian principle of prayer: the God to whom one prays is good. In his goodness Jesus forgives Christians their many sins, opening their way to union with him. Since he is their Saviour, they can gladly go to him in prayer.

The titles Erasmus gives to Mary in the *Paean* and the *Obsecratio* he confers in the *Precatio* upon her Son. Now Christ is 'our only hope,' the 'sole author of salvation.'[23] Erasmus calls upon him as 'my delight,' 'my protection,' 'my reward,' 'my solace,' 'the joy of my heart.'[24] In hailing Christ as his 'peace' and 'tranquillity,'[25] Erasmus establishes the unbreakable bond between peace and piety, a union that will express itself in his requirements for the spiritual dispositions for prayer, in his expositions of the Lord's Prayer, and in his prayer book, the *Precationes aliquot novae*, to which he added the *Precatio ad Virginis Filium Jesum*.

Erasmus was not the only one to like the *Precatio*, for it managed to influence two very different people. According to Paul Althaus, Cornelius Crocus (d. 1550), a Dutch humanist and theologian who eventually joined the Society of Jesus, found inspiration in this early prayer of Erasmus for his own *Precationes in passionem Jesu Christi*. Crocus' *Precationes* were first printed in 1531 but also quite appropriately appeared in an appendix to a 1561 edition of Erasmus' prayer book published in Cologne. The story does not end here, however. Through Crocus the influence of Erasmus' prayer extended to the Silesian Sacramentarian,

Kaspar von Schwenkfeld (d. 1561). The latter, obviously touched by Crocus' meditations on Christ's passion, reproduced them almost verbatim.[26] Thus the significance of the *Precatio ad Virginis Filium Jesum* lies not only in its manifestation of essential elements of Erasmus' conception of prayer but also in the irenic quality of prayer to unite in devotion Catholics and Protestants, who steadfastly refused to agree on doctrine.

Erasmus published his first three prayers with the *Enchiridion* in 1503. The latter work laid the foundations of his mature religious thought. His view of Christian life as perpetual warfare against Satan and vice; the importance he attaches to baptism as an oath of allegiance to Christ; the primacy of the spiritual sense in his interpretation of Scripture; his fundamental concept, borrowed from Saint Paul, of the church as the body of Christ; and his campaign to subordinate ceremonies, the outward manifestations of piety, to the inner, invisible realm of the spiritual – all these characteristically Erasmian religious views and values come to light for the first time in the *Enchiridion*. What he has to say about prayer fits into the conceptual framework of Christian warfare and of the fifth and most important rule for Christian soldiers: that they understand perfect piety to consist in the constant effort to advance from the visible to the invisible, from the material to the spiritual.

Having argued that life is an unceasing war against vice and the temptations of devils, a war that Christians can only win with the help of Christ their Head, Erasmus advises his Christian soldiers never to be without their weapons. They must always be ready to repulse the enemy, whose strategy includes surprise attacks. Prayer and knowledge are the two chief weapons that keep them on their guard 'against the whole horde of vices, principally the seven deadly sins.'[27] Erasmus explains: 'Devout prayer raises our desires to heaven, a stronghold inaccessible to the enemy, and knowledge in turn fortifies the intellect with salutary opinions so that the one will not be lacking to the other.'[28]

Prayer is not self-sufficient because it requires the help of knowledge, which indicates what one should pray for. Erasmus insists not on any piety whatever but on a learned piety. The knowledge associated with this piety in general and with prayer in particular is essentially a knowledge of Scripture, most specifically the ability of arriving at the spiritual sense of a scriptural passage. Yet here knowledge, or 'human industry,' cannot succeed without 'frequent prayer.'[29] Piety requires learning; learning requires piety.

Although prayer and knowledge operate in tandem, the former 'is the more effective of the two, since it is a conversation with God.'[30] Erasmus does not elaborate on what he means by this reason for the superiority of prayer. Perhaps he believes prayer to be the more effective because conversing with God is the surest refuge and bulwark against temptation. In the *Modus orandi Deum*, Erasmus describes prayer as the 'most secure armour' against the demons, the flesh, the world, and the evils that accompany human life or that result from human wickedness. Human weapons often fail, but with the shield of prayer a Christian's armour is complete.[31]

In recommending prayer as a necessary weapon in the battle against evil, Erasmus is aware that through abuse prayer can become ineffective and futile. By subordinating the invisible to the visible, the access to God as one's heavenly stronghold will deteriorate into an empty religious observance. On several occasions, Erasmus rails against measuring piety according to the number of psalms one rattles off.[32] Implicit in his criticism is an objection to the perfunctory recitation of the divine office by monks and their lay imitators, who often did not understand the Latin words they were saying. One should not, moreover, seek 'the power of prayer' in 'a multitude of words.' To do this means to cleave to the letter, to external ceremonies. Those who confine themselves to the letter 'have not grown up into the maturity of the spirit.' Erasmus reminds his readers of Christ's teaching in Matthew 6: 7 against using many words in prayer and of Paul's belief that speaking five words with understanding is better than pronouncing ten thousand words in ecstasy (1 Corinthians 14: 19).[33]

Ceremonies do not piety make. Charity does not consist in 'being an assiduous churchgoer, prostrating yourself before the statues of the saints, lighting candles, and repeating a certain number of prayers.'[34] Charity involves the devotion of 'all your resources, all your zeal, all your care to this one end, that you benefit as many as you can in Christ.'[35] Genuine prayer is born not of the loud noise of the lips but of 'the ardent desire of the mind that like some piercing sound strikes the ears of God.'[36] True charity, true prayer, true piety: these are fundamentally spiritual. Erasmus announces: 'God is spirit, and he is moved by spiritual sacrifices.'[37]

Prayer should be a spiritual sacrifice, offered up not as a concatenation of words but as an earnest plea for God's help against evil. Spiritual, invisible worship finds greater favour with God than visible ceremonies. He desires neither sheep nor fragrant incense; the sacrifice that pleases him most is 'a pure prayer coming from a pure heart.'[38] The Gospel has rendered obsolete the sacrifices of the Mosaic Law. No sacrifice has been so carefully handed down by Jesus or so religiously embraced by his disciples as prayer, the 'calves of our lips,' in Erasmus' quotation from Hosea 14: 2,[39] the greatest of spiritual sacrifices.

In 1503, Erasmus had not yet reached the height of his fame. The *Enchiridion* only became a great success in 1518 when he reissued it with the now famous preface addressed to Paul Volz, the abbot of Hugshofen. By then, Europe acknowledged Erasmus for what he was, the greatest scholar of his day. Two years previous to the new edition of the *Enchiridion* Erasmus had published his edition of the works of Jerome as well as the fruit of many years of labour, the first printed edition of the Greek New Testament, complete with a fresh Latin translation and annotations. Between 1519 and 1535, he published four more editions of the New Testament and produced editions of Cyprian, Hilary, Ambrose, Augustine, John Chrysostom, and Basil, to name but the most prominent Fathers he edited.

Hand in hand with his scriptural scholarship and editorial work went Erasmus' promotion of piety. The New Testament was the source of knowledge of Christ's teaching; Erasmus endeavoured to help his contemporaries put that teaching into practice. Beginning with the Epistle to the Romans, Erasmus wrote his *Paraphrases on the New Testament* between 1517 and 1524, the most prominent of which were on the four Gospels and the Acts of the Apostles. In 1523, he published his paraphrase of the Lord's Prayer, the *Precatio Dominica*. The following year, in which Erasmus debated the freedom of the will with Luther in the *De libero arbitrio*, the *Exomologesis sive modus confitendi, De misericordia Domini concio*, and *Modus orandi Deum* issued forth from Johann Froben's printing press in Basel.

Soon after he wrote this last work, Erasmus found among the works of Chrysostom two homilies on prayer that had not yet been translated into Latin. (Erasmus suspected that the second homily was not genuine. Migne in his patrology classifies both homilies as dubious.) Erasmus could have destroyed his own book, so much did it pale in comparison with his discovery.[40] In Cologne in 1525, Eucharius Cervicornus published Erasmus' translation of the two homilies along with the *Modus orandi Deum*.[41]

Erasmus' interest in prayer is evident not only in the *Precatio Dominica* and the *Modus orandi Deum* but also in his other works on piety. The treatise on confession teaches that sinners cannot supply themselves with the desire for conversion, for this is a free gift from God. Nevertheless, they must seek this gift from God 'with tears, prayers, almsgiving, and other pious undertakings.'[42] Erasmus in his *Christiani matrimonii institutio* (1526) says that God bestows good fortune on those couples who begin married life with holy prayers.[43] Prayer remains important for those bereaved of their spouse. Erasmus advises Christian widows 'that it is singularly appropriate to widows to devote themselves to constant prayer.'[44] The passages in the New Testament that touch on prayer give him many opportunities to make some point on prayer in the *Paraphrases*, which serve as an important source for Erasmus' conception of piety in general and of prayer in particular.

The *Modus orandi Deum* is the centrepiece of Erasmus' teaching on prayer. He regarded this book as a work of his old age – Erasmus was in his mid-fifties in 1524 – a work with which he was obviously pleased, for it caused him little trouble to write and was especially conducive to piety.[45] Léon Halkin declares that the *Modus orandi Deum* is 'Erasmus' principal contribution to the art of piety' and recognizes its 'pastoral character.'[46]

In February 1525, Duke George of Saxony informed Erasmus: 'Your book on prayer is being read everywhere.'[47] Given this comment and the history of the book's dissemination, Erasmus did not exaggerate when at the end of March 1525 he wrote that everyone had browsed through the *Modus orandi Deum*, and not without approval.[48] Froben published a first edition in October 1524 and a second edition, which contained a few corrections and interpolated some more material, the following March. Between December 1524 and the end of 1525 printers in Strassburg, Cologne, Nürnberg, Krakow, Venice, and Antwerp produced ten new impressions of the first edition. This edition was reissued five more times between 1529 and 1540 in Lyon, Paris, and Cologne. It appeared in German translation in 1525 and in Dutch in 1616.[49]

As with the *Precatio Dominica*, dedicated to Josse Ludwig Dietz, secretary to King Sigismund I of Poland, the *Modus orandi Deum* also has a Polish connection. In 1520, the young Polish nobleman Hieronim Laski met Erasmus in Brussels and in Cologne. Four years later, he visited him in Basel and presented him with a silver flask and a polemical work written against Luther by Andreas Krzycko (Cricius), the bishop of Przemysl.[50] In October of that year, 'as a token of a mutual spirit,'[51] Erasmus expressed his gratitude to Laski by dedicating to him the *Modus orandi Deum*. Apart from being published in Krakow, the *Modus orandi Deum* also enjoyed the favour of the cathedral chapter of that city, which in preparation for a synod in 1551 recommended the treatise on prayer along with the *Enchiridion* for the edification of the Polish clergy.[52]

Erasmus does not seem to have had many forerunners in the genre of treatises on prayer. The *De oratione* of Tertullian (d. c.220), the first surviving Christian treatise on prayer, contains a brief explication of the Lord's Prayer as well as comments about other subjects, such as the necessity of being at peace with one's neighbours, the washing of hands, physical posture, women's dress, and times for prayer.[53] Erasmus would not have read the *De oratione*, for it was first printed in 1545, nine years after his death.[54] He may also have been unaware of Origen's *Peri euches*, which he did not include in his posthumous 1536 edition of Origen's *Opera* or mention as a lost work.[55] In his treatise on prayer,[56] Origen (d. c.254) considered, among other things, the problem of human freedom and God's foreknowledge and the benefits of prayer. He devoted about half of his treatise on prayer to the Lord's Prayer. Written around 412, Augustine's letter (Epistle 130) on prayer to the noble widow Proba enjoyed great influence in the Latin West.[57] Thomas Aquinas often referred to it in his own scholastic analysis of prayer in the *Summa Theologiae*,[58] and Erasmus used the letter to Proba as a source for the *Modus orandi Deum*.

As John O'Malley observes, Erasmus' book is, despite its title, 'more a treatise about the nature and qualities of prayer (or prayers) and an incitement to it than a practical, "how-to" manual.'[59] As such, the *Modus orandi Deum* is somewhat of a literary first, creating a genre that over the past five centuries has had and still has today a large number of successors in the many books that explain and encourage prayer. This genre did not catch on right away, however. The exposition of the Lord's Prayer in the catechism served as the basic source for teaching prayer in the sixteenth century and was probably overtaken by the *modus orandi* only in the twentieth century. Nevertheless, Erasmus soon had a literary heir in Thomas Becon (d. 1567?), a prolific propagandist for the cause of the Reformation in England.[60] In 1542, Becon published his treatise *The Pathway unto Prayer*. He was convinced that 'no man hath as yet perfectly entreated of this matter, neither in the Greek, Latin, nor English tongue that ever I could see.'[61] Becon, who does not mention Erasmus' book, may not have deemed it perfect, but he had obviously read it. He quotes a sentence from the *Modus orandi Deum*, the influence of which appears in a few other places in Becon's book. Erasmus' friend John Fisher (d. 1535) most likely wrote his *Tractatus de necessitate orandi* before the publication of the *Modus orandi Deum*. Perhaps completed around 1520, the *Tractatus* was first published in English in 1560 and then again in 1576 in a Latin edition.[62]

Although the *Modus orandi Deum* cannot match Fisher's *Tractatus* or Becon's *Pathway* in clarity and neatness of organization, it certainly does not deserve this assessment: 'It had no real beginning or ending, no introduction or conclusion, and it rambled along without making clear its major objectives.'[63] Erasmus clearly begins with a consideration of the various types of prayer and then analyses petitionary prayer under four categories. He examines the nature of God, the one to whom one prays; the sort of person one has to be in order to pray; what one should pray for; and how one should pray.[64] The 'objectives' of the *Modus orandi Deum* are therefore evident, even if Erasmus' presentation digresses at times, especially in a long excursus on prayers to the saints. After discussing Erasmus' attitude towards liturgical prayer, I shall present Erasmus' fundamental principles of prayer according to the essential themes of the *Modus orandi Deum* and with frequent references to his *Paraphrases on the New Testament*.

Prayer may be private or public, and public prayer may also be called liturgical prayer. Given his critique of ceremonialism, it is not surprising that Erasmus did not focus his attention on the promotion of liturgical piety. His suspicious attitude towards ceremonies, however, was not unique in his day. Liturgy in late medieval Europe had fallen into disrepute. As Jean-Pierre Massaut has pointed out, the proliferation of vocal prayers recited in a mechanical way, the superstitious and magical practices that resulted from an ignorance of the meaning and purpose of ritual, the predominantly external and juridical conception of worship that militated against the interior spiritual dimension of liturgy – all of these things alienated the humanists of the late fifteenth and early sixteenth centuries.[65] A notable exception was Josse Clichtove, the Flemish humanist, theologian, and reformer of the clergy, whose voluminous book, the *Elucidatorium ecclesiasticum ad officium ecclesiae pertinentia planius exponens* (1516), aimed at teaching priests the spiritual and theological meaning of the prayers of the divine office and of the Mass.[66]

Although Erasmus makes the interior, private, or as he would say, invisible aspect of devotion his first priority, this does not mean that he repudiates liturgical worship. Erasmus did not want to create, in the words of Renaudet, a 'religion d'un pur esprit,' a purely internalized religion without external manifestations; rather, the goal of his religious reform was to foster a 'religion d'un esprit pur,' a genuine piety rooted in faith, hope, and love. His reform was spiritual, not spiritualizing. He did not condemn the daily celebration of Mass, but the sort of celebration that lacked any spiritual basis. Priests who celebrate Mass and yet selfishly give no thought to the misfortunes of their neighbours celebrate unworthily. Should they, however, when offering sacrifice, consider themselves to be one in spirit with Christ and members of his body, love nothing but Christ, and esteem the common good more than their own interests, then they celebrate 'with great profit,' for they do so spiritually.[67]

Erasmus perhaps may be criticized for not integrating and harmonizing external worship and interior devotion as Clichtove did, but he cannot be accused of contempt for liturgy. In 1523, he composed prayers for a Mass in honour of the Virgin of Loreto.[68] The previous year in a notice to the pious reader that prefaced the *Paraphrase on Matthew* Erasmus had even proposed a new type of ceremony. After private instruction in the essentials of the faith, baptized youths should publicly renew their baptismal vows with ceremonies that are 'dignified, appropriate, chaste, earnest, and even magnificent.'[69]

The *Modus orandi Deum* shows that Erasmus cared enough about liturgy to have his own sense of what was liturgically appropriate. He believes that the liturgy should be the same among all Christian peoples and not be unduly long, for there is nothing worse than having too much of the best things.[70] He dislikes the ostentatious performance of music at Mass:

> No one should think that God takes delight in the empty bellowing of voices, the modulated neighing of musicians, or the organs with which churches everywhere nowadays resound. Not that I would condemn corporeal music if it is performed in a restrained manner, soberly and in keeping with the divine liturgy, but I would point out that that sort of music is nothing if it lacks the silent inner sense of devotion towards God (*tacitus ille pietatis affectus in Deum*) which is the song that pleases God most even if no din of voices is added to it.[71]

Worthy attendance at Mass requires a 'silent inner sense of devotion towards God,' and, what is more, the absence of all licentiousness, desire for gain, flattery, and other feelings inappropriate to the liturgy.[72]

The subject of flattery brings Erasmus to offer advice on the saying of prayers for princes at Mass. If Christians are fighting one another – and as Erasmus wrote the *Modus orandi Deum* Charles V was at war with Francis I – it is unbecoming for a priest to offer prayers for the victory of his own country and for the death of the enemy since sometimes both sides have offended God. It is even less fitting to hear the glorious titles of a prince, 'most victorious,' 'unconquered,' and 'most triumphant' spoken at the altar. Still less seemly is the slavish and undignified flattery with which people adore the prince for whom the Mass is being offered. In their prince Christians should wish for a good mind worthy of God, wisdom, and piety rather than triumph and glory. To pray for one's own prince is permissible, but in public prayers it is better to pray for all Christian princes, and it is better to pray for God's mercy on the Turks and on the other enemies of Christianity than for their destruction.[73]

Another Erasmian liturgical predilection is the opinion that public worship should be in the vernacular. Declaring in the *Paraclesis*, one of the prefaces to his first edition of the New Testament, that 'Christ desires his mysteries published as openly as possible,' Erasmus expressed his own wish that the Gospel and Pauline Epistles would be translated into the languages of all people 'so that they could be read and understood not only by the Scots and Irish but also by the Turks and the Saracens.'[74] A vernacular liturgy followed logically from vernacular translations of the Bible. Why should Christ want his mysteries published as openly as possibly, if he did not also want them to be celebrated as openly as possible?

Erasmus first seems to advocate vernacular liturgies three years after the *Paraclesis* in his *Paraphrase on 1 Corinthians* (1519). In 1 Corinthians 14: 14–19 Paul discourages the Corinthians from speaking in tongues, in unintelligible utterances inspired by the Holy Spirit. Erasmus' paraphrase of the text[75] criticizes the saying of public prayers in a language, Latin no doubt, that the common faithful cannot understand. Whereas Paul simply writes: 'if I should pray in a tongue' (*si orem lingua*, Vulgate) Erasmus paraphrases: 'if I should pray in a tongue unknown to the people (*si precer lingua populo ignota*), say, in Persian among the Greeks, or indeed if ... I should discourse in a language of which I have no more knowledge than others.' His emphasis clearly is on 'a tongue unknown to the people.' Prayers 'in a tongue' benefit neither whom we must assume to be the presiding priest nor the congregation. The former prays without profit to his soul and becomes a burden to others and an object of ridicule. The latter cannot genuinely affirm a prayer of thanksgiving with the customary 'amen' when they do not understand what they are affirming, when God's praises are sung out in a language unknown to all. Paul becomes Erasmus' spokesman when in the *Paraphrase* he says to the person who likes to pray in tongues: 'What you say is holy and perhaps even of some benefit, but in the meantime the people do not at all become better.' Prayer's purpose is to transform the faithful, to make them better, more devout people; yet this purpose remains unfulfilled if they cannot understand the prayers at Mass. To use the terminology of the *Enchiridion*, the weapon of prayer is useless to Christian soldiers if unaccompanied by the weapon of knowledge.

Erasmus espouses a vernacular liturgy much more explicitly in the *Modus orandi Deum*. In ancient times, the faithful could understand the collects recited by the priest at Mass because Latin was the language of the people. Now that there has been a change in language, yet without any corresponding change in ritual, Erasmus wonders whether the old form of worship should be scrapped or renewed. Refusing to become an innovator of custom, Erasmus nevertheless recommends that the people daily read in their own language the collects, the lessons from the Gospels and from the Epistles, and the Lord's Prayer.[76] This cautious proposal eventually gives way a few pages later to the desire that the entire liturgy should be performed in the tongue of the people.[77]

Although Erasmus does express himself on liturgical matters, his main concern in the *Modus orandi Deum* is to guide his readers in their private devotions. He begins his treatise with a discussion of prayers of praise and thanksgiving. He calls the psalms hymns, and as such they praise God. Erasmus quotes from the psalms to illustrate his point: 'Praise the Lord, my soul; I will praise him all my life; I will sing psalms to my God as long as I live' (Psalm 145 [146]: 1). The opening verses (1–3) of Psalm 83 (84) proclaim the soul's longing to free itself from the body and enjoy eternal life: 'How lovely are your tabernacles, Lord of hosts. My soul longs and faints for the courts of the Lord. My heart and my flesh exult in the living God.'[78] Whereas hymns attribute to God the glory that is his due, prayers of thanksgiving celebrate God's goodness more than his greatness. We give thanks to God when we sing: 'Acclaim the Lord for he is good, for his mercy lasts for ever' (Psalm 117 [118]: 1).[79] Erasmus endows hymns and prayers of gratitude with special theological significance when he links them to the Eucharist and Christ's redemptive death: 'Praise and thanksgiving therefore are a perpetual sacrifice of all Christians, but especially when at the consecration of the sacred bread and of the mystical cup we recall (*repraesentamus*) his death, by which he redeemed us, and moreover the society of the mystical body.'[80] Christians should remember the redemption, the sacrament of the Eucharist, and the church's unity, which the sacrament symbolizes, as special reasons for which to give God thanks and praise.

Praise and thanksgiving are not confined to this life; perfected, they continue for ever in the next life. Petitionary prayer, however, is confined to this side of eternity, for in heaven all needs are fulfilled. When Erasmus speaks of prayer, he most often means the requests presented to God. His short definition of prayer refers to petitionary prayer: prayer is a 'raising of the mind unto God with the fervent desire of asking something from him.'[81] This traditional definition of prayer goes back to the Eastern Church Father John Damascene (d. 749), who called prayer 'the ascent of the mind to God.'[82]

The mind's ascent to God is a form of discourse. In Erasmian terminology prayer is a *colloquium cum Deo*, a colloquy or conversation with God. This notion appears as early as the *Enchiridion*. Prayer is a more effective weapon than knowledge because it is a conversation with God: 'precatio quidem potior, ut quae cum deo sermones misceat.'[83] Perhaps Erasmus' earliest characterization of prayer as a colloquy with God appeared in 1516 in the first edition of his *Annotations on the New Testament*. At Ephesians 1: 16, Paul writes that, remembering them in his prayers, he always give thanks for the Christians at Ephesus. The Vulgate reads: 'non cesso gratias agens pro vobis, memoriam vestri faciens in orationibus meis.' Erasmus believes that the expression *mentionem facere*, not *memoriam facere*, more accurately translates the original Greek since when we pray we converse with God: 'quandoquidem orantes cum deo colloquimur.'[84] Similarly, he disagrees with the Vulgate's translation at Romans 1: 9: 'sine intermissione memoriam vestri facio.' Erasmus prefers to translate Paul's statement that he remembers the Romans without ceasing as 'indesinenter mentionem vestri facio.'[85] In the 1519 edition of the *Annotations*, he justifies his translation with the observation that to pray is nothing other than to converse with God: 'orare nihil aliud est quam colloqui cum deo.'[86]

His choice of *colloquium* as a term for prayer appears in the *Paraphrases* and in the *Modus orandi Deum*. In the *Paraphrase on Matthew*, he writes: 'It is a pious thing to converse with God (*cum Deo colloqui*) by means of pious prayers.' Paraphrasing 1 Thessalonians 1: 2, he has Paul say to the Thessalonians: 'We always give thanks to God for you ..., mentioning all of you by name whenever we converse with God by means of holy prayers (*quoties cum Deo sacris precationibus colloquimur*).'[87] In the *Modus orandi Deum*, he sometimes employs the verbs *loqui*, to speak, and *colloqui*, to converse, when he writes of prayer. He advises: 'Even if you are not weighed down by the burden of sins, still, when you go to pray, cast aside for a while your shabby, little worries when you speak (*loqueris*) with the Most High.' Scripture associates prayer with vigils and sobriety because 'extravagance and lethargy weigh down the mind that desires to converse with God (*cum Deo colloqui*).'[88] Erasmus, moreover, found a kindred spirit in Pseudo-Chrysostom, who also understood prayer in terms of a conversation with God. His translation of the latter's homilies on prayer renders the expressions 'Theōi dialegesthai' and 'pros Theon homilia' as 'colloquium miscere cum Deo' and 'colloquium cum Deo.'[89]

The use of the words 'colloquy' or 'conversation' to characterize prayer is an interesting one, as it is a favourite literary term of the Renaissance humanists. For Erasmus, the author of the *Familiaria Colloquia*, a colloquy teaches and arrives at truth in a much more spiritually stimulating and peaceful way than the acrimonious bouts of logic-chopping in the disputations of European theological faculties. His humanist concept of education therefore is integrated within his promotion of piety. It is unclear, however, what exactly Erasmus means by *colloquium*, for, unlike Ignatius of Loyola, he never elaborates on it. Ignatius' *Spiritual Exercises*, completed in 1535, direct retreatants to have colloquies with God whereby they conjure up an image, say of Christ crucified, and speak to God as they imagine him. In the first exercise, Ignatius explains: 'The colloquy is made properly by speaking as one friend speaks to another, or as a servant speaks to his master, now asking some favor, now accusing oneself for some wrong deed, or again, making known his affairs to Him and seeking His advice concerning them.'[90] In his *Pathway unto Prayer*, Becon expresses a similar view: 'For what other thing is prayer than a familiar communication with God, wherein we may freely pour out the troubles of our hearts, and declare all our matters boldly to him, as the child doth unto his father, and obtain at his hand all good things?'[91]

Erasmus could easily subscribe to these statements. His use of *colloquium* to characterize prayer as a conversation with God suggests a pleasant familiarity between human beings and their divine Father, as when 'one friend speaks to another.' On one occasion towards the very end of his life, Erasmus saw prayer as a conversation with God that would shelter him from all his troubles. In the preface to the *Ecclesiastes*, Erasmus allows us a glimpse into his own spiritual life. He yearns to replace his labours with 'peaceful leisure' and 'to converse alone with the Alone who once proclaimed – and he has not changed his message today – : "Come to me all you who labour and are heavy laden, and I will give you rest."' When he considers how turbulent his times are, he confesses that there is nothing 'in which my mind more gladly finds rest than in this mysterious conversation (*in hoc arcano colloquio*).'[92]

Erasmus' humanism expresses itself in his study of words as well as his choice of words. The leading philologist of the New Testament of his day, he cannot resist a discussion of the meaning of the three types of entreaty mentioned at 1 Timothy 2: 1: 'obsecrationes, orationes, postulationes,' that is, 'supplications, prayers, intercessions' (RSV). The corresponding Greek words are *deēsis, proseuchē,* and *enteuxis.* Following the scholia of the Greek interpreters, Erasmus notes that by *deēsis* we pray for liberation from the evils that oppress or threaten us, by *proseuchē* we desire good things, and by *enteuxis* we complain about those things that hurt us or, in the opinion of Theophylact, we intercede for the conversion of those who harm us. Erasmus explains that *deēsis* is related to the verb *deomai,* which means 'I need' or 'I ask for,' and therefore is a verb of supplication. *Proseuchē* is related to the verb *euchomai,* which means 'I wish for' and to the noun *euchē,* which means 'a wish.' *Enteuxis* connotes an intercession or a plea (*interpellatio*) by which someone mediates between a person who has been offended and the person who has given offence.[93]

Beyond defining various modes of petition, Erasmus indicates in the *Modus orandi Deum* why someone should ask something of God at all. Prayer recommends itself for several reasons. We should always pray to God, Erasmus writes, so that he might deliver us from oppressive wickedness, increase his gifts within us and wish them to belong to us for ever, and perfect in the future life of heaven what he has begun in us.[94] Prayer possesses great dignity, for the angels pray, inasmuch as they converse with God, sing his praises, and intercede for us to him. Prayer is supported by the authority of God, who gave it to us as a refuge, and by the example of the patriarchs, prophets, kings, and priests. Christ has approved their example, and the apostles have handed it down to us. Thus we should pray because God wants us to pray and because the actions of the heroes of the Bible and the teaching of Christ and of his apostles move us to pray. Prayer, moreover, is useful to us. If we do not pray, God will bestow nothing on us, but through prayer there is nothing that God does not give us. Prayer provides us with a sense of spiritual protection, 'for with this single weapon we are safe against everything which a hostile power can threaten.'[95]

The most compelling incentives to pray are the authority of the teaching and example of Christ and of his apostles as well as the example of the famous figures of the Hebrew Bible. Abel offered his sacrifices with prayers, and Abraham built an altar and called upon the name of the Lord when he first heard of the promised land. Moses' prayers brought down God's wrath upon Egypt, helped win the day for Israel against the Amalekites, and placated God, whose anger was kindled against faithless Israel. Joshua prayed that the sun and moon should stand still, and barren Hanna became the mother of Samuel after silent prayer. Erasmus also mentions Aaron, Solomon, Elijah, Elisha, Hezekiah, Nehemiah, Tobias and his wife Sara, Judith, Esther, Daniel, and Jonah.[96]

Among the apostles, Paul teaches Christians to pray without interruption (1 Thessalonians 5: 17), and he desires that they pray with pure hands and without anger and quarrelling (1 Timothy 2: 8). Peter admonishes his readers to be sober and vigilant (1 Peter 5: 8), and Erasmus applies this command to prayer. James orders that Christians should pray for the sick and for each other (James 5: 14–16).[97] Erasmus supplies many examples from the Acts of the Apostles that show the first Christians at prayer, and, as an admirer of Paul, 'that wonderful defender of the Gospel,'[98] he lists the many times that Paul prayed. Since Paul's letters usually greet his readers with a prayer, such as 'Grace and peace to you,' Erasmus believes that Paul did not write the Epistle to the Hebrews, for it does not begin with a prayer.[99]

Of course, the greatest teacher and exemplar of prayer is Christ, 'our prince.'[100] Jesus issued no commands about the external trappings of religion, vestments, food, drink, and fasting, but he did hand down a formula of prayer, the Pater Noster. He told his disciples to seek, and they would find; reassured them that should they ask the Father anything in his name, the Father would grant it (Matthew 7: 7); and he commanded them to watch and pray (Mark 13: 33).[101] According to Jesus' teaching, prayer should be earnest and assiduous. With the parable of the widow who constantly pestered the wicked judge to give her justice (Luke 18: 1–8) he admonishes his followers to be steadfast in prayer. We learn the same lesson from the parable of the person who, with his impetuous clamour for bread, rouses his neighbour from bed at midnight (Luke 11: 5–8).[102] In the *Paraphrase on Matthew*, Erasmus has Jesus tell his apostles in the Garden of Gethsemane that it is not time for slumber but for 'vigilant and earnest prayer.' By praying three times that the Father, if it be his will, let the cup pass him by, Jesus 'teaches us that we must pray persistently and impetuously whenever the storms of temptation threaten us.'[103]

Erasmus remains faithful to his interpretation of the principal feature of Jesus' teaching about prayer. Whenever Erasmus speaks of prayer, he usually describes it as something that must be done diligently, constantly, urgently, even importunately. In his *Paraphrases on the New Testament*, he communicates any special emphasis on the act of praying in the original text by using the adjective *assiduus*, or the verb *interpellare*, which means to interrupt, disturb, importune, or appeal. Thus the angel mentions Cornelius' 'assiduous prayers' (Acts 10: 4), and Paul tells the Colossians (1: 9) that he and his companions implore God on their behalf with earnest prayers (*assiduis precibus interpellantes Deum pro vobis*). Where the Vulgate at 1 Thessalonians 5: 17 renders Paul's command to pray always as 'Sine intermissione orate,' Erasmus writes: 'indesinenter interpellate Deum precibus vestris.'[104]

Erasmus' insistence on praying earnestly manifests itself in his other pastoral works. In the *Enchiridion*, he urges his Christian soldier to ask God with 'most ardent prayers' for the wisdom to know himself.[105] The need for a 'pious and true pastor' to guard the secrecy of confession will encourage him to pray with greater urgency, Erasmus notes in the *Exomologesis*.[106] In the *Vidua christiana*, he tells widows that God has placed great value on 'assiduous prayer.'[107] Only with assiduous prayers, as his readers learn in the *De praeparatione ad mortem*, can one obtain from God faith, charity, and hope, virtues important for a good preparation for death.[108] In the *Ecclesiastes*, Erasmus states that among the important qualities of a preacher are modesty, sobriety, and constant prayer. With ardent and assiduous prayers the faithful should ask Christ to send preachers into the harvest of souls. Christians should also earnestly beseech God with diligent prayers to convert the hearts of princes and priests to the things that please Christ.[109]

Christians must persevere in prayer because this is what Christ taught them, but also because only through persistent, diligent prayer do they obtain from God what they need. God does not hear those who pray 'sluggishly,' Erasmus has Jesus say in the *Paraphrase on Matthew*. Whoever seeks will receive; whoever searches eagerly will find what he is looking for; whoever knocks persistently, for him doors will open. Jesus' followers should not distrust God's kindness but know that he will grant their needs, if only they persevere in prayer, if they appeal to his kindness with 'burning and persistent prayers.'[110] When it seems that our prayers remain unanswered, we should not lose hope, as Erasmus writes in the *Vidua christiana*, for God 'sometimes delays answering our prayers so that our sense of need might be stronger.' In that case, Erasmus urges: 'Let us not cease to implore him, let us not cease to cry out to him loudly, until he takes pity on us and delivers us from our adversary.'[111] As on the boat the apostles woke up Jesus to silence the wind and sea, so also when we are rocked by temptation, we must rouse Christ 'with fervent and pressing prayers.' Erasmus advises in the *Paraphrase on Mark*: 'If he does not immediately hear you when he is called, do not desist, poke him, pluck him until he awakens. And tranquillity will return instantly through him.'[112] We need not worry that Christ will be vexed by our unceasing entreaties, for he 'loves even those who importune him with untimely prayer.'[113] Through the voice of Saint Paul Erasmus assures his readers in the *Paraphrase on Philippians* that although God knows 'what is in your interests even if you ask for nothing,' nevertheless 'he loves to be roused by pious prayers and, as it were, to be compelled by them.'[114]

Jesus' own example of praying is as impressive as his teaching. They both encourage Christians to pray. In Luke 3: 21, we learn that Jesus was praying after his baptism in the Jordan. In his *Paraphrase on Luke*, Erasmus writes that Jesus did this in order to teach us that, 'after the restoration of innocence through baptism, we might directly turn to those spiritual pursuits among which prayer holds first place.'[115] Jesus often withdrew to pray alone, and Erasmus in the *Modus orandi Deum* interprets this as a lesson for pastors. Jesus 'taught pastors that they must frequently pray to the Lord for those whom they have been charged to rule, knowing that if heavenly favour does not inspire it, their work of teaching and admonishing will bear no fruit.'[116] Paraphrasing Luke 5: 16, Erasmus takes Jesus' withdrawal into the wilderness for prayer as an opportunity to argue that nothing more invigorates a preacher or strengthens him against every seduction of this life than frequent withdrawal from the crowd. Such a with-drawal should not be for the sake of idleness, gaming, pleasures, or the riches of this world, but 'for the reading of Sacred Scrip-ture, for pure prayer, for thanksgiving, for the contemplation of heavenly things, in short, for the purification of the soul.' Too much human intercourse is not good for the pastor because familiarity with his flock usually breeds contempt. Once the preacher has fed the people with the food of the Gospel, he should withdraw into solitude. Fortified by sacred studies and by the 'divine colloquy' that is prayer, he can return to do a better job of helping his neighbours.[117] Taking the lead from Jesus' invitation to his apostles to rest in a lonely place, Erasmus similarly comments in his *Paraphrase on Mark* that 'men who undertake the apostolic task are obliged to have dealings with strong men and weak, learned and unlearned, good and bad alike, so that losing some of that perfect composure is at times unavoidable. When that happens they must turn their minds to concentrated, private prayer, to the pure contemplation of heavenly things, so that they may regain their spiritual strength and soon return to aid their brothers.'[118]

Although God wants Christians to pray, and Christ teaches his followers to do so, this does not mean that God needs human prayers. Prayer is for our benefit, Erasmus insits in the *Modus orandi Deum*, not for God's. We do not pray to tell God our needs as if he did not know them; on the contrary, we pray to realize how much we need God. The purpose of our obligation to praise and thank God is not that we contribute something pleasant to God, but that in our weakness we come to fear and revere God's greatness and to love his goodness more and more. We must pray frequently 'not so that God may learn from us what we lack but that we accustom ourselves to hope from him all that we need and that the desire for life everlasting will continue to grow in us.'[119] In his treatise on restoring peace to the church, the *De sarcienda ecclesiae concordia* (1533), Erasmus writes that God desires assiduous prayers 'not so that he might be issued a reminder, but that we by asking might make ourselves worthy for him to bestow his blessing on us all the more generously.'[120] Prayer, moreover, does not seek to control or manipulate God. The function of our praise is not to mollify him, nor do we rumi-nate over our sins to win God's favour, nor do we exhort God in our prayers in order to wake him up. We praise God to learn of his greatness; we recall our sins because we wait on his mercy; and we clamour to him so that we may seek with urgency what we do not merit unless we ask for it insistently.[121]

Although Erasmus stresses the need for insistent, assiduous, and constant prayer, he distinguishes between earnest and verbose prayers.[122] The latter sort of prayer provokes his scorn and ridicule. He disagrees with the view that lengthy prayers form part of the sum of piety, castigates prolixity in prayer as pharisaical, pokes fun at monks who have no time to seek wisdom because of their many prayers, and complains that priests are burdened by rules that prescribe the saying of 'excessively prolix prayers.'[123] Yet if Christians are to pray constantly, how can they reconcile Jesus' command to pray always and Paul's exhortation to pray without ceasing, with Jesus' prohibition in Matthew 6: 7 of *multiloquium* (or *battalogia* in Greek), of verbosity in prayer? The key to the answer lies in Erasmus' belief that Christians pray for their own edification, for the growth within them of the desire for eternal life. Prayer does not ultimately consist of words, but of desire, for it is desire (*affectus*) that moves God, not noisy lips.[124] Not to cease from praying means to desire one's whole life long the supreme good of the future life. Devout people therefore direct all their actions to this goal, whether it be in eating, drinking, or sleeping.[125] The 'ardent and earnest inner disposition of a person at prayer' does not contravene Christ's prohibition of *multiloquium*.[126]

Erasmus' distinction between prayer as enduring desire and as spoken words recalls the traditional reconciliation of the command to pray always with the condemnation of wordy prayer that goes back to Augustine. In his letter to Proba, Augustine points out that 'we pray always by continuous desire' and associates Paul's injunction to pray without ceasing with the desire for eternal life. Lengthy prayer should not be confused with *multiloquium*, for much talk is not the same thing as a long-lasting desire. In verbose prayer, to speak at length means to ask for necessities with 'superfluous words.' Prayer, however, is ultimately affective, not verbal. Constant prayer does not consist of words but of a 'long and pious stirring of the heart.' Prayer expresses itself more in sighs and tears than in speeches or in utterances.[127]

Having resolved the problem of *multiloquium*, Erasmus continues his discussion of prayer in the *Modus orandi Deum* by considering two further questions: first, 'to whom do you pray?' and second, 'who are you that prays?' The first question is in effect a question about what God is like. Erasmus begins his discussion of God's nature by emphasizing God's majesty. Seeking to instil a sense of reverence for God, Erasmus directly addresses the reader with rhetorical questions that employ the rhetorical device of *quanto magis*. This device drives home a point through a comparison of two realities of lesser and greater significance, where if something holds for the former it holds all the more (*quanto magis*) for the latter.[128] Through the use of this type of comparison, Erasmus reprimands his readers for the inconsistency of paying respect to the majesty of human royal authority while neglecting the more important majesty of God.

If anyone has to speak with the emperor, with what care does he attend to his composure so that he does not offend the emperor's eyes in ceremony, body, or word? Yet this is merely the case of one man petitioning another, and often the one who asks is a better person than the one whom he asks. Who, therefore, takes care not to offend God's eyes when he comes before the throne of divine majesty? You do not speak to a king unless on bent knee, and yet, Erasmus asks with puzzled indignation, you speak to God standing up straight, not physically, but in your arrogance? You do not dare to call upon a human king without wearing fine clothes, combing your hair, and washing and anointing yourself, and you call upon the Lord in so many ways with a sordid conscience? Reverence for the lofty position of princes makes you speechless and captivates your mind, and you speak with your God with yawns as if you were doing something else?[129]

Erasmus' criticism aims at urging his readers to take prayer seriously because it is communication with God, to whom they owe honour and reverence. He does not, however, want to present them with a formidable and fearful God. God's majesty should not deter them from prayer, and thus to promote prayer Erasmus emphasizes that God is above all good.

God's goodness is a hallmark of Erasmus' theology and a central theme of his pastoral writings. We have already observed his emphasis on God's goodness in the *Precatio ad Virginis Filium Jesum*. The *Enchiridion* bids Erasmus' Christian soldiers to trust in the goodness of their divine helper as they struggle against sin and vice.[130] Although God is powerful, his power is not opposed to, nor, as Ernst-Wilhelm Kohls points out, should it be separated from, his goodness towards human beings.[131] Erasmus assures the readers of the *Enchiridion*: 'God alone is truly powerful, who can neither harm even if he wished to, nor wishes to do so even if he could, since his nature is to do good.'[132]

At the outset of the *Enchiridion*'s remedy against 'the promptings of avarice,' Erasmus dissuades his readers from their inclination to love money by reminding them of the ground of their human dignity, that they 'were born and redeemed for one thing only, to enjoy forever the sovereign good.'[133] God is the *summum bonum* and appears as such in other early works on piety by Erasmus. The *Concio de puero Jesu* (1511) encourages schoolchildren to think of Jesus as the 'ocean of all good things,' as the 'utmost good from which all good things flow.' Jesus is the 'sum of every good'; we should therefore 'love him alone, than whom nothing can be better.'[134] In the *Enarratio in primum psalmum* (1515), Erasmus calls Christ the 'source of all good things' and asks: 'For what is it that truly brings peace to the soul if not the supreme good? But is there any supreme good, indeed anything which is entirely good, if not God himself?'[135] The idea of the *summum bonum* also appears in the *Paraphrases on the New Testament*. At Romans 11: 36, Erasmus takes the opportunity to point out again that 'whatever is good proceeds from God as from its source and is conferred through him as through its author.' He begins his paraphrase of James 1: 17: 'As God in his very nature is purely and supremely good, so nothing proceeds from him unless it is good.'[136]

The *Paraphrases* sing out God's goodness. Where Paul's epistles usually end with a wish that the 'grace of our Lord Jesus Christ be with you,' Erasmus renders the Vulgate's *gratia* as *favor* and adds a reference to Christ's goodwill (*benevolentia*) or kindness (*beneficentia* or *benignitas*).[137] His expansion of Paul's farewell in 2 Corinthians 13: 13 reads: 'The favour of our Lord Jesus Christ, and the love of God the Father, and the communion of the Holy Spirit be with you, so that in recognizing the kindness of the Son; the charity of the Father towards you, who so loved you that he gave up his only Son for you; and the goodness of the Holy Spirit, through whom [the Father] imparts to us all his gifts, you may live according to the example of the three persons in concord, purity, and perfection.'[138] This passage shows that, for Erasmus, the divine *summum bonum* is not merely a philosophical principle; it also has a soteriological dimension. The Father's love manifests itself in the sacrifice of the Son. Justification, moreover, 'is given freely by the divine goodness,' righteousness comes through Christ's kindness.[139] The incarnation and the redemption are unthinkable without God's love and goodness. The *Paraphrase on Romans*, from which we have just quoted, explains: 'For unless God had deeply loved us with a kind of supreme tenderness, never would his only Son Jesus Christ by the will of the Father have come down to the earth, assumed a mortal body, and died for us.'[140] Having spoken of Christ, who became incarnate and died for the salvation of humankind, Erasmus in the *Paraphrase on Mark* continues: 'For God, who is merciful and kind by nature, wished in this manner to declare his supreme and inestimable kindness towards the human race – greater kindness one could not ask or dare to expect.'[141]

The subject of divine mercy affords Erasmus the occasion for his most sustained treatment of God's goodness in the *De misericordia Domini concio*, published two months before the *Modus orandi Deum*. God's goodness and mercy manifest themselves everywhere. Every page of Scripture tells of God's mercy. It is a mistake to claim that the God of the Old Testament is not identical to the God of the New, as if the former were just but not good or the latter were good but not just.[142] God's mercy is the origin of all we are and all we possess. The body and soul, the mental faculty of memory, and all the natural human endowments are 'in actual fact the gifts of divine mercy.'[143] His creation of the human race was an act of goodness, but more wonderful was his plan to redeem humanity through Christ's life, teaching, miracles, passion, cross, resurrection, ascension, and through the descent of the Holy Spirit.[144] So 'excessive and immoderate' is God's mercy that whenever we sin we need only repent, and God invites us back into his family, into his bedchamber of charity.[145] Erasmus calls us to trust firmly in God's forgiveness but not without forgiving our neighbours. He believes that it is worse to despair of God's mercy than to deny his existence.[146] In the *Exomologesis*, he writes that to neglect God's goodness seems to offend God less than to deny that he is good and merciful by despairing of his mercy.[147]

This excursus on Erasmus' belief in God's goodness provides the context for and the significance of the image of God that the *Modus orandi Deum* conveys. The parable of the widow who through her untiring persistence obtains justice from the judge who respected neither God nor human beings demonstrates that, if the judge answered the widow's request, God, who is kind by nature, will listen to our prayers all the more. Alluding to Matthew 7: 11, Erasmus observes that the wicked grant the needs of their children; yet the Father in heaven surpasses the natural piety or kindness of the wicked. He who is good and generous by nature and who showers ineffable charity upon his children answers their prayers. Indeed, God is so good that he would bestow his favour upon his children even if they had not petitioned him for it.[148] Elsewhere in the *Modus orandi Deum*, Erasmus comments that prayer always obtains new graces from a most kind God,[149] and who could be kinder than God?[150]

Christians should not fear God when they come before him in prayer. He is their Creator, Erasmus teaches, but he also is their Redeemer. The Lord of all is the same God who is the Father of all who believe in him. God is the supreme judge, but he is the one who surrendered his only Son to death to save all and condemn no one. Although God is a judge, during this earthly life there is still time for mercy, and since God is just, he who promised to deny nothing to those who petition him with faith in the name of his Son will not go back on his promises.[151]

Erasmus' message about God's goodness does not support Jean Delumeau's depiction of religious culture and pastoral care in medieval and early modern Europe. According to Delumeau, these centuries of 'sin and fear' were characterized by a contempt for the world and for the human body, by a morbid fascination with and terror of death and damnation, by a religious culture of guilt. Pastoral care, both Catholic and Protestant, instilled an enduring sense of guilt into sinful humanity. An 'evangelism of fear' was supposed to frighten Christians into repentance; the image of God that it mediated was a 'terrifying image of God as Judge,' a God who took vengeance on sinners, a God whose justice overshadowed his goodness.[152]

Undoubtedly, some preachers may have tried to mould the faith and conduct of their audience through fear, but this was not part of Erasmus' pastoral enterprise. The God of Erasmus is not a God of terror and vengeance. In the *Paraphrase on James*, he writes that God 'is good by nature, desiring of his own accord to do good to all. Whoever asks of him does not ask in vain. He wants to do good to all, and he is able to do whatever he wants.'[153] The purpose of Erasmus' assiduous portrayal of God as good is quite clear. He wishes to encourage his readers to pray, making them feel at ease with God. Far from engaging in any pastoral terror tactics, he offers believers an image of a God whom they can love and trust, a God whose very nature is goodness, a God who in his kindness gave his only Son over to death to redeem the human race. God's justice, moreover, does not contradict his goodness but inspires people to pray with confidence, for their just God will not renege on his promise to grant their prayers.

It is abundantly clear that the God to whom one prays is good, but how does Erasmus understand those who pray? Having declared God's goodness, Erasmus reminds his readers that they are sinners: 'You approach God's throne as a poor little man. Nothing can be imagined more sublime than God, but what can be more lowly than man? For even if one is pious by human standards, nevertheless, the purity of all human beings is impurity when compared to the divine purity.'[154] Erasmus should not be accused here of propagating a dim view of humanity. Above we noted that in the *Enchiridion* Erasmus says that human dignity is grounded in being 'born and redeemed for one thing only, to enjoy forever the sovereign good.' God created the world so that everything would serve the needs of humankind.[155] An often quoted passage from the *Paraclesis* bears witness to the goodness of humanity: the philosophy of Christ is a rebirth, a restoration of nature – and one assumes that Erasmus here means human nature – created in goodness (*instauratio bene conditae naturae*).[156] In the *Modus orandi Deum*, Erasmus insists that, since the Holy Spirit has been given to all Christians, those who pray have the dignity of being priests and prophets.[157] 'Christians, acknowledge your dignity,' he writes in his commentary on Psalm 14 (15), the *De puritate tabernaculi sive ecclesiae christianae* (1536). Erasmus addresses himself to men and women, the young and the old, the poor and the rich, the nobility and those of humble origins, kings and peasants, tailors and weavers, anyone who has been reborn in Christ: 'you are a king, you are a priest, you are holy.'[158] This is an allusion to 1 Peter 2: 9: 'you are a chosen race, a royal priesthood, a holy nation' (RSV).

Erasmus' comparison of sinful human beings with God does not seek to fill his readers with contempt for themselves but aims at preserving their reverence for God and at teaching them that they must be humble when they pray. Given the gulf between human imperfection and divine excellence, what should Christians do when they pray? Erasmus teaches in the *Modus orandi Deum* that they need to raise themselves up on high so that they can speak with the one who dwells in the heavens or rather dwells above the heavens. Yet they do this by humbling themselves, for the more they cast themselves down the closer they come to God. The Pharisee who remembered all his good deeds and felt disgust for other human beings was indeed far away from God in his prayer, but closer to God came the publican, even though he stood farther away from the altar than the Pharisee (Luke 18: 10–14). Quoting Psalm 137 (138): 6, 'the Lord is high and regards lowly things, but lofty things he knows at a distance,' Erasmus explains that God scorns the haughty but has regard for and does not reject the prayer of the humble. In Sirach 35: 21, we read that 'the prayer of the person who humbles himself will pierce the clouds, and he will not be consoled until God draws near, nor does he yield until the Most High takes thought for him.'[159] Perhaps we can detect Erasmus' influence on Becon's *Pathway unto Prayer* when the latter, in proving that the 'humiliation of ourselves helpeth greatly to the avancement [sic] of our prayer,' employs references to the same three scriptural passages and in the same order as Erasmus does.[160]

Some people obviously do not take the importance of humility in prayer to heart, for, as Erasmus complains, proud laypeople fight their way into the priests' choir stalls, while princes are given golden tents near the altar. Some people are so arrogant that they think God owes them something for gracing the divine service with their august presence. The common folk nudge each other out of the way to get closer to the altar, as if they are closer to God than those who stand farther away or as if their prayers will be more quickly heard.[161]

A fanatical and proud attachment to ceremony will not accomplish anything. In his explanation of the meaning of the first verse of Psalm 85 (86), 'Incline, O Lord, your ear and hear me, for I am needy and poor,' Erasmus urges in the *Concionalis interpretatio in Psalmum LXXXV* (1528): 'Let us incline our ear to his commandments so that he [i.e. God] may be pleased to incline his ear to our prayers. In short if we wish his loftiness to incline to us, our pride should incline to him.' To be sure, God does not listen to those who boast of their own merits. By what right may someone ask that God incline his ear? The answer lies in being 'needy and poor.' The needy and poor realize that all they have comes not from their own merits but from God's gratuitous kindness.[162] A humble dependence upon and trust in God's goodness will no doubt assure Christians that God will listen to their prayers.

In the *Modus orandi Deum*, Erasmus demands humility of the sinner. 'Cast off the burden of sin,' he admonishes, and follow the example of the publican in the temple, of Mary Magdalene, and of Peter. Throw yourself upon the ground and beat your breast; weep at the feet of Jesus; go out with bitter tears as if unworthy of Christ's presence.[163] The more they humble themselves through contrition and rejection of their faults, the more sinners can draw near to God.

It is, of course, not enough for Christians to prostrate themselves before God physically; they must also do so spiritually. Their spiritual prostration shows that they recognize their sinfulness and beg God's pardon. Having humbled themselves, they leave behind the allurements and cares of the world and raise themselves up to God by flying to him, for prayer is a sort of flight of the soul (*volatus animae*).[164] The dove, a bird of innocence, should be their model. 'You are a dove,' Erasmus explains, 'if you do not think ill of anyone, if you judge no one, if you do not suspect anyone falsely.' The dove's two wings represent the contempt for worldly things and the desire for heavenly things. The one wing takes Christians away from whatever smacks of the flesh, the other brings them to God's throne.[165]

God does not pay attention to prayers that are not made in the spirit of humility. He also is deaf to them if one prays without faith. Faith itself is a form of humility because it demands the abandonment of reliance upon one's own capabilities and the placing of all one's trust in God's help. His help, which he has promised to us 'if we implore it with ardent and earnest prayers,' is a most sure defence against evil.[166] In the *Modus orandi Deum*, Erasmus quotes Paul, who tells the Philippians (4: 6): 'Do not be anxious about anything, but in every prayer and entreaty with thanksgiving make your petitions known to the Lord.' Erasmus comments that the anxious, those who distrust heavenly help and put their faith in human might and talent, will not be heard when they pray.[167] In his paraphrase of the passage from Philippians, Erasmus has Paul say: 'Depend on him [i.e. Christ] with all your hearts. But if you are in need of anything, do not put your trust in the protection of the world, but importune God with earnest prayers.'[168]

Erasmus' insistence that his readers put their faith in God and in no one else recurs throughout the *Paraphrases*. He concludes the story of how Jesus saved his disciples from the storm at sea (Matthew 8: 24–7) with a lesson. In this episode, Jesus taught that 'whenever the storms of temptation and persecution rage against us, we should seek help from no other person than him.'[169] In the *Paraphrase on Mark*, Jesus says: 'If you want to flourish, have faith, not in your strength, but in God ... He who doubts will have no effect. For he who doubts either believes that the Father cannot grant it – when he can do anything with a word – or that he does not wish to grant what is rightfully sought.'[170]

When Paul at 2 Corinthians 12: 9 asks three times that the thorn in his flesh be removed, and God answers that his grace should be sufficient for Paul, Erasmus also has God assure Paul that under his divine protection he will be safe and invincible. When Satan and the world oppress weak humanity, the spreading of the Gospel should rely on God's power, not on human aid.[171] We read in the *Paraphrase on James* that it is a mistake to put a half-hearted trust in God by not abandoning the search for human assistance, or to implore God's help but have no faith in him, as if he does not sufficiently desire the welfare of humanity, or cannot bring it about, or does not keep his promises.[172]

Along with faith, Jesus in Mark's Gospel makes the forgiveness of one's neighbour a prerequisite for genuine prayer. In the *Paraphrase on Mark*, we learn that our prayer accomplishes nothing if we ask God to forgive us our trespasses and do not wish to pardon others. Jesus expostulates: 'when you set yourself to pray, forgive in your heart anyone who has offended you in any matter; on this condition your Father who is in heaven will pardon your sins. For if you are unwilling to forgive your neighbour the wrong committed against yourself, your heavenly Father will not be indulgent towards the sins committed against him.'[173] Jesus imparts this teaching not only with words but also by the example of his life. 'Desiring to serve as the most perfect exemplar of supreme forbearance,' he prayed on the cross that the Father forgive those who reviled him. The 'holy prayer of our high priest on the altar of the cross' was not without effect, for, as Erasmus remarks in the *Paraphrase on Luke*, many of those who put him to death professed his name after hearing the preaching of the apostles.[174] In the *Modus orandi Deum*, Erasmus advises his readers that when they speak with the Most High they must purify their hearts of any grudge they harbour against their neighbour.[175] In his commentary on Psalm 85 (86), he repeats that God will listen only to the humble, to the 'needy and poor.' What effrontery it is to refuse to forgive a neighbour while expecting God to hear one's prayers! Erasmus writes: 'Your neighbour has sinned against you and cries: "Forgive me, I have sinned," and you do not put aside your anger. In vain you, too, will cry to God: "Incline your ear."'[176]

Erasmus also makes his point in his paraphrase of 1 John 5: 14. The original text, referring to Christ, reads: 'And this is the confidence which we have in him, that if we ask anything according to his will he hears us' (RSV). In the *Paraphrase on 1 John*, Erasmus does not limit himself to writing: 'Indeed the Spirit of Christ shows you this confidence, that you will obtain whatever you ask of the Father in the name of the Son.' He believes it is necessary to add a condition. You will obtain what you ask for, 'provided that you ask according to his [i.e. God's] will.' Praying according to God's will means in part to be 'pure of all fraternal hatred, for he, from whom his neighbour does not obtain pardon for his faults, will obtain nothing from God.' To pray in conformity with God's will also means to ask for the chief spiritual object of human desires: whatever pertains to eternal life and the glory of Christ.[177]

Pardoning the sins of one's neighbours is an important duty of Erasmus' Christian soldier. In the *Enchiridion*, Erasmus stresses forgiveness as a remedy against anger and the desire for revenge. He encourages his Christian soldier to see extenuating circumstances in the actions of those who offend him. Perhaps the person who hurt him is young and inexperienced. He will also more readily forgive the slight sins of his neighbour when he considers the many times he has gravely offended God.[178] However Christians wish to understand those who sin against them, they cannot escape the obligation of forgiving them. Their prayer is futile if they refuse to forgive because in denying others their forgiveness they refuse to improve themselves spiritually, and thus they refuse to become like the merciful God to whom they pray.

Mutual forgiveness is a great sign of Christian concord. For Erasmus, the peacemakers whom Jesus pronounces happy are the people who forgive those who offend them. Jesus calls these peacemakers the sons of God (Matthew 5: 9), and they are worthy of this title, as we read in the *Paraphrase on Matthew*, if they forgive their brothers in imitation of the heavenly Father, who, in pardoning all sins, invites all human beings to peace and friendship with him.[179] Jesus' confirmation that 'if two of you agree on earth about anything they ask, it will be done for them by my Father in heaven' (Matthew 18: 19, RSV) provides Erasmus with the opportunity to advocate the necessity for human concord in prayer. In the *Paraphrase on Matthew*, Jesus says that our 'consensus,' our agreeing with one another, will not only take effect in forgiving one another our sins, but also will be proved 'if at least any two people are found on earth who are truly of one heart (*concordes*) with my spirit, that is, who are not influenced by human desire but in harmony (*concorditer*) love divine things, whatever they ask, they will receive from my Father who is in heaven. So much does the Father love the holy concord of the Gospel.' We may beseech the emperor, who may not be able to grant our requests right away, if at all, but, Jesus concludes, 'there is nothing so difficult or unbelievable which my Father cannot bestow upon you if you petition him in harmony with one another (*concorditer*).'[180]

This human concord is, more specifically, the concord of the church, of which the apostles praying together with the women, with Mary, Jesus' mother, and with Jesus' brothers (Acts 1: 14) are an image. These are the first Christians, the first members of the church, who have come together in Jerusalem, which in Hebrew means 'vision of peace.' No one lives in Jerusalem, Erasmus maintains in the *Paraphrase on Acts*, who makes his home in this world, whose mind is made restless by worldly desires, who does not long for the peace of eternal life. Erasmus then describes the beginnings of the church in Jerusalem. The first Christians do not waste their time on quarreling or on useless talk, but 'all persevere with one mind (*unanimiter*) in holy prayers,' for 'the church of Christ is not found where there is no unanimity.' God takes no pleasure in prayers said without fraternal concord, when one person prays for wealth, another for the death of his enemy, another for long life, and another for royal power. Where different people pray for different things that are not in the common interest, where there is no unanimity of purpose in prayer, there one cannot find Christian prayer, the prayer of the church.[181]

Christian concord, therefore, is an essential ingredient of Christian prayer. Without concord, moreover, prayer will have no effect. If peace does not bind Christians together, their petitions will not be answered. In the *Paraphrase on Jude* (1520), Erasmus writes: 'Accordingly, by constantly imploring God's help with pure and spiritual prayers, keep each other safe in mutual concord and in mutual charity. For God does not listen except to those who are of one heart (*concordes*).'[182] On one occasion when the early Christian community was at prayer, the place in which they were staying was shaken (Acts 4: 31). Erasmus explains in the *Paraphrase on Acts* that the tremor was a sign that God had heard and approved the prayer and remarks: 'There is nothing so efficacious as the prayer of the church in agreement with itself.'[183]

Erasmus' association of prayer with peace indicates that those who pray, pray as members of the church. Peace is a necessary requirement for the church's existence. 'Remove peace,' Erasmus warns in the *Querela pacis* (1517), 'and the whole community of Christian life is destroyed.'[184] To Justus Jonas, the German humanist and a supporter of Luther, he points out in 1521 that the word 'church' is emptied of meaning if it does not include the notion of concord and asks: 'For what is our religion, if not peace in the Holy Spirit?'[185] In the preface to his edition of the works of St Hilary, the church father, Erasmus states categorically in 1523: 'The sum and substance of our religion is peace and concord.'[186] According to James Tracy, from Erasmus' point of view to find tranquillity one must look for it in the church,[187] and only in the church, for Erasmus believes: 'outside the confines of the church there is no peace.'[188] True to the example and teaching of Christ, in whom it has its origin and goal,[189] the church must also live in peace with itself. Christ is the church's preceptor in the way of peace as well as of prayer. In the *Modus orandi Deum*, Erasmus recalls Jesus' angry avowal to the buyers and sellers in the temple at Jerusalem that God's house will be called a house of prayer, and he goes on to state: 'The church is the house of God.' Anyone who passes his life within that house, and that means every true Christian, is 'not obliged to do anything other than to pray.'[190]

Having made this remark, Erasmus proceeds to say: 'For prayer is the never-failing dedication to live a consistently pious life.'[191] Becon quotes this sentence in *The Pathway unto Prayer* without attributing it to Erasmus.[192] We have already noted Erasmus' belief that to pray always means constantly to desire God's promise of eternal life. When we pray, when we desire our heavenly inheritance, our lives become spiritually transformed, for a pious life and prayer are the same thing. Prayer cannot simply be confined to words; it cannot be divorced from essential spiritual virtues such as humility, faith, and concord, or from pious actions. In the *Ecclesiastes*, Erasmus instructs preachers to seek wisdom not only with 'assiduous and at the same time ardent prayers' but also with good works. The same goes for preachers when they ask God for the gifts of fluent speech, a sonorous voice, firm lungs, a reliable memory, and a knowledge of Scripture.[193] Erasmus uses Cornelius, the devout centurion, as a scriptural example of his point about the necessary link between prayer and action. Two things prove that Cornelius was worthy of becoming a Christian: his great generosity in helping the needy and his constant prayer to the Lord. The angel in Erasmus' paraphrase of Acts 10: 4 tells Cornelius that God has heard his prayers, 'for your ears have not been deaf to the poor.'[194]

Erasmus practised what he preached. In 1523, he writes to Joost Vroye of Gavere, a friend who taught at the University of Louvain, of his struggle 'to form in my mind a state of perfect confidence in my own salvation.' This is the subject of much inner debate and of conversations with learned friends. Neither Lutherans nor anti-Lutherans can put his mind to rest. The best remedy lies in prayer and good works, yet at the same time Erasmus acknowledges that trust in God's goodness is more efficacious than confidence in his own accomplishments. Erasmus concludes: '... the wisest course seems to me to be to seek security on this point in every way I can from Christ by prayers and by doing good up to the last day of my life, and then leave the decision on this point too to him, but with the feeling that just as I have the least possible hope from my own merits, so I have great confidence from his immense love towards us and his most generous promises.'[195]

In the *Modus orandi Deum*, Erasmus interprets Jesus' words, 'Not everyone who says to me Lord, Lord, will enter the kingdom of heaven, but the one who does the will of my Father who is in heaven' (Matthew 7: 21), not as a deterrent to prayer but as a way of uniting the striving for a pious life with prayer. Without this dedication to piety prayer becomes a mockery. Those who say 'Lord, Lord' and are not afraid of neglecting God's commandments throughout their lives hold him in derision. Yet it is not possible for those who pray from the heart to remain long in their sins or easily to fall back into them.[196] This prayer from the heart transforms Christians, for it cannot but improve them spiritually.

Erasmus proceeds to employ again the combination of rhetorical question and comparison, this time to make the incongruity of impiety and prayer very clear. Prayer leads away from sin; it must not and cannot lead to sin. When someone has an appointment with the emperor and feels superior by virtue of speaking with him, he disdains the company of base people. Yet why does he quickly return to Satan's household after conversing with God? Whoever asks the emperor's pardon makes sure not to offend him again, and whoever desires a special favour of the emperor takes care to remain in his good graces. Yet how can a person pray to the most merciful Lord to forgive all his sins only to return to them right away? Or who has obtained through prayer so many spiritual gifts and still has shown no gratitude for God's great generosity? Continuing his attack on hypocritical prayer, Erasmus moves from exposing the disparity between respect for superiors and disrespect for God to commenting on the incompatibility between the unkind treatment of one's neighbour and devotion to God. How can anyone intercede to God for his brothers and then slander his neighbour or daily sing God's praises and heap calumny upon him for whom the Son of God died?[197]

Erasmus' series of rhetorical questions reveals that he took the setting of prayer within a pious life very seriously and that he wanted his readers to do likewise. Pseudo-Chrysostom also attached great importance to the theme of prayer and a person's spiritual transformation, and this surely contributed to Erasmus' admiration of the two homilies on prayer. Pseudo-Chrysostom compares the soul to a house: what the foundation is to a house, prayer is to the soul. We should lay within our souls the foundation of prayer upon which we can build 'modesty, gentleness, justice, care for the poor, in a word, all the laws of Christ.'[198] Everyone knows that it is simply impossible to live virtuously without prayer. No one, furthermore, can practise virtue without imploring it from the one who bestows every virtue on human beings. The Ninevites, who hearkened to Jonah's warning, show the transforming power of prayer. As soon as the zeal for prayer took hold of them, it made them just, and they immediately reformed the city, which had wallowed in lust and wickedness. Prayer brought with it temperance, kindness, gentleness, concern for the poor; it filled the Ninevites with every form of justice, motivating them to practise virtue and shun vice.[199]

Erasmus fully agrees with Pseudo-Chrysostom: prayer transforms Christians. Prayer leads them to humility, engenders within them a trust in God and a desire for everlasting life, and requires them to love our neighbours. Prayer, in short, makes Christians pious, and that is why Erasmus can call it 'a certain principal part of piety.' Piety comes about through prayer, but a pious life is also the necessary context and condition for prayer. Each nourishes the other.

Given the old and still-enduring interpretation of Erasmus as a moralist who understood Christianity merely as a means to promote virtue, it is important to see that the transformation that prayer brings about is, for Erasmus, decidedly a *spiritual* one. It is incorrect to claim that the 'moral function of prayer was uppermost' in Erasmus' mind or that he subordinated prayer or meditation to morality. To argue that prayer's goal was a 'moral transformation' or 'moral elevation' and was designed 'to establish and maintain higher moral ideals and motivation'[200] is, while beating the old moralist drum, to misunderstand and misrepresent Erasmus' concept of prayer. Prayer does not primarily signify a promotion of virtue but a discourse with God. The supreme object of prayer is to attain a share in God's life, to enjoy eternal salvation in heaven. A virtuous life on earth is a means to that end, but not the end in itself of prayer.

'God is spirit' (John 4: 24), Erasmus reminds his readers in the *Modus orandi Deum*, 'and no one can converse with him unless he speaks in spirit.' Those who associate with good men will become better people by virtue of their association. Therefore, how can it be possible to converse with God and not to become like him, than whom nothing is more pure, sublime, free from care, and peaceful? Someone might object that there are priests and monks who pray all day and night and are not the better for it. Yet they are not really praying because they have not undergone any spiritual change or transformation. They have not really spoken with God because they have not become like him.[201]

Thus, prayer raises Christian minds to God and helps them to become more like God. They do not acquire the virtues that prayer instils within them for the sake of virtue but for the sake of continuing their conversation with God. To pray constantly does not mean to desire virtue but to desire God. In supplying the qualities that maintain the desire for God, prayer transforms Christians spiritually.

We should not reduce the Erasmian conception of prayer to a means for personal moral reform; nor should we exaggerate the spiritual transformation brought about by prayer to the heady heights of mystical union with God. In his close reading of the conclusion of the *Praise of Folly*, M.A. Screech speaks of what he calls Erasmus' 'theology of ecstasy' and 'ecstatic piety.'[202] At one level we can agree with Screech. Erasmian piety is, according to Screech, characterized by 'the reality of the spiritual over and above the material,' by the soul's desire to be liberated from the body that imprisons it, and by the striving for God, the Supreme Good.[203] In the *Modus orandi Deum*, Erasmus writes that in this life the soul is weighed down by the mortal body, and thus the knowledge of the greatness of God's goodness as well as the ability to praise him is imperfect. Life on earth is an exile from the heavenly homeland.[204] At the beginning of the treatise, Erasmus recalls Paul's desire 'to be dissolved and to be one with Christ' (Philippians 1: 23).[205]

Nevertheless, Erasmus does not promote contemplative prayer, the prayer of mystical union with God. Prayer, in the context of Erasmus' discussion, involves neither ecstasy nor rapture. The closest verbal correspondence between Erasmus' understanding of prayer and the argument that he espoused an ecstatic piety occurs on the opening page of the *Modus orandi Deum*. Here Erasmus establishes the following definition of hymn: 'A hymn is when the soul, reflecting upon the sublime nature of God, is caught up (*rapitur*) into his praise, to whom alone all glory is due.'[206] Erasmus does not, however, elaborate on the meaning of the soul's rapture, which in any case he does not identify with ecstatic union. Neither here nor in his comparison of prayer to a flight of the soul up to God on the two wings of the disdain for worldly things and the desire for heavenly things does he guide his readers how to arrive at the point of rapture. For the sake of clarity, it is important to distinguish between the desire for God and union with God. We may interpret the *volatus animae*, the soul's flight to God, as a metaphor for the former and not for the latter, given the lack of a specific ecstatic function of prayer in the *Modus orandi Deum*. Folly says that the pious 'sometimes experience a certain flavor or odor' of the reward of heavenly immortality but admits that 'it happens to *very few.*'[207] In his treatise on prayer, Erasmus speaks to all of Christendom, not to a few individuals. The spiritual tranformation that he requires of all Christians makes them like God, but it is not intended to make them attain an experience, if ever so brief, of ecstatic oneness with God.

Now that we have examined Erasmus' conception of the nature of God and of the identity of those who pray, it is time to move on to his third and fourth categories of analysing prayer: what one ought to pray for, and how one should pray. Since the goal of prayer is spiritual transformation, it is not surprising that the *scopus* or chief object of Erasmian prayer is spiritual. First and foremost prayers must be offered for whatever 'applies to God's glory and to the eternal salvation of humankind.'[208] In conformity with the patristic and medieval heritage, Erasmus believes that the words of Psalm 26 (27): 4 sum up the *scopus* of prayer: 'One thing have I asked of the Lord, this I will seek after, that I may dwell in the house of the Lord all the days of my life.'[209]

Next in importance to praying for God's glory and for salvation come petitions for the public good, which are superior to requests for private needs. Erasmus does not prohibit prayers for temporal needs or comforts, provided that one have nothing else in mind than the 'goal of eternal salvation.' Thus, if anyone asks God for physical health, he does so in order to avoid being a burden on his brothers or in order to benefit his neighbours all the better. When someone prays for a long life for his bishop, he wishes that the bishop's teaching and moral conduct should glorify God and profit the good of the flock. 'We rightly ask for life for our children,' Erasmus writes, 'not so that we may glory in them, but that, after a holy upbringing, they may make progress in the Christian religion.'[210]

Erasmus' *Paraphrases* bear witness to the primacy of salvation as the *scopus* of prayer. He does not confine himself simply to report that Jesus prayed, but, amplifying certain pertinent passages from the Gospels, he portrays Jesus as praying for the salvation of the human race. At Matthew 3: 16, we read that Jesus, having been baptized, emerged from the water and that the Spirit of God descended upon him as a dove. Borrowing from the parallel passage of Luke 3: 21, which adds that Jesus was praying as the Spirit descended, Erasmus supplements Matthew's account. After his baptism, Jesus kneels, raises his hands towards heaven, and prays that 'the Father will desire that the task of saving the human race, which he has begun, will turn out favourably and fortunately for all.'[211] Jesus, as Mark 6: 46 records, left his disciples to pray on a mountain. Erasmus explains that Jesus 'quietly withdrew to the mountain where in solitude he prayed to the Father that the business of the Gospel, having begun well, might progress in like manner.'[212] At Luke 21: 37 we read that, after teaching the people in the Temple, Jesus spent his nights on the Mount of Olives. There, Erasmus imagines, he prayed to the Father 'without interruption for the salvation of the world.'[213]

Luke's Gospel tells the story of the encounter in the temple at Jerusalem between the angel Gabriel and the priest Zechariah, destined to be the father of Jesus' herald, John the Baptist. Erasmus imagines the content of Zechariah's prayer. At one time he frequently importuned God to free his wife from the reproach of a barren womb and himself from the hardship of having no children. Now that he thinks that having a child is an impossibility, he asks God with ardent prayers for the long-awaited public redemption of the people. Assuring Zechariah that the Messiah will soon come, Gabriel tells him that his prayers will be answered: 'You have asked for a Redeemer, you will also receive the Redeemer's herald.'[214] The lesson of Erasmus' paraphrase is clear: it is more important to pray for salvation, for spiritual values, than for the fulfilment of our own emotional and material needs. He uses the story of blind Bartimaeus to convey the same point. The blind man calls out: 'Jesus, son of David, have mercy on me' (Mark 10: 48), yet the many people who 'cry out to Jesus even today' with these words intend something else: 'One says: "Make me rich." Another: "Let me obtain an office." A third: "Give me a wife with a dowry." Yet another: "Give me prowess."Another: "Give me long life." And another: "Let me be avenged on my enemy."' Erasmus points out: 'But these things Jesus often takes away from his beloved people because it is better for their salvation.' In addition, he gives a spiritual interpretation of Bartimaeus' request for Jesus to restore his sight: 'Disregarding everything else, he wished nothing but vision to discern God and his Son, Jesus. To know him is to have eternal life. To know is to see. O truly evangelical prayer! How few words in it and how much faith! Indeed this is the short prayer that reaches heaven.'[215]

Erasmus not only esteems prayers for spiritual goods more than those for material goods; he also warns against the impiety of petitions for private needs if they are not subordinated to prayer's primary object. In the *Enchiridion*, Erasmus remonstrates:

> You pray to God that you may not suffer a premature death rather than pray that he grant you a better frame of mind so that wherever death overtakes you it will not find you unprepared. You give no thought to amending your life, yet you ask God that you may not die. What is the object of your prayer? Obviously that you may go on sinning as long as possible. You pray for riches, but you do not know how to use them. Are you not praying for your own undoing? You pray for good health and you abuse it. Is not your piety really impiety?[216]

Requests for the necessities of this life are not genuine unless they are made with some higher, pious or spiritual purpose in mind. In the *Modus orandi Deum*, Eramus gives the example of David, who prayed for the gift of understanding so that he might learn God's commandments (Psalm 118 [119]: 73). Erasmus criticizes the man who asks for physical health to please the sweetheart whom he loves worthlessly, or for strength to take vengeance on an enemy, or for long life to prolong his enjoyment of this world. The soldier prays that he may return home laden with booty taken from the churches he has pillaged; desiring greater earnings, the impious doctor asks that many people fall sick and stay sick for a long time; someone looking for legacies prays for the death of his relatives. It is a sin, Erasmus declares, to pray for wealth and health more frequently and more insistently than for our principal needs, for faith, charity, and a knowledge of Scripture, things appropriate to mention in our prayers. The common people have the wrong priorities, however, for many do not even ask for the things for which one ought to pray, but, departing from Christ's teaching, they ask God to fulfil their impious requests or seek to harm their neighbours.[217]

Prayers for the necessities of life must also submit to God's will. We make our petitions, Erasmus teaches, upon the condition that God should will it and that it should be conducive to our salvation. To illustrate his point Erasmus composes a prayer for a sick person: 'Lord, health of all the living, if it is possible, take from me this burdensome illness. But may your will be done, not mine. If you, from whom nothing escapes, judge this illness to be necessary for eternal salvation, deal with me as is pleasing to your holy will. Only give me firm strength that I may be able to endure, and in time of temptation grant success that I may be able to continue on.'[218] When Saint Paul persisted in his plan to go to Jerusalem, his friends no longer tried to dissuade him, and, as Acts 21: 14 records, they said: 'The will of the Lord be done' (RSV). Erasmus comments in his paraphrase on the passage: 'This is truly the saying of Christians. It ought to be always in every heart, even if it is not verbally expressed, whatever happy or sad situation is at hand: "May the Lord's will be done."'[219] Jesus supplies the best example of subordinating personal desires to God's will when in Gethsemane he prays for deliverance from his impending passion and death but nevertheless prefers his Father's will to his own. In Erasmus' view, expressed in the *Paraphrase on Mark*, Jesus does this with great confidence, for he trusts that the Father's will 'wants nothing but what is best.'[220] Since God's will is good and wills what is best for Christians, they need not hesitate to allow it to be the judge of the validity of their requests.

Having established that his readers' prayers should never lose sight of a spiritual focus, Erasmus still has to discuss how they are to make their prayers. He begins to answer this question in the *Modus orandi Deum* by considering with which words they should pray. First, they should pray the words that Jesus taught to his disciples, the Lord's Prayer, the greatest of all prayers. Erasmus agrees with the church fathers that one should ask of God only for what is contained in the Lord's Prayer, and thus he instructs that all prayers conform to the seven petitions of the Our Father.[221] Following Augustine, he holds that all the prayers in Scripture, especially the Psalms, correspond to the seven petitions of the Lord's Prayer. Although they differ in wording, in terms of their content these prayers are the same as the petitions of the Pater Noster. In his letter to Proba, Augustine matched these petitions with quotations from Old Testament prayers, most notably from the Psalms.[222] Erasmus does the same in the *Modus orandi Deum*, combining some of Augustine's examples with his own scriptural selections. For example, in Erasmus' estimation the request in Psalm 85 (86): 11, 'Lead me, Lord, in your ways, and I will walk in your truth. May my heart rejoice so that it may fear your name,' is another way of saying to God: 'May thy will be done on earth as it is in heaven.'[223]

Since all scriptural prayers echo some part of the Lord's Prayer, Erasmus, in the second place, recommends using the words of Scripture to converse with God. Someone in need of help against the vice of disparaging and base speech may ask in the words of Psalm 119 (120): 2: 'Lord, deliver my soul from perverse lips and from a deceitful tongue.' Provided that scriptural passages inspire prayer, one need not quote Scripture verbatim. Erasmus takes Jesus' promise, 'If anyone loves me, he will keep my word, and my Father will love him, and we shall come to him and make our home with him' (John 14: 23), and turns it into the following prayer: 'Impart to me, Lord Jesus, your Spirit, so that I may love you and keep your words, that I may deserve to be loved also by your Father and be considered worthy for you to come and dwell together with me for ever.' Grounded in Scripture, prayer can successfully obtain what it seeks because God gladly recognizes his own words.[224]

The ancient collects of the church provide the inspiration for a third way of wording prayers. A collect is the prayer that concludes the entrance rite of the Roman Mass.[225] Through a brief structural analysis of the collects Erasmus shows his readers how to compose their own collect-like prayers. He suggests that they are ideal for imploring help against temptation, obtaining pardon for sins and an increase of faith and charity, and for praying for public peace and the progress of the Gospel. After recommending collects together with prayers inspired by Scripture and the Lord's Prayer, Erasmus leaves his readers free to devise their own prayers, provided that they pray in Jesus' name and that what they ask for does not conflict with the *scopus* of salvation or the petitions of the Our Father. They need not worry about the way they word their prayers because God, who is best of all, takes all in good part and is not offended by solecisms as long as they pray with a sincere mind.[226]

Although Erasmus has nothing against prayers with stylistic and grammatical flaws, he writes that nothing stands in the way of outlining a theory of prayer taken not so much from the precepts of the experts in rhetoric as from the examples of Scripture. He thus embarks on a brief, informal rhetorical analysis of prayer. A prayer should begin by attracting the attention of its listener, namely God. Praise, the sort of complaint (*conquaestio*) that curries favour, and sometimes thanksgiving, a genus of praise, all accomplish this purpose. Praise sometimes expresses itself through a title of respect such as, 'Our Father who art in heaven' (Matthew 6: 9) or 'Lord, you who know the hearts of all' (Acts 1: 24). Since *conquaestiones* can be found throughout Scripture, Erasmus provides no examples of these, but he does give a sampling of *expostulatio* or a remonstration, which often appears together with complaints. Jeremiah (20: 17) exclaims: 'Lord, you have misled me, and I was misled; you were stronger than I, and you have prevailed.' The prophet adds a hint of flattery (17: 17) when he asks God: 'Do not be a terror to me, you, my hope in the day of affliction.' Erasmus calls the thanksgiving of the poor 'ambitious' (*petax*), for 'the one who thanks a very rich donor for past kindnesses is implicitly aiming at a new one.' Prayer also captures God's attention through earnest entreaty. Psalm 101 (102) begins: 'Listen, Lord, to my prayer, and let my cry come to you.'[227]

After we have God's attention, we make a case for whatever we ask, and this is called the *argumentatio*. This part of the petition principally takes four things into account: that God is able, wills, is accustomed, and has a duty to answer our prayers. God is all-powerful; he can do whatever he wills. His will is determined by his goodness and mercy. That God is in the habit of answering our prayers is evident when we recall the examples of others or the benefits that he has often bestowed upon us. God must answer our prayers not because we deserve it but because he has promised to do so. Erasmus points out that in Scripture truth is often associated with mercy as in Psalm 88 (89): 15: 'Mercy and truth go before your face.' It is called mercy because we do not deserve what we ask for, and truth because in a certain way God owes it to us because of his promise. At the end of his rhetorical analysis, Erasmus cautions that the rhetoric of prayer, with its praises, its ways of winning God's attention, its appeals to his promises and to Christ's charity, death, and resurrection, is for our benefit and not for God's. We need to remind ourselves of God's glory, goodness, and faithfulness, of the God from whom we have our salvation.[228]

Having made suggestions to guide his readers in the way to compose prayers, Erasmus takes into account a few questions before bringing the *Modus orandi Deum* to a close: (1) Is it necessary to pray aloud, or will silent prayer suffice? (2) When should one pray? and (3) Where should one pray? He also devotes attention to the prayer of princes and magistrates and to the problem of unanswered prayers.

Erasmus considers it a matter of personal freedom whether to entreat God's mercy with vocal or silent prayers, but he shows his preference for silent prayer when he adds that 'often silent sighs and tears obtain more than loud cries.' He thinks, however, that those who have not yet had much experience in praying should sing aloud holy prayers as they learn how to pray, since the desire of the soul sometimes comes to birth through vocal practice. Thus, as with other 'ceremonies,' vocal prayers are useful inasmuch as they lead us through things visible to the realm of the invisible. For busy people, Erasmus, following Augustine, recalls the example of the early Egyptian monks and recommends short, quickly uttered, vocal prayers, which he calls 'eiaculatae precatiunculae.'[229]

Any time is appropriate for prayer, but we should especially pray at dusk, at night, in the morning, before and after meals, on feast days when the church calls everyone to worship, and in time of affliction or temptation.[230] In the *De praeparatione ad mortem*, Erasmus passes on what he considers some excellent advice. Every person should examine his conscience every evening before going to bed. If a person is conscious of any sin, he should beat his breast and with tears beg God's forgiveness. Having implored God for help, he is ready to emend his life.[231] Occasions for prayer, moreover, constantly present themselves. Erasmus tells the readers of the *Modus orandi Deum* that when sadness weighs down upon them, they should pray. After a happy occurrence they should give thanks to God, seek his forgiveness upon committing a sin, and ask him to increase his gifts within them if any virtuous act has been performed. If they see a person of outstanding virtue, they should ask God that he would have many people be similarly virtuous. If they notice someone whose bad morals are conspicuous, they should pray that God grant him a better mind and preserve them from turning out like him. If anyone becomes a magistrate, he should ask for the gift of wisdom, and upon leaving office, he should pray that he be succeeded by a better man.[232]

As with all times, so also, Erasmus notes in the *Modus orandi Deum*, are all places suitable for prayer: the bedroom, the kitchen, the workshop, on a ship, in a cart, on horseback, the baths, and even the lavatory.[233] In the *Paraphrase on 1 Timothy*, Erasmus writes: 'For Christians every place is pure and also holy for offering up the sacrifices of prayer ... From whatever place people pray to him God will listen.'[234] In the *Modus orandi Deum*, Erasmus' readers learn that the Christian's very heart is God's temple, the place where he finds God's favour and presence. Erasmus teaches: 'The more you withdraw within yourself, the more you enter the sacred inner shrine, the closer you become to God.' This temple should remain pure. If the mind becomes polluted, it should be cleansed with prayer.[235]

Erasmus, who commanded the respect of Europe's crowned heads, devotes a few pages to advising princes and magistrates on the relationship between the spiritual life and public office. Before they undertake any official task, they should ask for God's help, but their prayers should be short. A king about to meet with his council should quietly pray to God in this way: 'O God, without whose Spirit nothing is done rightly, favour this council with your presence so that nothing will be decided that offends your majesty.' While taking his seat in court, a judge may silently pray: 'Lord, may your wisdom, which governs all things, be present so that no innocent person may suffer what he does not deserve and no injury may come to anyone while I preside as judge.'[236]

The piety of a Christian prince in part consists of performing his office with God's help and in God's presence. Prayer should help princes in performing their duties well; it should not interfere with them. Erasmus is aware that many princes, in imitation of the clergy, like to say the divine office, even if they do not understand the words they speak. He does not condemn this practice, but he prefers princes to spend less time in reciting psalms and more time in discharging their responsibilities to their people. If they do have any leisure, they would profit more from thoroughly learning God's commandments or from reading works such as Aristotle's *Politics*, Cicero's *De officiis*, Plato's *Republic*, or even Erasmus' *Institutio principis christiani* or his argument for peace and against war, the essay on the adage *Dulce bellum inexpertis*, than from saying the office.[237]

Erasmus brings the *Modus orandi Deum* to a close with a consideration of the problem of unanswered prayers. He does not want his readers to give up on prayer because they do not receive what they ask for. Unanswered prayers are the result of divine providence or of human sinfulness. If God denies what we pray for, he does it for our own good, just as a father denies the request of a beloved son when he realizes that the son's petition is harmful. When our prayers go unanswered, we should embrace God's goodness and believe that he has something better in store for us, or that there is some just cause, especially an offence against a neighbour, that disqualifes our prayers. Erasmus underlines the latter explanation: 'Unkindness (*inhumanitas*) towards a neighbour closes the ears of God.' Erasmus attacks the hypocrisy in those who refuse to help others and who cannot understand why God will not help them: 'You turn a deaf ear to a needy brother who begs you for help, and he does not murmur against you; and if he does murmur, you cannot bear it. And you find fault with God if he does not immediately give you what you ask?'[238] Prayer is a form of piety, but it is only truly pious and therefore genuine and efficacious when it is accompanied by a pious life. God will only listen to those who call upon him if their piety combines prayer and love of neighbour.

While discussing ways of attracting God's attention in prayer, Erasmus admits in the *Modus orandi Deum* that it does not matter much to which person of the Trinity one addresses one's petitions. Nevertheless, he thinks it is more fitting (*aptius*) to ask the almighty Father for help against enemies and demons, more appropriate (*accommodatius*) to pray to the Son to reconcile the Father to us, and more suitable (*congruentius*) to seek an increase within us of divine grace from the Holy Spirit.[239] Here Erasmus explicitly applies the principle of accommodation to prayer. Prayer, like all discourse, is amenable to rhetorical analysis, and, like all good discourse, it should demonstrate propriety. Throughout the *Modus orandi Deum*, Erasmus teaches what is appropriate to the sacred rhetoric or divine colloquy of prayer. That is the purpose underlying the book's four categories of analysis. In his accommodation or pastoral service to western Christendom, Erasmus shows his readers how to accommodate themselves to or converse appropriately with God.

In the twenty-five years that separated the writing of the three prayers for Lady Anna van Veere and her son and the publication of the *Modus orandi Deum*, Erasmus' concept of prayer did not undergo any drastic changes. Over time he elaborated on ideas already evident in 1499, namely that prayer has a Christocentric aspect, requires and brings about a spiritual transformation, assumes a good and merciful God as its recipient, and seeks eternal life as its goal. He also developed his concept of prayer by adding new elements to it. The *Enchiridion* introduces the idea of prayer as conversation with God, an idea that demonstrates the interplay between Erasmus' humanism and his promotion of piety, as do his philological discussion of *deēsis, proseuchē,* and *enteuxis,* and his rhetorical analysis of prayer in the *Modus orandi Deum.* In the *Enchiridion,* Erasmus also for the first time mentions prayer as a weapon with which Christians fight against vice and the devil, against anything that would separate them from God. Prayer's ally is knowledge. Through the *Modus orandi Deum* and other writings, such as the *Paraphrases on the New Testament,* Erasmus, as a pastor for western Christendom, provides the fundamental knowledge required to pray well.

He teaches his fellow Christians about silent and vocal prayer, gives advice about the time and place of prayer, and shows where to seek inspiration for prayer. That Scripture provides the best teaching about and examples of prayer and that it should be the principal source of inspiration for appropriate discourse with God indicates what lies at the heart of Erasmus' pastoral programme. Christians must read Scripture and live according to its teachings. The scriptural nature of prayer emerges as another fundamental Erasmian principle of prayer. It is closely linked with the Christocentric nature of prayer. For the teachings of Scripture are the teachings of Christ, and prayer becomes Christocentric if Christians conform themselves to Christ's teaching and to the way he prayed.

Since prayer is human discourse with God, it is no surprise that the focus of Erasmus' thinking and teaching about prayer is on the relationship between God and human beings. God's majesty and power are to be revered and praised, but in God these two attributes neither oppose nor overwhelm his goodness. By nature God is good, kind, generous, and merciful. Christians always have reason to hope that God will give them a favourable hearing as long as they prove worthy to be heard. God will hear them if they make salvation their primary petition and if their prayer proves to be a constant effort to live piously. Humility, faith, forgiveness, concord, and a heart-felt concern for one's neighbour are the forms of piety that prayer engenders within Christians. They are also the necessary prerequisites for any genuine and sincere conversation with God. Thus Erasmus' primary pastoral aim is to instil within his contemporaries the right spiritual disposition for prayer. This is what the *Modus orandi Deum* is all about. In writing about prayer, Erasmus demands that his readers become spiritually transformed. He wishes to cultivate in them a loving desire for God manifested within a pious life.

TWO

Critique, Reform, and Defence of Prayers to the Saints

※

Writing in 1531 to Jacopo Sadoleto, bishop, humanist, and his most fervent supporter in the Roman curia, Erasmus complained of the 'great conflict' over prayers to the saints and the reverence shown to images.[1] This conflict arose in the wake of the Protestant Reformation. Indeed, a year before Erasmus wrote his letter to Sadoleto, Lutherans and Catholics had crossed theological swords over the invocation of saints at the Imperial Diet of Augsburg. Chapter 21 of Philip Melanchthon's Augsburg Confession undermined the practice of invoking the saints by denying it any scriptural justification. Arguing from Scripture and tradition, the Catholic Confutation of the Augsburg Confession upheld the practice. Melanchthon's refutation of the Catholic position, the Apology for the Augsburg Confession, accused the Catholics of denying that Christ was the sole mediator of redemption. By claiming that the saints were intercessors for humankind, the Catholics made the saints into co-redeemers with Christ or even replaced Christ with the saints.[2]

The controversy over the place of the saints in Christian devotion provoked more than debate and polemics among theologians. It often broke out into the violence of iconoclasm, which itself may be interpreted as an expression of a popular theology. Through the destruction of church furnishings and of images of Christ and of the saints many ordinary people asserted their own theological conviction about what was most important to them: God's presence. Iconoclasts were convinced that 'God and Christ could not be "present" through the images in the churches.' Christ was to be found 'not in things, but in acts of brotherly love, gestures, relations, behavior, and in the culture that would structure the lives of evangelical Christians – the Reformed communion service, the cadences of the Christian year, and preaching.'[3] Erasmus, of course, could not draw the same conclusion. For him, violence was antithetical to theology and piety.

In January 1522, shortly before Luther returned to Wittenberg from the Wartburg, Andreas Bodensee von Karlstadt, a theologian at the University of Wittenberg, preached that all images should be removed from the town's churches. Although the town council decided to consent to Karlstadt's demand, an impatient crowd 'pulled down and burned many images.'[4] In Zwingli's Zurich, a new wave of iconoclasm began in September 1523. At the end of October, the Second Zurich Disputation concluded with a condemnation of images and of the Mass. After some temporizing, the town council on 15 June 1524 ordered the removal of images from the churches. Sometimes as in Bern and in Sankt Gallen in 1528 the destruction of images came on the heels of municipal ordinances.[5] In Basel, however, when on 9 February 1529 the town council proved reluctant to give in to the demand for the abolition of the Mass and the elimination of the images, a Protestant mob vented its frustrations in the cathedral. The image-breaking forced the council to concede the Protestant demands and compelled Erasmus to leave his beloved Basel for the Catholic town of Freiburg im Breisgau.[6]

The cult of the saints, which had become a matter of such dispute, began with the reverence for those who witnessed to the Christian faith with their blood, the martyrs. The first written piece of evidence that we have of the cult comes to us from AD 160 in an account of the martyrdom of Polycarp of Smyrna. The Christian community at Smyrna relates that it has acquired his bones, treasures more valuable than precious stones and gold, and has interred them in an appropriate place. There they will gather to celebrate 'with joy and gladness' the anniversary of Polycarp's martyrdom.[7] With the elevation of Christianity to the official religion of the Roman empire, the ranks of the saints came to include, after the apostles and martyrs, the confessors, ascetics, popes, bishops, priests, monks, doctors of the church, founders of religious orders, and important kings.[8]

From its earliest beginnings the cult of the saints emerged as popular religion *par excellence*. Peter Brown advises that we should not conceive of popular religion as 'popular superstition' or within the framework of a 'two-tiered' mode of Christian society comprising the 'enlightened few' who tolerated the less refined devotional practices of the 'vulgar.'[9] Brown's admonition about understanding popular religion holds not only for late antiquity but also for the Middle Ages. Eamon Duffy is convinced that in late medieval England 'no substantial gulf existed between the religion of the clergy and the educated elite on the one hand and that of the people at large on the other.' Duffy urges: 'We should resist any simplistic division of late medieval religion into high against low, élite, churchly, or official against popular.'[10] The cult of the saints was popular religion precisely because it enjoyed the support of all Christian people, clergy and laity, the literate as well as the illiterate. Ambrose made much of acquiring the relics of Saints Gervasius and Protasius for his basilica in Milan, Augustine established the cult of Saint Stephen in Africa, and, a millenium later, Jean Gerson (d. 1429), the chancellor of the University of Paris, vigorously promoted the cult of Saint Joseph, who by the fifteenth century had still not achieved a special place in Christian devotion.[11] Thomas More, defending pilgrimages to the shrines of saints, avowed in 1529: 'And surely I byleue this deuocyon so planted by goddes owne hand in the hertes of the hole chyrche that is to wyt not the clargye onely but the hole congregacyon of all crysten people that yf the spyrytual-tye were of the mynde to leue it yet wolde not the temporaltye suffre it.' More could not really imagine, however, that the clergy would want to abandon pilgrimages. He was 'very sure that many an holy bysshop and therwith excellently well lerned in scrypture and the law of god haue had hygh deuocyon therto.'[12]

The cult of the saints was popular not only in terms of its adherents but also by reason of its pervasiveness. The saints were everywhere. Churches were dedicated to them, and altars contained their relics. The saints' physical remains were placed on display in reliquaries. In honour of the saints, medieval people went on pilgrimages to local shrines and to distant places, especially to Rome, the city of Saints Peter and Paul, and to Compostela, where Saint James was believed to be buried. A saint was considered to be especially present and powerful at his or her earthly resting place. Relics were not the only aids for devotion to the holy men and women of the past. Duffy reminds us that by the late Middle Ages the focus of devotion had shifted from relics to images. 'The men and women of late medieval England,' he writes, 'were busy surrounding themselves with new and refurbished images of the holy dead, laying out large sums of money to provide lights, jewels, and precious coverings to honour these images.'[13] Of course, the very days of the year also reinforced the commemoration of the saints, whose feasts were celebrated within the liturgy of the church and often by public parades. The saints deserved great honour in part because they could exercise a great deal of influence with God by interceding for their devotees. Kingdoms, towns, and guilds sought the patronage or protection of specific saints: 'Patron saints personified the communal identity of their city, town, village, and nation; they cast their protective mantle across generations; they brought the faithful together in processions to commemorate past favors and implore future ones.'[14] Yet the saints' protection was not limited to political, social, or economic groupings. During the Middle Ages, people prayed to the saints for protection from crop failure, plague and disease, blindness and physical pain such as toothache, and sudden death.

Even before Luther entered the monastery in 1505, Erasmus had begun criticizing popular piety in the *Enchiridion* (1503). The cult of the saints, or rather the superstition that had become part of it, became one of his important targets. The author of the *Enchiridion* would be inclined to disagree with Brown, since in Erasmus' opinion 'most Christians are superstitious rather than pious.'[15] For Erasmus, popular piety verged on popular superstition. Paying attention to the external trappings of religion, the unwashed multitude has reduced devotion to a series of mechanical observances robbed of any sort of spirituality. People mumble psalms without knowing what they are saying, they take delight in ceremonies but do not grasp their spiritual significance, they put on a great show of outward devotion without demonstrating any signs of spiritual growth. Erasmus warns the Christian soldier: 'Do not be swayed by the fact that you observe the majority of mankind living as if heaven and hell were some sort of old wives' tales, bugbears, or childish enticements.'[16] The sixth rule of the *Enchiridion* states that 'the mind of one who aspires after Christ should be in complete disaccord with the actions and opinions of the crowd and his model of piety should be Christ alone and no other.'[17] Erasmus explains: 'The common crowd has long been a poor model of life or judgment.' He compares them with 'those in Plato's cave, who, chained by their own passions, marvel at the empty images of things as if they were true reality.'[18] It is necessary therefore to 'hold the common crowd with its opinions and actions in complete contempt.'[19] Suggesting the creation of a vernacular liturgy in the *Modus orandi Deum*, Erasmus concedes that he is not entirely sure whether the time has come to change from the Latin, for 'it is the nature of the multitude to revere what it does not understand.'[20]

Erasmus' low opinion of the common people manifests itself in his ecclesiology. In the preface to the third edition (1518) of the *Enchiridion* and in the *Ratio verae theologiae*, Erasmus portrays the church, 'the whole people of Christ,'[21] as a social hierarchy consisting of three concentric circles with Christ as the common midpoint. Closest to the midpoint in this hierarchy is the first circle, which contains the clergy. The priests and bishops must pass on Christ's purity to the members of the second circle, the secular princes. Farthest away from Christ in the third circle stand the common people.[22]

Despite their lack of cultivation, the common people nevertheless belong to the body of Christ. As inferior members of that body – shins, feet, and privy parts – they 'must be given more indulgence, but in such a way as to invite them, as far as possible, to follow the things that Christ approves.' Erasmus' disdain for the unrefined majority of Christians thus does not signify utter rejection. He is willing to accommodate himself to them. Although the common people may be the least in the Christian republic, they are still its members and require special attention from their pastors. Erasmus believes that the people 'in their weakness must be tolerated and fostered with paternal indulgence, following the example of Christ, who so gently tolerated and fostered his disciples, until by degrees they grow to maturity in Christ.'[23] The Christian soldier, while remaining separate from the common crowd, must not be like the Cynics who snarled 'indiscriminately at the beliefs and deeds of others.' No, Erasmus advises in the *Enchiridion*, 'You, too, must be all things to all men, so that you may win everyone to the side of Christ, as far as it is possible, without giving offence to piety. Adapt yourself to everyone exteriorly, provided that interiorly your resolution remains unshaken. Exteriorly let your friendliness, affability, good nature, and obligingness win over your brother, who should be attracted to Christ in an appealing manner and not put off by harshness of behaviour.' Nevertheless, one must not make too many concessions to the weakness of the common people so as to lack 'the courage to defend the truth vigorously when the occasion arises. Men must be corrected, not deceived, by kindness.'[24]

Thus, from the *Enchiridion* we can discern Erasmus' fundamental pastoral approach towards the shortcomings and excesses of popular piety in general and of the cult of the saints in particular. In principle, superstition must be condemned. In practice, the pastor must take into account the weakness of the flock but without failing to witness to the truth and against falsehood. Although in his kindness the pastor must correct and not deceive, his correction must be kind and not severe. Erasmus unfailingly criticizes the superstitious elements of praying to the saints, but he does not reject the practice completely. His pastoral accommodation encompasses not only relentless criticism but also a genuine desire to reform and even defend the cult of the saints. He provides his contemporaries with a valid way of honouring the saints by redirecting it to an imitation of the virtues of the saints and by keeping Christ as the focus of piety. When the Protestant reformers call for the suppression of the invocation of the saints, Erasmus refutes their arguments and is even ready to tolerate superstition if it cannot be corrected without violence.

The young Erasmus, as a 'man of the Middle Ages,'[25] was influenced by medieval popular piety, specifically by the cult of the saints. In Paris, he occasionally preached on saints' feast-days[26] and became a devotee of the city's patron saint, Geneviève. In January 1497, he writes an older friend at Steyn that he has recovered from a bout of quartan fever 'not by a physician's help (though I had recourse to one) but by the aid of Ste Geneviève alone, the famous virgin, whose bones, preserved by the canons regular, daily radiate miracles and are revered: nothing is more worthy of her, or has done me more good.' Erasmus also reports that Paris had been subjected to almost unceasing rain for the past three months. The saint who had helped the Augustinian canon also came to the rescue of her city. Her shrine 'was brought from its usual place of keeping to Notre Dame. The bishop and the whole university went forth to meet it in solemn procession, led by the canons regular, then the abbot, and all his monks walking barefoot.' Erasmus' concluding remark witnesses to the efficacy of the invocation of the saint: 'Now the sky is perfectly clear.'[27] In 1500, he relies again on the patroness of Paris. He tells his friend Jacob Batt of his fear that another attack of fever will finish him off. Yet Erasmus does not despair, 'for I trust in Ste Geneviève, whose ready help I have more than once enjoyed.'[28]

In the years preceding the *Enchiridion*, Erasmus shared with his contemporaries the commonly held beliefs about the saints. They exercised a localized patronage, they brought healing to those who prayed to them, and the veneration of their relics resulted in miracles. Since they successfully intervened in human affairs, the saints were worthy of one's trust and devotion.

Devotion to the saints also manifested itself in Erasmus' early poetry, written in the 1490s. His conversion from poet to theologian had not yet been completed, for the secular letters of the great writers of Latin antiquity still held first place in his heart.[29] Yet, without restraining his enthusiasm for the pagan Latin authors, he was ready to make religious themes, the 'praise of holy men and of holiness itself,' a subject of his verses.[30] Erasmus praised Gregory the Great, the only holy man whom he celebrated in verse, and wrote poems in honour of the three archangels, Michael, Gabriel, and Raphael, and all the angels, of Saint Anne,[31] and of the Virgin Mary. In honour of Mary, he composed a short paraphrase of the *Salve Regina* and a lengthy ode.

According to Harry Vredeveld, Erasmus wrote the *In laudem beatissimi Gregorii papae* in the winter of 1490–1 for his monastery of Steyn, which was dedicated to the famous pope.[32] He invites heaven and earth to celebrate the happy feast of Gregory, and praises the pope for his humility and his dedication to the pastoral care of his flock. Before ending with a Trinitarian doxology, Erasmus asks Gregory, 'greatest of bishops,' to protect his people and to keep the devil from carrying off anyone from the pope's flock.[33]

Erasmus published the ode *In laudem Michaelis et angelorum omnium* along with his poem on the house of Jesus' birth (*Carmen de casa natalia Jesu*) in Paris in 1496, but he seems to have written it five or six years earlier.[34] He did not like the poem in praise of the angels very much. In 1523, he remembered that he had written it 'not of my own choice, but driven to it by the appeals of a certain great man who presided over a church dedicated to St Michael.' Erasmus refused the remuneration of his 'generous patron,' namely 'money to buy a pint of wine – which was about what the poem was worth.'[35] He addresses petitions to Michael, Raphael, and all the angels. Through his prayers Michael should 'make the mild king of heaven take pity on us and sheathe his avenging sword, make him grant us a holiday, and give the weary world a rest.'[36] Raphael receives the request to heal our bodies and minds and to 'drive from the earth the plague which rages, alas, so fiercely against your charges.'[37] Erasmus reminds us that all the angels bring our prayers to God and return with gifts. This is how we thank them: 'our muse remembers to sing hymns of thanksgiving and we bring offerings to the churches dedicated to you. When the year brings around your feast-days, here we envelop your images with solemn incense, here the choir prays to you earnestly, raising its hands in supplication.' We ask that 'our prayers may always penetrate to the ears of our Father on high and that they may be validated by you, O patrons and blessed guardians of the family of Christ.'[38]

In 1501, Erasmus informed Lady Anna van Veere: 'I am sending you a version of yourself – another *Anna* – in the shape of a poem, or rather a set of verses which I threw off when I was a mere boy; for ever since my earliest years I have burned with eager devotion to that saint.'[39] Given Erasmus' desire to maintain Anna's patronage, one probably should take his long-standing 'eager devotion' to Saint Anne with a grain of salt. Nevertheless, it was in keeping with the times to honour Anne, revered as the mother of the Virgin Mary and the grandmother of Jesus. In the West, her cult took root in the fourteenth and blossomed in the fifteenth century. It developed in part as a result of the growing acceptance of the doctrine of the Immaculate Conception of Mary. Several German humanists, among them Rudolf Agricola and Johannes Trithemius, sang the praises of Anne. In 1519, Jacques Lefèvre d'Etaples was one of the first writers to challenge the medieval legend, the so-called *trinubium*, that, after the death of her husband Joachim, Anne was married two more times. This challenge provoked a refutation from Noël Béda, the prominent watchdog of theological orthodoxy at the University of Paris.[40] Erasmus must have known Agricola's poem, *Anna mater*, first published in 1484, as well as Baptista Mantuanus' *Parthenice Mariana* (1481), whose first two books tell the story of Anne and Joachim 'at epic length,' since he mentions to Lady Anna that her patron saint is 'celebrated in the eloquent works of Rodolphus Agricola and Baptista Mantuanus.'[41]

Erasmus probably wrote the first version of the poem, the

Rhythmus iambicus in laudem Annae, aviae Iesu Christi, in the winter of 1490–1 and augmented it later for presentation to Lady Anna. The poem first appeared in print in the *Epigrammata*, a collection of his poetry published in 1518.[42] Erasmus greets the saint, 'blessed in having a holy spouse, an even more holy daughter, a most holy grandchild,' who is 'the Word of God and God himself.' The prayers of the elderly and barren Anne and Joachim are answered when an angel prophesies that they will have a child. Anne gives birth to a daughter, 'and not just any daughter, but a daughter who would be fertile and give birth while still remaining a virgin.' The end of the poem assumes a chain of intercession that begins with Anne, continues through Mary and Jesus, and ends with God the Father:

> O mother blessed, thrice blessed and more, give aid – for you can – to the prayers of us mortals who honour you devoutly on this holyday, for under your patronage there is nothing we do not hope to obtain, as long as you wish it and your daughter also wishes it; and when she asks for anything, her little boy will not know how to refuse her. The Son loves his mother, nor will his Father refuse his Son, for he, too, loves his Son. Amen.[43]

Probably written in 1499, although never published in Erasmus' lifetime, were his paraphrase of the *Salve Regina* and his long sapphic ode, *Paean divae Mariae, atque de incarnatione verbi*. The paraphrase closely adheres to the original prayer, although it does not appeal to Mary as 'our advocate' (*advocata nostra*). Vredeveld argues that the lack of this title is entirely due to the fact that *advocata*, a trochaic word, cannot fit into the poem's elegiac metre.[44] The *Paean* recalls the title of the prose prayer, *Paean Virgini Matri dicendus*, also written in 1499. Vredeveld points out the thematic parallels between the ode and the prayer.[45] The two paeans correspond in their exuberant praise of Mary. She seems to become an object of worship when Erasmus addresses her in the poem: 'For you are the unique glory of the highest heavens; you alone, O divine lady, had the power to revenge our death and to take vengeance for the life that was stolen from the whole world.'[46] As the 'greatest of goddesses' she placates God the King for 'fearful sinners.' By virtue of being the mother of Christ, Mary is a most effective intercessor for human beings in trouble:

Can your son, O mother, refuse you anything you ask for, and is there anything you can ask for that he does not have the power to provide for you, whom one so great has singled out and venerated with such a great honour?

Therefore all mortals rightly wear you out with their complaints and prayers, whenever they are crushed by any kind of suffering, fearing the countenance of their terrible judge.[47]

After 1499, Erasmus the poet became a theologian, and as a pastoral theologian he subjected popular piety to criticism. He treats the cult of the saints within the context of the fourth and fifth rules of piety that he propounds in the *Enchiridion*. An expression of Erasmus' Christocentrism, the fourth rule states: 'place Christ before you as the only goal of your life, and direct to him alone all your pursuits, all your endeavours, all your leisure time and hours of occupation.'[48] Learning and the pursuit of knowledge, material possessions, 'honours, pleasures, health, and even the life of the body,' the exercise of a trade, family life, fasting, and the desire to become a priest – all of these things must have Christ as their goal.[49]

That piety too must be Christocentric is what Erasmus has in mind when he begins to consider 'those who honour certain saints with certain specific ceremonies.' People invoke and worship Christopher to avoid a violent death, Roch to remain free of the plague, Barbara or George so as not to be captured by enemy soldiers. Fasting in honour of Apollonia prevents toothaches, visiting statues of Job relieves itching, and lighting candles to Hiero restores lost property. The result of all these ceremonies is that 'we have appointed certain saints to preside over all the things we fear or desire.' What is more, these saints do not exercise the same power in all places, for their efficacy depends on the country in which they are invoked.[50]

The object of most prayers to the saints is pure folly. That is the argument of the goddess of that name in the famous *Praise of Folly*. She observes that none of the votive tablets to the saints in churches commemorate an escape from folly or an increase in wisdom. Folly chuckles at those who believe they were helped by the intervention of a saint:

One saved his life by swimming. Another was stabbed by

an enemy but recovered. Another, with no less luck than bravery, fled from the battle while the rest were fighting. Another who had been hung on the gallows fell down by the favor of some saint friendly to thieves, so that he could proceed in his career of disburdening those who are sadly overburdened by their riches. Another escaped by breaking out of jail. Another, much to the chagrin of his physician, recovered from a fever. For another, a poisonous potion, because it worked as a purge, was curative rather than fatal, though his wife (who lost her effort and expense) was not exactly overjoyed at the result. Another, whose wagon had overturned, drove his horses home uninjured. Another, buried by the collapse of a building, was not killed. Another, caught by a husband, managed to get away.[51]

In his apology for the *Praise of Folly*, a letter written in 1515 to the Louvain theologian Maarten van Dorp, Erasmus argues that his criticism of the cult of the saints was not intended to overthrow the cult but was 'confined to the superstition of those who do not venerate saints in the way they should.'[52]

The purpose of the *Enchiridion* and the *Praise of Folly* is, according to Erasmus, one and the same, the only difference being that he uses humour in the latter work to guide, help, and improve others.[53] In both works, he charges that the contemporary devotion to the saints borders on the superstitions of ancient paganism. In the *Enchiridion*, he comments that if the devotion to particular saints for particular benefits is not 'redirected towards Christ,' then it is not very different from offerings made to individual pagan gods for personal gain. 'The names may have been changed,' he writes, 'but the purpose remains the same.' In the *Praise of Folly*, he draws a parallel between Saint George and Hercules. In this saint, misguided Christians 'have discovered a new Hercules ... They all but worship George's horse, most religiously decked out in breastplates and bosses, and from time to time oblige him with some little gift. To swear by his bronze helmet is thought to be an oath fit for a king.'[54]

Erasmus' recipe for reform calls for a spiritual transformation of the cult of the saints: devotion to the saints must divest itself of the pursuit of material favours and must reorient itself towards Christ.[55] Expounding the important fifth rule of the *Enchiridion*, Erasmus shows how this transformation can take shape. In his fifth rule, he seeks to reform piety by subordinating the external manifestations of piety to their underlying, inner meaning. Here the motto is: 'per visibilia ad invisibilia.' In the case of the cult of the saints this slogan for reform demands an imitation of the saints' virtues. 'You venerate the saints,' Erasmus observes, 'and you take pleasure in touching their relics. But you disregard their greatest legacy, the example of a blameless life.' True devotion to Mary requires above all an imitation of humility, to Peter and Paul an imitation of the former's faith and of the latter's charity. The best way to honour Francis is to 'despise sordid gain and covet the goods of the mind.'[56]

Erasmus' insistence on imitating the saints is genuine. In the *Vidua christiana*, for example, he recommends Mary to widows as a great example of virginity.[57] On three occasions, he praises Elizabeth of Hungary, a sainted queen who lived in the early thirteenth century. In her dedication to her husband, to Christ, and to matters of church and state, she not only avoided 'becoming tainted by any contagious evils but she also inspired many others to the love of God.' From Elizabeth widows can learn to avoid making a show of their piety and to come to the aid of the poor.[58]

Although Christ is the exemplar of all piety, Erasmus concedes in the *Enchiridion* that 'if you take great delight in worshipping Christ in his saints, then make sure you imitate Christ in his saints and in honour of each saint eradicate one vice or strive to attain a particular virtue.' Thus Erasmus' reformed cult of the saints places Christ at the centre of the devotion to his saints. The transformation at which the reformed cult aims is more than a moral one; it is spiritual, for it serves Christ. If Christians become transformed to be more like Christ through their devotion to the saints, Erasmus will 'not be averse' to its 'external manifestations.'[59]

We can safely assume that he would include invocation among these external manifestations, for he himself invoked the help of saints. He not only prayed to Saint Geneviève, but he also, at least on one occasion, appealed to Saint Paul. In the summer of 1514 on the road to Ghent, Erasmus' back became wrenched with pain when his horse shied. His servant helped him dismount, but Erasmus found it too painful to remount and finish the journey. He wrote to his English patron, Lord Mountjoy: 'I made a vow to St Paul that I would complete a commentary on his Epistle to the Romans if I should have the good fortune to escape from this peril.' Soon the injured scholar had the strength to remount and ride into Ghent. Feeling much better the next morning, he 'returned thanks to God and St Paul.'[60] The saint would have to wait three years, however, for Erasmus to publish his *Paraphrase on Romans.*[61]

Ten years after the journey to Ghent, Erasmus wrote in the *Modus orandi Deum* that the cult of the saints comprises mainly three things: imitation of their lives, honour, and invocation.[62] In the sermon that he added in 1525 to the liturgy in honour of the Virgin of Loreto, he teaches that 'the cult of the most holy Virgin consists especially in four things, in praise, honour, invocation, and imitation.'[63] Since imitation does not exclude invocation, it is incorrect to conclude: 'In place of the intercessional *cultus divorum* of the medieval Church, Erasmus proposed an emulatory piety. The only way to honor the saints was to follow their example.'[64] Although he emphasized imitation, Erasmus did not advocate the abolition of invocation. Indeed, calling upon the saints in prayer can accompany imitation. Simple people should be taught to remember in their prayers the virtue for which a particular saint was famous. To the Virgin Mother they should pray: 'Obtain for me from your Son the gift of your chastity and modesty.' They should ask Saint Paul: 'Bravest herald of the Gospel, commend me to Christ so that by the grace of his help, I might be able to put into practice what he taught us through you.' Those who pray to Saint Martin should say: 'Help me with your prayers so that in enduring wrongdoing I might be able to imitate your gentleness.'[65]

While Erasmus offered sound pastoral advice in order to reform the cult of the saints, he continued to expose and poke fun at superstitious practices associated with the cult. Throughout the 1520s and 1530s the ever-expanding editions of the famous *Colloquies* became the prominent outlet for his satire. Yet here, as with the *Praise of Folly*, his ridicule should not be considered in isolation from his desire to reform piety. Walter Gordon, who links Erasmian satire to reform, contrasts Luther with the author of the *Colloquies*. Whereas the former believed that a reformer should attack abuses 'with great authority and seriousness,' Erasmus 'had great confidence in the curative powers of congenial laughter in leading men to a point where they are convinced of their erroneous ways. Comedy provides the honey to the medicine of reprimand.'[66] Franz Bierlaire has described the *Colloquies*

as a 'guide for the Christian life.' Erasmus might not be exactly
what one would call a saint, but the type of Christian that his *Colloquies* seek to portray is not far from being one.[67] Erasmus, who
made no pretensions to being a saint, saw the *Colloquies* as conducive to teaching the 'elements of piety.'[68]

In *Confessio militis* (1522), a soldier, Thrasymachus, tells his
friend that on the battlefield he put his trust in Saints Barbara and
Christopher. Barbara indicated her favour with a slight nod of
the head of her statue. Christopher's image, drawn with coal on a
tent, provided Thrasymachus with a source for daily contemplation.[69] Two Franciscans, Bernard and Conrad, visit an inn in *Ptochoplousioi* or *The Wealthy Beggars* (1523). After the innkeeper
overcomes his distrust of them, he wishes that Conrad would
stay to preach the following day, the feast of Saint Anthony. This
is a special day for the village swineherds, who are convinced
that Anthony guards their pigs and who would not neglect the
saint for fear of his wrath. Conrad wishes that the swineherds
would truly honour the saint and, echoing a familiar Erasmian
theme, explains to the innkeeper: 'Whoever imitates the saints
pays them the most holy form of devotion.' Unfortunately, the
villagers, as the pagans once feted Bacchus, celebrate Anthony
with drinking bouts, dances, games, and fights.[70] *Alcumistica*
(1524) is the story of a priest and charlatan who manages to get
the financial backing of the learned but gullible Balbinus for his
gold-making enterprise. With Balbinus' money the alchemist
makes offerings to the Virgin Mother in order to secure her blessing. Mary's patronage does not, of course, bring success to the
production of gold, yet it does prove useful when the priest-turned-lover, having entreated Mary on his knees, escapes from
the bedroom of the wife of an angry courtier.[71]

Ichthuophagia or *A Meal of Fish* (1526) is Erasmus' longest colloquy. After the butcher and fishmonger have exchanged stories of
the superstitions of monks and of simple folk, they ridicule popular devotion to the saints. Many people put more trust in the Virgin Mother or Christopher than in Christ. Sailors in a storm
appeal to these two or any other saint before they ask for Christ's
help, and they sing the *Salve Regina* to the Virgin, a hymn they do
not even understand. Soldiers act in the same way. They think of
George or Barbara before Christ. As for imitating the deeds of the
saints, they all reject this form of devotion, pleasing as it is to
Christ.[72] The butcher and fishmonger also deride those who think

they find safety in the robes of the Benedictines or the Franciscans,[73] while in *Exequiae seraphicae* (1531), Philecous and Theotimus turn the practice of being buried in the cowl of a Franciscan into an occasion for laughter. In this colloquy, Erasmus exposes the superstition that one must take care not to provoke the anger of the saints above. It matters little that Francis was the most innocent of men or that, while they lived on earth, no one was kinder than Cornelius, gentler than Anthony, or more patient than John the Baptist. 'But now,' explains Theotimus, 'how terrible are the diseases that they inflict, unless they are properly honoured.'[74]

The most extended treatment of the cult of the saints in the *Colloquies* appears in *Naufragium* (1523) and in *Peregrinatio religionis ergo* (1526). The 'cruel' satire of the former tells the story of how various people react as a storm at sea breaks apart their ship. In the latter, a 'merciless text,' a pilgrim recounts his experiences at Compostela, Walsingham, and Canterbury.[75]

Naufragium scorns the extravagant trust that the common people put in the saints. In singing the *Salve Regina* and in imploring Mary by titles not found in Scripture, such as star of the sea, queen of heaven, mistress of the world, and harbour of safety, the sailors of the unhappy ship have replaced Venus with the Virgin as their protectress. These men were sincere in their superstition, unlike the fellow who at the top of his voice promised Christopher a veritable mountain of a candle in the largest church in Paris but in private admitted that, if he got to shore, he would not even offer the saint a mere tallow candle.[76] Adolph, the principal interlocutor and a passenger on the ship, refused to cut a deal with the saints. Instead, praying a *Pater Noster*, he went straight to God the Father, for God hears petitions more quickly and grants them more gladly than any saint.[77]

In the *Peregrinatio*, Ogygius, the pilgrim, relates that Saint James at Compostela was uncommonly frigid since 'this new persuasion which has made its way far and wide around the world has brought it about that he is greeted more infrequently than usual.' Pilgrims no longer bring donations, but only greetings, insisting that it is more appropriate to give the money to the poor.[78] A similar vein of Erasmian sarcasm comes to the surface in Ogygius' account of his visit to Canterbury. It does not make sense that so many treasures should accumulate at the shrine of Thomas Becket, who in this life was 'most generous towards the poor.'[79] The popular propensity for venerating relics also becomes the subject for ridicule. At Canterbury, Ogygius kissed the rusty sword that killed Saint Thomas, as well as his bones, pallium, and bloodstained handkerchief,[80] while at Walsingham he venerated three suspiciously large finger bones of Saint Peter and gazed upon 'the heavenly milk of the Blessed Virgin.' His interlocutor Menedemus marvels how alike mother and son were. Jesus poured out so much blood for us, while Mary left behind so much milk that it was hard to believe that a mother of one child could have had as much milk as she did, even if the baby had nothing of it to drink.[81]

As the 'new persuasion' of the Reformation tried to eradicate praying to the saints, Erasmus continued to hammer away at the familiar themes from the *Enchiridion*. In the *Colloquies*, he attacked popular devotion to the saints for having nothing to do with Christ and for not leading to an imitation of the saints' lives. His biting sarcasm did not, however, amount to an alliance with the 'new persuasion,' a persuasion that Menedemus calls 'impious.'[82]

Menedemus suspects that all the saints are threatened by the same plight of Saint James: a decline in devotion, if not real neglect. Ogygius recites a letter concerning the 'new persuasion' from Mary, the mother of Jesus, to Glaucoplutus, an alias for Zwingli. She thanks this 'follower of Luther' for arguing for the superfluity of the invocation of the saints. Previously, she had been worn out by the perverse petitions of mortals who asked all sorts of things of her, as if her son were still a baby and would not dare deny a request from his mother. Although the onslaught of silly prayers has subsided, Mary is still not content, for a greater evil has befallen her. Now hardly anyone honours her, and Glaucoplutus is casting out of the churches whatever belonged to the saints. The saints will not allow the attack on their cult to go unpunished. For her part, Mary warns that if she must go, her son, whom she holds in her arms, goes with her. Glaucoplutus should carefully consider whether he wants a church without Christ.[83]

In 1526, in the *De utilitate colloquiorum*, an apology for the *Colloquies*, Erasmus defended himself against the charges that he had mocked praying to the Blessed Virgin or to the other saints. His ridicule is confined to those who ask of saints what they would not ask of a good man, to those who think that one saint will or can grant prayers more quickly than another or even than Christ himself. With justification Erasmus points to his *Pietas puerilis* (1522).[84] Gaspar, a youth obviously schooled in Erasmian piety, likes to stop in at Saint Mary's Church to pay his respects to Christ and to some saints, especially to the Virgin Mother and to his patrons, Paul, Cyprian, Jerome, and Agnes. He asks that his patron saints commend him in their prayers to Christ and bring it about that he might eventually join their heavenly company.[85] Gaspar's devotion keeps Christ at its centre and seeks the highest spiritual good, eternal salvation, as its goal.

More evidence that Erasmus did not reject the invocation of the saints may be found in another colloquy he published in 1522, the *Apotheosis Capnionis*, a sort of eulogy on the famous German Hebraist, Johannes Reuchlin, whose last name in Latinized form was Capnio. Reuchlin had died in 1521. Brassicanus tells Pompilius of the vision of a certain Franciscan who saw Reuchlin's wondrous entry into heaven. Although Reuchlin has not yet been canonized by the Roman pontiff, the two interlocutors agree that the recently deceased scholar should be included in the calendar of the saints. Promising to hang up his image in their chapels and libraries, they see him as a patron saint of the humanists, of those who study and love languages and literature, especially Scripture. Brassicanus believes that Reuchlin, while his memory is held holy and his name is praised, should often be greeted with these words: 'Oh holy soul, show favour to languages and to those who study them. Promote holy discourse, and do away with wicked discourse, infected by the venom of hell.'[86] Brassicanus then recites a collect of his own composition. It recalls that God through his servant Johannes Reuchlin has renewed the gift of tongues once given through the Holy Spirit to the apostles for the preaching of the Gospel. Brassicanus asks God to grant that all people in every language and in every place, tell of the glory of his Son Jesus to the confusion of the false apostles, who plot to build an impious tower of Babel to obscure God's glory.[87]

In 1521, Erasmus had similarly canonized his old friends, John Colet, the dean of Saint Paul's Cathedral in London (d. 1519), and Jehan Vitrier (d. 1521?), the scholarly Franciscan of the monastery at St Omer in Artois. They were 'truly and sincerely Christians.' Erasmus advises Justus Jonas not to hesitate 'to add the names of both to the calendar of saints, although no pope may ever write them into the canon.' He concludes his letter to Jonas with the following prayer to his departed friends: 'O blessed souls, to whom my debt is so great, assist by your prayers your friend Erasmus, who is still struggling with the evils of this life, that I may find my way back into your society, never thereafter to be parted from you.'[88]

In the canon of the saints, the Virgin Mary occupied the pre-eminent place; she was always the first to be invoked in the litany of the saints. The declaration of the Council of Ephesus (431) that Mary was the *Theotokos*, the mother of God, gave impetus to a special devotion to the Virgin that developed and grew over the subsequent centuries. Medieval Europeans honoured Mary with images and statues, poetry and song. They dedicated countless shrines, churches, and abbeys to her and showered upon her a panoply of titles. They hailed her as their mother and queen and, under the titles of 'mediatrix' and 'redemptrix,' associated her with the salvation accomplished by her son Jesus. Medieval theology developed the doctrines of the Assumption and of the Immaculate Conception, although the latter continued to be a source of controversy. By the end of the Middle Ages, Mary exercised a universal patronage over Christendom. Artists depicted her as the 'Schutzmantelmadonna,' the patroness under whose cloak all orders of society found refuge.[89]

Erasmus felt uncomfortable with many of the manifestations of the cult of Mary. He had nothing against the old custom of daily prayers commemorating 'the Virgin Mother who can never be praised enough.' Yet he seemed to regard as excessive the many daily offices that constituted the Hours of the Blessed Virgin Mary, the staple of the medieval Books of Hours.[90] In the *Modus orandi Deum*, he writes that he prefers the daily recitation of 'the liturgy of the Virgin Mother' to the superstitious and magical prayers that some people say. Unacceptable, however, is the twisting of scriptural texts about the church as the spouse of Christ or about the wisdom of the Father to refer to Mary. The opening hymn of the Hours of the Blessed Virgin, the *Memento rerum conditor*, asks Mary: 'Protect us from the enemy and receive us at the hour of death.' Erasmus objects that such a petition is more appropriately addressed to the Virgin's son.[91]

Another form of devotion that provoked Erasmus' displeasure was beginning a sermon with a prayer to Mary. Like many other preachers, Jean Gerson, who has been called 'one of the greatest preachers of the Middle Ages, perhaps the greatest preacher at the beginning of the fifteenth century,' commonly began his sermons with an *Ave Maria*.[92] The butcher in *Ichthuophagia* complains that those who expound Scripture from the pulpit prefer to invoke the help of the Virgin Mother rather than Christ or the spirit of Christ. Anyone who dares to mutter against this so-called praiseworthy practice falls under the suspicion of heresy.[93] At the outset of his sermon on God's mercy, Erasmus notes that some priests customarily greet the Virgin Mother when they preach, but he feels that it would be more appropriate for his hearers to join him in a prayer to Jesus Christ, 'the almighty Word (*Sermo*) of the Eternal Father,' asking that they might more fully understand Christ's mercy, give thanks for it, and show mercy towards their neighbours.[94]

Erasmus took no firm stand in the debate over the doctrine of the Immaculate Conception of Mary. Yet, according to Léon Halkin, he believed that it was 'more favourable' and 'more probable' to hold that Mary was conceived without original sin.[95] To Noël Béda, his main adversary in the faculty of theology at the University of Paris, Erasmus points out in 1527 that he was never aware of believing that the Virgin was conceived in original sin, and, moreover, that for almost thirty years he had subscribed to the opposite opinion. Although it is impious to take away any praise rightfully due to the Virgin, Erasmus none the less warns that it is far more dangerous to make any creature equal to Christ.[96] Béda had accused him of holding that Christ alone was free of sin.[97] Erasmus assures Béda that the Virgin Mother would be pleased if the decision about how to honour her would be left to her son.[98] Given his dislike of the burdening of Mary with honorific titles and Folly's exclamation that so few people imitate Mary's 'chastity, her modesty, her love for the things of heaven,'[99] Erasmus' additional comment to Béda makes perfect sense: 'If only the most holy Virgin had as many imitators of her virtues as exaggerators of her dignity.'[100]

The main problem for Erasmus with the popular cult of Mary, as with that of all the saints, is that it stands in the way of a Christocentric piety. As Halkin notes, Erasmus 'ferociously' opposes any teaching that 'places Mary side by side with Christ, if not ahead of him.'[101] Folly remarks: 'Some saints have a variety of powers, especially the virgin mother of God, to whom the ordinary run of men attribute more almost than to her son.'[102] The fishmonger in *Ichthuophagia* complains that, while people honour

Mary with images, candles, and canticles, they offend Christ with an impious life.[103] In the colloquy *Concio sive Merdardus* (1531), Erasmus ridicules one of his critics, the Franciscan preacher Metardus or Medardus, who in 1530 attacked his Latin translation from the Greek of the *Magnificat*. Hilarius, indignant at the preaching of 'Merdardus,' sarcastically explains that it is only right to honour the Virgin with a sermon on Saturday and Christ with a sermon on Sunday so that the Mother may take first place.[104]

Erasmus certainly severely criticized the popular cult of Mary, yet it is insufficient simply to dwell on Erasmus' criticisms and unduly hostile to claim that he cleared the path for 'Lutheran errors.'[105] He did not reject devotion to Mary; he tried to reform it in his own way. The wit who ridiculed the pilgrimage to the Virgin of Walsingham himself visited this Marian shrine as a pilgrim. On 9 May 1512, not long before setting out for Walsingham, he informed his friend Andrea Ammonio, the Italian humanist: 'I have taken a solemn vow for the happy outcome of the church's affairs. I see you approve my piety already! I am to pay a visit to Our Lady of Walsingham, and I will there hang up a votive offering of a Greek poem. Look for it if ever you visit the place.'[106] Erasmus' poem appeared along with the *Enchiridion* in the 1515 edition of the *Lucubrationes*.[107] It salutes the 'blessed mother of Jesus, unique among women as the virgin mother of God.' Some people may offer her gold, silver, or precious stones, but Erasmus, 'a poet well disposed though poor,' presents verses, 'for that is all I have.' Indeed, what could be more appropriate from a humanist scholar who lived by his pen? Erasmus not only draws a contrast between the gifts of other pilgrims and his own gift; he also indicates that their petitions are quite different from his own. While some people pray for health, wealth, offspring, and a ripe old age, Erasmus begs the Virgin 'for a great prize: a devout heart, completely free for once from sin.'[108] At the same time his poem both criticizes popular piety and suggests a way to reform it. It shows that a pious desire expressed in a prayer makes a better gift for Mary than glittering treasures. To ask to be free from sin is to pray for the ability to imitate the Virgin's sinless life as well as for one's own spiritual transformation. Such a request is superior to the desire for material comforts.

Ogygius also knows how to pray like Erasmus. He addresses this prayer to Mary after being shown some of her milk: 'Virgin

Mother, you who were worthy to nurse with your virgin breasts the Lord of heaven and earth, Jesus your son, we ask that, purified by his blood, we may also advance towards that happy childhood of dovelike innocence, which, unaware of malice, fraud, and deceit, eagerly desires the milk of Gospel teaching, until it grows into the perfect man, in the measure of the fullness of Christ, whose happy company you enjoy for ever with the Father and the Holy Spirit.'[109] Ogygius conforms his piety to the fifth rule of the *Enchiridion* by subordinating his reverence for the visible mother's milk to a prayerful consideration of the invisible and metaphorical milk of the Gospel. In another prayer to the Virgin, he fulfils Erasmus' demand that a devotion to the saints requires an imitation of their virtues in order to draw closer to Christ. We come to the most pure Virgin, Ogygius confesses, as impure devotees, and we ask her: 'May your son grant that in imitating your most holy character we may merit through the grace of the Holy Spirit to conceive the Lord Jesus within the womb of our soul and never to lose him once he is conceived.'[110]

The most conspicuous evidence of Erasmus' Marian devotion is the Mass he composed in 1523 in honour of the Virgin of Loreto, a shrine consisting of Mary's house in Nazareth miraculously transported by angels, as it was believed, to Italy in 1295.[111] He wrote the *Virginis matris apud Lauretum cultae liturgia* at the request of Thiébaut Biétry, the parish priest of Porrentruy in the Swiss canton of Bern. The liturgy won the approval of Biétry's ordinary, Antoine de Vergy, the archbishop of Besançon, who on 20 April 1524 issued a diploma decreeing that Erasmus' Mass be celebrated in the churches of his diocese and remitting forty days of imposed penance to all who celebrated it with religious sincerity.[112]

Into the second edition of the liturgy (1525) Erasmus inserted a sermon whose main theme was the necessity of imitating Mary's virtues for a proper devotion to her. Furthermore, whatever is worthy of imitation in the Mother is ultimately a gift of her son.[113] The sequence of the liturgy is a hymn in praise of Mary's virginity. It asks the Virgin to turn away the wrath of God,[114] who in the other prayers of the Mass does not at all appear as an angry God to be placated. The *secreta* or secret, the prayer said over the bread and wine at the end of the offertory, invokes Jesus as the 'source of all good things,' and the final prayer of the liturgy refers to worshipping God in his kindness.[115] Erasmus addresses the opening collect to God the Creator, who is glorious in all his saints, especially in Mary, and who rejoices in being glorified at Loreto by the many miracles performed through her. Through this collect Erasmus reminds those who venerate the Virgin of Loreto that Christ must be the centre of their devotion. The celebrant of the Mass asks God that 'those who devoutly worship you in the Son and the Son in you, and who venerate the Son in the Mother and the Mother because of the Son, may be freed through heavenly protection from all evils.'[116]

While Erasmus pilloried the superstitious abuses of the cult of the saints and indicated how to reform the cult, he also defended praying to the saints from the attacks of the 'new persuasion' of Protestantism. To Alberto Pio, the deposed prince of Carpi and 'the toughest of his Catholic detractors,'[117] he insisted that he had published the *Liturgia* 'against the detractors of the Virgin.'[118] Erasmus also tried to persuade others of his Catholic credentials by linking his *De libero arbitrio*, published in September 1524, to the *Modus orandi Deum*, which appeared in print the following month. Three letters from Basel bear witness to this. In October 1524, Erasmus wrote to Gian Matteo Giberti, an official in the papal curia and the bishop-elect of Verona: 'Recently I sent [you] the book, *De libero arbitrio*; now one about the invocation of the saints and and about some other themes is being printed.' This second book was the *Modus orandi Deum*. In February 1525, Erasmus mentioned to Jean Lalemand, secretary to Charles V, the hostile 'Lutheran faction': 'It was raging most furiously at me before I wrote anything against Luther. Now with the publication of the books *De libero arbitrio* and *De modo orandi* it is not safe enough for me to remain here any longer.' In March 1525, Erasmus informed Jean, cardinal of Lorraine: 'I am now sending you the book *De libero arbitrio*, which I have written against the teaching of Luther. If I feel that this interest of mine pleases you, I will soon send you the book *De modo orandi Deum*, in which against the same man I have asserted the cause of the invocation of the saints.'[119] Indeed, Erasmus devoted a long section of the *Modus orandi Deum*, roughly one-fifth of the text in the second edition, to responding to the Protestant critique of the invocation of the saints.

Over the preceding fifteen centuries, very few people had doubted the legitimacy of praying to the saints. Augustine defended the cult of the martyrs from the charges of idolatry made by Faustus, his old Manichean mentor. Christians, stated Augustine, commemorated the martyrs to imitate them, to associate themselves with their merits, and to be helped by their prayers, but they did not honour them with *latreia*, the sort of worship due to God alone.[120] Jerome, in a polemic against Vigilantius, a priest from Aquitaine, attacked the calling into question of the ability of the saints in heaven to pray for those below. If the apostles and martyrs were able to pray for others on earth, why should they not be able to do so all the more once they have entered their eternal reward?[121] Thomas Aquinas justified praying to the angels and the saints by distinguishing between praying to God for the fulfilment of some request and praying to the saints to obtain this request through their own prayers.[122]

Only with the advent of the Reformation did the cult of the saints become a real point of contention within western Christianity.[123] Yet as Georg Kretschmar and René Laurentin have pointed out, the cult did not prove to be a principal theme of controversy in the sixteenth century, at least from the perspective of the Reformation begun in Luther's Wittenberg.[124] Robert Kolb believes that in the northern regions of Germany that became Lutheran 'the pious had apparently never cultivated an intimate relationship with the holy departed precisely like that in most areas of Western Europe.' Since the cult of the saints was not firmly rooted in these areas, it comes as no surprise that Protestantism never subjected it to major attacks. 'Luther,' comments Kolb, 'wrote no *On the Veneration of the Saints* comparable to his *On Monastic Vows*.'[125] Indeed, not only the reformers in Saxony but also those in Franconia, Switzerland, and Strassburg devoted more effort to abrogating the Mass, closing monasteries, devising new services of worship, and debating the presence of Christ in the Eucharist than to writing polemics against praying to the saints and venerating their relics.

The Reformation did not, of course, ignore the issue of the invocation of the saints. In 1530, ten years after burning the papal bull that threatened him with excommunication, Luther claimed that tearing himself away from the saints was a bitter experience, for he had been thoroughly inebriated with devotion for them.[126] His repudiation of prayers to the saints did not coincide with the Ninety-five Theses of 1517; it occurred a few years later. Indeed, Peter Manns shows that in writings of 1519 and 1520 Luther both held and provided a theological justification for the doctrine of the intercession and the invocation of the saints.[127] In his *Sermon von Bereitung zum Sterben* (1519), Luther bade the dying person to find solace in calling upon all the saints, especially his guardian angel, the Mother of God, and the apostles. In his exposition of the *Magnificat* (1521), he advised that one should invoke Mary so that through her God will grant our requests. For the same reason, one should invoke all the saints so that the work may remain God's alone.[128] Luther's acceptance of prayer to the saints, however, did not prevent him at the same time from doubting the reliability of the legends of saints' lives; denouncing the canonization of saints; attacking the view that each saint possessed a special power that could alleviate a specific complaint; and criticizing pilgrimages to shrines, the veneration of relics, and the belief in the miracles attributed to the saints.[129]

In 1522, Luther showed the first signs of rejecting the invocation of the saints. Writing at the end of May to Johann Lang, a friend and one of the pastors of Erfurt, he expressed his astonishment that the 'whole world' was asking questions about the cult of the saints. He wished that such an unnecessary issue, by which Satan leads people away from faith and charity, would go to sleep. 'Content with Christ alone and with God the Father,' the Luther who in the previous year had encouraged the invocation of Mary and all the saints could no longer remember when he had stopped praying to the saints.[130] In July, Lang received Luther's *Epistel oder Unterricht von den Heiligen*, some advice for the pastors of Erfurt. Having repeated his claim that honouring the saints was unnecessary, Luther counselled the pastors to tolerate the weak and to allow them to invoke the saints, provided that they put their trust in no saint, but in Christ alone. The faithful should learn 'to abandon unnecessary things and to grasp Christ as the only necessity, for we must at last abandon the saints and ourselves, so that we know nothing other than Christ.'[131]

Karlstadt's patience with the weak had already run out. On Christmas Day 1521, he celebrated the first Evangelical Mass, reading the words of the institution of the Eucharist aloud in German and administering communion in both species to the laity. In the long preface to his treatise on monastic vows, *Von gelubden unterrichtung* (1521), Karlstadt also argued against praying to the saints.[132] By 1523, Luther, who attacked Karlstadt for his radical ideas and practices, was also scarcely willing to tolerate the weak and their old religious observances. Martin Brecht notes that, 'without further consideration for the weak,' Luther strongly advocated the receiving of communion in both kinds. He called for the abolition of private Masses, and his appeals for the reform of the Roman Mass with its self-styled nature as a sacrifice grew in angry forcefulness.[133] In one of his macaronic sermons of 1523, Luther scowls that he would have devotion to Mary eradicated solely on account of its abuses.[134]

The canonization in Rome on 31 May 1523 of Benno, bishop of Meissen (1066–1106), a diocese in neighbouring Albertine Saxony, provoked Luther's wrath against the old faith. Shortly before the exhumation and reburial of the saint's bones on 16 June 1524, Luther attacked the canonization of Benno in *Wider den neuen Abgott und Teufel, der zu Meissen soll erhoben werden*.[135] It was obvious from this angry blast that Luther no longer would make concessions to the weak as far as the cult of the saints was concerned.

By no means one of the reformer's important writings, *Wider den neuen Abgott* nevertheless contains the essential elements for his condemnation of praying to the saints. First, just as the newly canonized Benno is an 'Abgott' or idol, so the cult of the saints is a form of idolatry. It diverts people away from God's grace and Christ. Those who invoke the saints do not praise God but blaspheme him. In putting their trust in the saints, they abandon faith, deny God, and turn the saints into idols.[136] Second, Scripture provides no basis for devotion to the saints. It says little or nothing about the saints in heaven but speaks only of the saints on earth, the people, for example, to whom Paul addresses his letters. Luther asserts: 'If we want to live according to Scripture, we must turn away from the deceased saints in heaven and turn towards the saints on earth and extol and honour them. This is God's pleasure and command.' Honouring the saints on earth means helping one's neighbours.[137] Finally, praying for the saints' intercession with God contradicts Scripture, which at 1 Timothy 2: 5 refers to Christ as the sole mediator between human beings and God. Luther rejects the scholastic distinction between a mediator who makes satisfaction for sins, who is Christ alone, and mediators as intercessors, who comprise the saints.[138]

Some or all of these three criticisms appear in Luther's later writings.[139] In the *Schmalkaldic Articles* of 1537, his rejection of the invocation of the saints evinces the same polemical tone of *Wider den neuen Abgott*. Decrying prayer to the saints as 'one of the abuses of Antichrist,' Luther remonstrates that, even if the saints in heaven pray for us, it does not follow that we should invoke and adore them, hold fasts and celebrate Masses in their honour, dedicate to them churches and altars, and regard them as helpers in time of need and as our patrons. For all of this is idolatry.[140]

Luther's three principal arguments against the invocation of the saints were the common property of Protestantism, Lutheran and Reformed. The rejection of this form of piety found its way into the 'official' documents of the Reformation: Protestant catechisms, such as Luther's Large Catechism of 1529 and Calvin's Geneva Catechism of 1542, as well as Protestant confessions of faith, such as the Lutheran Augsburg Confession (as we have already seen), and the Calvinist Gallican Confession of 1559 and Belgic Confession of 1561. Protestant town councils also wanted to forbid the cult of the saints. In 1529, Bern outlawed the carrying about of rosaries. Violators of this ordinance were fined ten gulden.[141]

In the first half of the sixteenth century, a chorus of Catholic polemicists countered Protestant repudiations and came to the defence of the invocation of the saints. Catholic writers, often engaging in substantial apologies, took the controversy over the invocation of the saints far more seriously than the Protestants.[142] The Catholic campaign was under way by 1523. In that year, Josse Clichtove in his book *De veneratione sanctorum* proved why the saints were worthy of devotion and refuted the Protestant objections.[143] The following year, Jacob von Hoogstraten, the Dominican inquisitor who had hounded Reuchlin for his defence of the Torah, entered the lists against the 'Lutheran falsehood.'[144] In 1525, Johannes Eck, who had debated with Luther at Leipzig in 1519, devoted one of the longer chapters of his catalogue of Luther's heresies, the *Enchiridion locorum communium adversus Lutherum et alios hostes ecclesiae*, to the 'veneration of the saints.'[145] In 1544, Johannes Cochlaeus, the famous German Catholic polemicist, published his *De sanctorum invocatione et intercessione*.[146] In their exposition of the first commandment Catholic catechisms, such as Peter Canisius' *Summa doctrinae Christianae* (first published in 1555) and the authoritative Roman Catechism (1566), taught that invoking the saints was an acceptable form of piety and even a duty.[147] At its twenty-fifth session (3–4 December 1563), the Council of Trent confirmed the cult of the saints, decreeing that bishops should carefully teach the faithful about the intercession of the saints, their invocation, the respect due their relics, and the legitimate use of images.[148] The decree's import was primarily pastoral. An official dogmatic treatment of the cult of the saints as well as of Mary's place in the economy of salvation and in Christian devotion would have to wait for four hundred years when the Second Vatican Council devoted chapters 7 and 8 of *Lumen gentium* (1964), the dogmatic constitution of the Catholic church, to these subjects.[149]

Erasmus' defence of the invocation of the saints in the *Modus orandi Deum* rests on the answer to two questions: (1) Is the invocation of the saints pious? and (2) Should it be tolerated?[150] The second question sounds rather superfluous. If praying to the saints is a valid form of devotion, it is obvious that it should be allowed. What Erasmus really means to ask in the second question, as we shall see, is: Should one tolerate prayers to the saints when they bear the stamp of superstition?

Erasmus begins his apology by confronting the Protestant charge that Scripture gives no express sanction for praying to the saints. He prefaces his remarks with the statement: 'perhaps this is a good part of the Christian religion: to revere all things in divine matters, but to affirm nothing beyond which is expressly stated in Scripture.' Erasmus concedes that Scripture is silent on praying to the saints, although he does state that this form of devotion could be inferred from Scripture.[151] Clichtove, Eck, and the authors of the Confutation base much of their justification of the devotion by appeals to Scripture. A favourite text is John 12: 26: 'If anyone serves me, the Father will honour him' (RSV). If God honours the saints, then why should not human beings do the same?[152] For all his arguments from Scripture, Eck, however, agrees that Scripture does not explicitly teach the invocation of the saints.[153]

Erasmus responds to the Protestants not by firing off a barrage of scriptural passages but by accusing them of inconsistency. For the sake of argument, he grants that human rules cannot demand anything (presumably in matters of faith or worship) that is not expressly set forth in Scripture. Yet this doctrine does not hold as far as the perpetual virginity of Mary is concerned, a widely accepted belief that finds no basis in either Scripture or the Apostles' or the Athanasian Creed. Erasmus supposes that the very reformers who assert the principle of *sola scriptura* would not tolerate the repudiation of or at least the calling into question of the belief that Mary remained a virgin after the birth of Jesus.[154] The reformers did indeed retain this belief.[155] Erasmus' accusation of inconsistency not only revealed a chink in the armour of the Reformation's scriptural principle. His reference to the perpetual virginity of Mary also appears to have been rather timely. In 1523, Catholics in Nürnberg started to spread rumours that Luther had claimed that Mary had conceived Jesus by Joseph and that she had given birth to several sons after Jesus. Luther responded to these 'new lies' in the same year in his short work, *Daß Jesus Christus ein geborner Jude sei.*[156] Luther devotes the opening pages of the treatise to arguing for the virgin birth. He acknowledges, almost in passing, that although Scripture does neither affirm nor deny that Mary remained a virgin after Jesus' birth, one may still believe in her perpetual virginity.[157]

Mary's virginity is not the only example with which Erasmus challenges the Protestant scriptural principle. In the second edition of the *Modus orandi Deum,* he reminds his opponents that such Trinitarian dogmas as the consubstantiality of the Son with the Father and of the Holy Spirit with the Father and with the Son are not clearly expressed in Scripture. Indeed, not even the terminology of these dogmas is scriptural. Where, for example, does Scripture speak of three hypostases? All the same, Christians believe in the Trinity.[158] Associating himself with those who invoke the saints, Erasmus demands where the critics are who, in a matter of lesser significance, accuse 'us' of coming up with a new dogma, when Christians are required to accept the teachings on the Trinity, teachings that are not expressly formulated in Scripture yet can be inferred from it. He wonders what has happened to those who charge 'us' with a controversial dogma yet who claim one may freely act in any matter that Scripture neither commands nor prohibits. If they leave the eating of meat and fish to one's own free judgment, why do they not concede to 'us' the same freedom in imploring the intercession of the saints?[159]

The fact that Scripture makes no authoritative statement about praying to the saints means that one should be free to pray to them or not. Yet the practice of those who invoke the saints is not without foundation. Just as Erasmus is aware that not all doctrines in the Christian creed are contained in Scripture but are rather the product of an age-old tradition of scriptural interpretation, so too he recognizes that tradition legitimizes forms of devotion not enjoined by Scripture. He underlines the antiquity of tradition, to which he refers as the 'consensus.' The invocation of the saints, especially of the martyrs, was practised by the orthodox fathers of old. The church fathers upheld the perpetual virginity of Mary 'with a great consensus,' and 'with a similar consensus' they handed down the invocation of the saints. Erasmus asks those who brand this devotion as a long-established error to distinguish between the evolution of something in any manner whatsoever and the handing down by those who lived closest in time to the apostles of something that is by nature pious and approved 'by the great and enduring consensus of the whole Christian world.'[160]

The 'whole Christian world' is the church, which Erasmus defines as 'the consensus of the Christian people throughout the whole world' and 'the consensus of the entire Christian people.'[161] The way in which the church has believed and worshipped over the ages provides a compelling justification for the doctrines and pious practices that have developed over time but lack a firm basis in Scripture. In March 1524, seven months before the publication of the *Modus orandi Deum*, Erasmus invokes the 'consensus of the Christian people' in support of auricular confession.[162] In September, he calls Luther's attention to the host of church fathers, scholastic doctors, church councils, and popes that have upheld the freedom of the will, which, from the apostles until this very day, only the Manichees and John Wyclif have denied.[163] Erasmus implies to the town council of Basel in 1525 that Johannes Oecolompadius' book on the Eucharist contradicts the consensus of the church, from which it is dangerous to dissent.[164] The consensus prevents Erasmus from giving up his belief in Christ's real presence in the Eucharist. He asks Conrad Pellican, one of Oecolompadius' colleagues in Basel, why, with regard to the sacrament, he should abandon what the church has taught for so many centuries.[165] He cannot understand why that which the church fathers have taught and religiously preserved for so many centuries in times past – whether it concern fasting, singing in church, the sacrifice of the Mass, the Eucharist, the invocation of saints, statues in church, free will, or monasticism – the Strassburg reformers and others dare to call 'idolatry, blasphemy, an insult to Christ, and assaults upon Scripture.'[166]

Although ancient tradition, the consensus, can undergird belief and worship, it is, Erasmus concedes, not infallible. In the *Modus orandi Deum*, he admits that antiquity does not make something right that is not right in itself, but it is not permissible for this reason to condemn what is old, for in a probable matter the 'consensus of antiquity' exercises no little influence.[167]

The concept of the consensus is an important characteristic of Erasmus' irenic ecclesiology. We have already noted in chapter 1 that concord is an important spiritual disposition for prayer. Those who pray are members of the church, Christians who are of one mind and of one heart. Erasmus is not alone in invoking the authority of the consensus to justify prayers to the saints. Other Catholic apologists for the invocation of the saints combine appeals to Scripture with appeals to the consensus. Clichtove includes praying to the saints among the doctrines and devotions sanctioned by 'the antiquity of time with the public consensus of all.'[168] The 'custom of the entire church' and 'the holy fathers throughout all the Christian centuries' bear witness to the invocation of the saints, claims Eck, while the Confutation asserts that this practice is supported not only by 'the authority of the universal church' but also by 'the consensus of all the holy fathers.'[169] When the Council of Trent decreed that bishops should carefully instruct the faithful about the invocation of the saints, it understood that they should do so 'according to the custom of the Catholic and Apostolic church, received from the earliest times of the Christian religion, and to the consensus of the holy fathers and the decrees of the holy councils.'[170] Interestingly enough, the Tridentine decree makes no mention of the authority of Scripture.

Before he leaves the issue of scriptural justification of the invocation of the saints, Erasmus concedes that no scriptural passages openly teach that the prayers of the deceased saints have any effect on God. Nevertheless, he alludes to Revelation 6: 9–11, in which the martyrs, who cry out for the destruction of Satan's tyranny and for the fulfilment of the kingdom of the Gospel, learn that they must wait for the time appointed by God. In the meantime, the martyrs receive white stoles, which Erasmus interprets as the 'glory of miracles which they initially lacked.' Erasmus thinks that Jerome's riposte to Vigilantius is also worthy of note. If, while bearing about their mortal bodies, the pious were heard interceding for their brothers, one should all the more believe that, having shed their mortality, the saints can accomplish something with their prayer in God's presence. For one cannot doubt that they desire with ardent prayers the salvation of all who profess Christ's name. With their own weapons Erasmus assails those who respond that the merits of the saints are efficacious only in this life. What they claim is not expressly stated in Scripture.[171]

Having dealt with one scriptural problem, Erasmus moves on to another: the assertion in 1 Timothy 2: 5 that there is one mediator between God and human beings, Jesus Christ. Catholic apologists, to meet the Protestant objection based on this text, adduced the scholastic distinction between Christ as the mediator of redemption and the saints as mediators of intercession.[172] Erasmus takes a different, more humanist, approach based on textual interpretation. He objects to an exclusive reading of the crucial passage, to a reading that makes Christ the sole mediator and sole intercessor. If Jesus is the only intercessor between God and human beings, why should human beings ask one another to pray for one another? Christ gave his followers the Our Father so that they might pray not only for themselves but for others too. He also instructed them to pray for their enemies. Paul at 1 Timothy 2: 1 commands that Christians pray for all people, especially for kings and for those who hold public office.[173]

In Erasmus' opinion, when Paul calls Jesus the one intercessor, he does not exclude the intercession of the saints but declares that Christ died for all peoples and that one should place one's hope for salvation in no one except in Christ.[174] The apostle to the gentiles wants to counteract, according to Erasmus, the Jewish opinion that God is only the God of the Jews. Erasmus thus quotes the passage immediately preceding the statement that Christ is the one mediator, the passage that speaks of God 'who wants all human beings to be saved and to come to the knowledge of the truth' (1 Timothy 2: 4). Each nation had its own gods; only the Jews gloried in God as if he were not the God of all. Thus, Paul says that there is one God who cares for all, one reconciler between God and human beings who died for all without exception. The one intercessor is common to all.

If, Erasmus continues, the one Son of God can be said to have many brothers, who themselves are also sons of God, then the fact that there is one intercessor should not exclude other intercessors. Implicit in the notion of the 'other intercessors' is another ecclesiological dimension to the justification of the invocation of the saints. Alluding to his favourite image of the church, the body of Christ that has one head and many members, Erasmus states: 'All the saints are members of Christ.' If Christ was pleased to grant a favour through the hem of his garment touched by the woman with the haemorrhage (Matthew 9: 20–2 and parallel passages), should we be surprised that he grants favours through his members?[175]

In defending the idea that the saints can intercede for human beings with God, Erasmus vindicates the piety of invoking the saints and refutes the charge that such invocation is idolatrous. Why, someone may ask, does God accomplish through the saints what he can do by himself? Just as the Father wants to be glorified through the Son, replies Erasmus, so too the Son wishes to be glorified through the saints. It is, therefore, to our advantage all the more to acknowledge the communion of the saints, which embraces not only the living but also the pious souls of the deceased.[176]

Take the example of the person who commends his petitions to his guardian angel so that the latter may bring them to Christ. Erasmus sees no reason why such a person should be censured.[177] Indeed, earlier in the *Modus orandi Deum* Erasmus recalls that Scripture records examples of how the angels acted as 'internuncii,' messengers or mediators between human beings and God. Raphael said that he had brought Tobit's prayers to God (Tobias 12: 12). In Revelation 8: 3–4, an angel stands at an altar with a golden thurible from which rises to the presence of God a most pleasant smoke of incense, an incense, as the text says, mingled with the prayers of the saints.[178] In his paraphrase on Luke 1: 10, Erasmus says that angels brought Zechariah's prayers to God, for it is their role 'to carry up the prayers of the pious to the heavenly Power and in turn to bring down to us his generosity.'[179] The whole point of the intercession of the angels is to give us a greater awareness of God. Although an angel is an intercessor, it is 'nothing but a minister,' writes Erasmus. We make use of the ministry of the angels not as if we always needed these ministers but so that we can understand how much God cares for us, the God who has given us the angels as guardians and protectors.[180] God commends the angels to us because through their ministry he wishes his love for us to come to light.[181]

What obtains for the angels also holds for the saints. If we can speak piously to the angels, then our prayers to Peter and Paul are pious too. Indeed there is nothing impious about the invocation of the saints in itself. If it is pious and Christian to believe that the souls of the saints survive, live with Christ, and are most pleasing to him, and that Christ desires that their memory should be held sacred by us and that he be glorified through them, then it is pious to believe that God wishes to bestow gifts through the saints, through whom he has converted the world and through whom he will judge it.[182] The many miracles, moreover, wrought at the tombs of the martyrs and by the invocation of the saints, miracles attested to by the great consensus of ecclesiastical writers, demonstrate the piety of praying to the saints and the pleasure that God takes in these prayers.[183] Since appealing to the saints as intercessors is pious, it cannot be a form of idolatry, provided of course that it is free of all superstition. To look to the saints as intercessors or mediators does not obscure the glory of Christ, who is glorified in the saints. Honouring the saints does not detract from God's glory but rather increases it, for in the saints we venerate nothing except the gifts of God. The person who prays for the intercession of a saint prays to Christ but in a different way.[184]

Erasmus compares the invocation of the saints to the act of a person, conscious of his own unworthiness, who sends intercessors to a king in order to find favour with him. The emperor does not spurn the intercessor but loves the reverence of the person afraid to come before the majesty of a prince. The emperor neither hears nor sees the petitioner, but Christ hears and sees everything. The more someone humbles himself before his majesty, the more Christ is pleased by the one who prays.[185] Erasmus argues that inherent in the invocation of the saints is a pious fear of God. We implore their intercession, he says, because we judge ourselves to be unworthy to appeal to God himself and because we believe that God is pleased to bestow upon us many things through his saints.[186] The person who does not dare to call upon God does not consider the saint he invokes more likely to be appeased than God and therefore more favourable than God, but he acknowledges God's majesty and fears his justice all the more.[187]

Someone might say that a person who invokes the saints for these reasons is subject to weakness and error presumably because he fears God's justice more than he loves God's goodness. God, however, is pleased by this weakness and loves this pious error in us. If it is an error to dwell on one's own unworthiness in the face of God's justice, God prefers this modest error to a pharisaical self-confidence.[188] (This sounds like a subtle quip against those who boldly claim that they are justified by faith alone.) Perhaps the saints avail us nothing by their prayers; perhaps they cannot even hear our prayers. Yet all that counts is a 'pious disposition' (*pius affectus*) in those who invoke the saints. This pious disposition by which we venerate the saints for the love of Christ, or rather by which we venerate Christ in the saints, cannot but be most pleasing to God, Erasmus argues.[189] Some people ask for the wrong things, and they ask of the saints what only God can give. Yet, as Erasmus writes in 1530 in his *Concionalis interpretatio in Psalmum LXXXV*, provided that the devotees of the saints are free of an 'impious disposition' (*affectus impius*), the Holy Spirit, forgiving the human simplicity in them, corrects the error of their prayer and grants them what they need, and not what they ask for.[190]

Erasmus went to great lengths to uphold the invocation of the saints. A definite 'yes,' therefore, is his answer to the question whether one should tolerate the invocation of the saints. Error and superstition in a person's prayer to the saints do not necessarily mean that the person praying is impious. Erasmus concedes in the *Modus orandi Deum* that in his books he has frequently warned against superstitions in honouring and in invoking the saints. Nevertheless, since superstitions are part of the human condition, they should be tolerated as long as they do not lead to impiety, or they should be corrected, but without violence. Although a learned piety (*docta pietas*) desires the elimination of superstitions from the mores of Christians, it tolerates what cannot be set right except through tumult.[191] It is very important for Erasmus that reform or correction should proceed peaceably. Violence is not the way of Christ nor of his church, which is founded upon peace and concord. To use force in bringing about reform is tantamount to achieving a good end with evil means. Erasmus in 1523 tells Ulrich von Hutten, the warrior humanist, and through him the Protestant reformers, that although he does not approve of the corruption of the Roman curia, it would be better to let the sleeping evil be than to reform the curia with 'warlike tumult' and to throw everything into confusion.[192] John Colet appears to have inspired Erasmus to espouse the ideal of non-violent reform. Erasmus recalls that Colet, during their visit to Canterbury in 1512, advised that one should tolerate the superstitious practices at the shrine of Saint Thomas Becket until it was opportune to correct these without violence.[193]

Erasmus would also agree with Clichtove, who in his discussion of excessive devotion to the saints refers to the parable of the weeds and the wheat (Matthew 13: 24–30). The harmful weeds have become mixed in with the wheat, but one should not 'condemn' and 'reject' the wheat on account of the weeds.[194] One should not abolish the invocation of the saints simply because into this devotion have crept superstitions and 'perverse observances.'[195] One bad apple does not spoil the entire bushel. Erasmus similarly insists in the *Modus orandi Deum* that the foolishness of some people does not justify the condemnation of what is proper in its own right. The superstition of the many does not provide grounds for the complete repudiation of invoking the saints. Otherwise, one would have to ban both the reading of the Gospels, since from this practice the seeds of heresy are sown, and the invocation of Jesus' name, for magicians invoke it.[196]

A final consideration for tolerating an unreformed and thus superstition-ridden cult of the saints, a consideration that other Catholic writers would not likely include in their apologies, takes into account the origin of superstitions in the cult. It is much easier to put up with superstitions by regarding them as 'vestiges of ancient paganism.' Formerly, pagans paraded about with Bacchus, Venus, Neptune, and Silenus with the satyrs. The church fathers deemed the carrying about of statues of pious people, whose miracles showed that they were reigning with Christ, as a great improvement upon pagan practice. The fathers tolerated the absurdities in the cult of the saints not because they saw anything Christian in them, but because they believed that the strange observances could serve as stepping-stones to piety.[197] The point that Erasmus therefore wishes to make is that the Protestant critics should prefer the cult of the saints to paganism. The superstition of Christians, which is not necessarily impious, is superior to pagan cults.

Erasmus says that in the *Modus orandi Deum* he asserted the case for the invocation of the saints against Luther. His defence of the most popular of all forms of popular piety should not be interpreted exclusively as a means of demonstrating his allegiance to Rome at a time when one's position on praying to the saints served as an easy litmus test of one's religious loyalties. Nothing indicates that Erasmus was insincere. His apology is genuine and even spirited, especially when he refutes the charge that the silence of Scripture invalidates the invocation of the saints. The Christian humanist who teaches Christendom how to pray engages in more than polemics with his Protestant opponents, whom he never mentions by name. As he confronts the problem of praying to the saints, he demonstrates a pastoral awareness of a controversy that threatens a traditional form of devotion. By insisting on the piety of the cult of the saints, Erasmus ministers to those confused by the Protestant critique. His emphasis on tolerance is his pastoral advice to Protestants and perhaps also to kindred Christocentric spirits who have not rejected Rome but who prefer to pray to Christ than to pray to the saints. Mutual tolerance between Catholics and Protestants becomes the cornerstone of Erasmus' pastoral peace plan for healing the divisions within the church. In the *De sarcienda ecclesiae concordia* (1533), as in the *Modus orandi Deum*, he advises that one should be free to pray or not to pray to the saints. Yet he cautions those who reject the cult of the saints and who prefer to invoke God with a sincere and pure mind not to disturb those who implore the intercession of the saints without superstition. Beyond this he recommends that in the invocation and cult of the saints a 'pious and simple disposition' (*pius ac simplex affectus*) should be tolerated even if it is associated with some sort of error.[198]

The sincerity of Erasmus' apology does not prevent him from repeating in the *Modus orandi Deum* the familiar themes from his critique of the cult of the saints. He openly acknowledges that the practice of praying to the saints is still tainted by grave superstitions. Many people ask for the wrong things when they pray to the saints, for they ask of the saints what they would not dare ask of an upright person, and what is more, they use magic to try to bring about the granting of their petitions. They also regard the saints not as intercessors but as the bestowers of the things for which they pray.[199] At the beginning of the *Modus orandi Deum*, while explaining what it means to sing psalms to the Lord, Erasmus emphatically states that those who trust and glory in Moses, Francis, Benedict, Dominic, or Augustine do not sing to the Lord but to human beings.[200] Erasmus wants Christians to stop worshipping the saints. Imitation, not worship, informs a pious cult of the saints and, as we have noted above, becomes the object of petitions to the saints. That Erasmus at least in passing considers the possibility that the saints in heaven can do nothing for mortals on earth, if they can hear them at all, does not present him as the most ardent spokesman for the invocation of the saints. His characterization of prayers to the saints as the expression of the humble piety of sinners who are afraid of directly addressing a just God turns invocation into a concession to the weak. This seems to be an inferior type of piety, especially in the context of a book that urges Christians to cast off their sins and to soar up to their good God on the wings of prayer. Imploring the intercession of the saints is pious, to be sure, but conversing with God is a higher, more perfect form of piety. In a letter written in 1528 to John Longland, the bishop of Lincoln, Erasmus, while allowing for the cult of the saints, insists that 'it is more perfect to beseech Christ for whatever we want to obtain.' It is also safer for us to imitate Christ than to make the saints our exemplars. As Erasmus stated earlier in the letter: 'Most pleasing to the saints is the devotion whereby one imitates their life; nevertheless a surer model of life is sought from no one other than Christ himself. I advocate true devotion.'[201]

If a true, more perfect form of worship prefers Christ to the saints, Erasmus, the advocate of true worship, can nevertheless still agree with an inferior piety in his declining years. In 1532, in Freiburg im Breisgau, his Catholic city of exile away from Protestant Basel, he published his *Carmen votivum* to Saint Geneviève. Noting that the *Carmen* appeared by itself in its own quarto volume, Clarence Miller writes: 'It was the only poem Erasmus published all by itself, and he must have had a high regard for it to single it out in this way.'[202] The 'dutiful poet' presents the saint with verses in fulfilment of a vow he made to her for her help while he was sick in Paris thirty-five years earlier. At the end of the poem, he begs Geneviève, 'best of virgins,' 'that I suffer no harm because I put off fulfilling this vow for so long.'[203] Miller points out that a twofold advantage would accrue to the saint for having to wait so long: by 1532 Erasmus was able to provide her with a wider readership and a better poem than if he had kept his promise in 1497.[204]

In the opinion of Jean-Claude Margolin, Erasmus' poem 'plunges us into the atmosphere of piety that was characteristic of popular religion not only in the Middle Ages but also in the centuries that followed.'[205] The critic, whose spokeswoman Folly calls it 'nonsense when particular regions lay claim to a certain saint, when they parcel out particular functions to particular saints,'[206] refers on three occasions in the *Carmen votivum* to the patronage of Geneviève. He addresses the patroness of Paris: 'O Geneviève, most faithful protectress of your people, as far as France, divided into three sections, extends.' Paris, however, is the special object of her care. With the Virgin Mary she keeps Paris under constant protection, surveying the fields outside the walls, while Mary, her colleague, 'fondles the wretched in her bosom and hears the woeful cries of the poor in the midst of the city.' Within the city Geneviève protects 'true priests, and the parliament with its regal majesty, and above all the Christ-loving king.'[207]

Besides praising Geneviève, the patroness of France and of Paris as a chaste, modest, and merciful virgin, the *Carmen* renders her public thanks for hearing Erasmus' prayer and giving him 'the gift of recovered health.' He does not, however, forget to fit his prayer of thanksgiving into a Christocentric framework. The saintly virgin helped him, but the glory 'belongs entirely to its source, Christ; to him be the honor for ever and ever.' When she was alive, she was 'pleasing to God' by Christ's gift; by his gift she became 'the refuge of many sick people' after her death. Her patronage of the sick of Paris is not an independent power but exists by the pleasure of Christ. His are the gifts he gladly bestows through her, his is the honour he receives through her.[208] Miller concludes: 'Surely the implied message here is as much for the protestants as the catholics: if you reject what Christ performs through her and for his saints, you reject him.'[209] Although Miller may be right, it seems that Erasmus is most interested in showing that, in praising and thanking Geneviève, he is still within the bounds of what he calls in the *Modus orandi Deum* a 'pious and moderate from of devotion'[210] because it derives its validity from Christ, the object of true worship.

In the *Enchiridion*, Erasmus tends to equate popular piety with popular supersition, with the mindless devotion of most Christians. Yet Erasmus' early poetry, his invocation of Saint Geneviève in 1497, his Greek poem to the Virgin Mother of 1512, his vow to Saint Paul in 1514, his liturgy for the Virgin of Loreto of

1523/1525, his apology for the invocation of the saints in the *Modus orandi Deum* (1524), and finally his *Carmen* of 1532 all substantiate Peter Brown's claim about popular piety. What we call popular piety is not popular because it is the piety of the ignorant majority; it is popular because it is practised by the learned and simple alike. For all his ruthless satire of the superstitions of the common crowd, the erudite Erasmus practised, defended, and with the *Liturgia* and *Carmen* even promoted, albeit in a limited way, a reformed cult of the saints. Halkin justifiably asserts that Erasmus 'is not one of those aristocratic believers who, in order to practise an enlightened religion, shun the common path. He wishes and feels himself to be *in* the church; he aspires to be a Christian among other Christians, if not like other Christians.'[211] Erasmus, moreover, remained faithful to the pastoral ideal in the *Enchiridion*, to the goal of being 'all things to all men' so as to 'win everyone to the side of Christ.' Like a diligent pastor, he accepted what was good in the devotion of the flock and was prepared to bear with their superstitions, even if, contrary to his own advice in the *Enchiridion*, in the *Colloquies* he often sounded like a Cynic who snarled 'indiscriminately at the beliefs and deeds of others.'

Erasmus does not attack superstitions out of a 'primitivistic impulse' to return to the ways of the early church, or out of a narrow and uncompromising use of Scripture. His chief objective is to reform piety. Erasmus' critique, which Carlos Eire believes 'made a positive contribution to Protestantism,'[212] had the same purpose as, and perhaps even indirectly inspired, the fathers of the Council of Trent. They wished to eliminate all abuses and superstitions from the cult of the saints and to impose episcopal control on popular piety by subjecting to the approval of the local bishop the erection of unusual images and the acceptance of new miracles and relics.[213]

Like Trent, Erasmus wanted to reform the cult of the saints, not to abolish it. His reform sought to show people the foolishness of revering the saints as gods. The saints should not be treated as ends in themselves but as a means to spiritual transformation. The 'emulatory piety' that Erasmus proposes emphasizes the imitation of the saints' virtues as a way of ultimately imitating Christ. Yet this piety does not exclude the intercession of the saints, for Christians are to ask the saints to obtain for them the virtues that make them more Christ-like. Thus the reformed invocation of the saints is Christocentric. Indeed, praying to the saints is just a different way of praying to Christ, who takes great pleasure in the saints, and whose kind Father is most pleased by the piety of those who ask for their intercession.

THREE

Interpreting the Lord's Prayer

卐

Christians in the medieval West prayed not only to the saints but also to God the Father. The Lord's Prayer was as much a staple of medieval piety as prayers to the saints. Indeed, the prayer that Jesus taught to his disciples is the best-known and most widely used Christian prayer. Already in the second century of the Common Era, the *Didache* enjoined upon believers to pray the words of Jesus three times daily.[1] The Lord's Prayer has always held a prominent place in catechesis and liturgy, and, with a sort of unbroken apostolic succession, it has served as a 'catechism on prayer.'[2] Since the catechetical lectures of Cyril of Jerusalem, delivered in the middle of the fourth century, the Our Father has always been explained in Christian catechesis, including Erasmus' own catechism, and has also given birth to hundreds of sermons and commentaries.[3]

Erasmus puts himself within the unbroken tradition that considers the prayer from the Sermon on the Mount as the prayer of prayers. In the *Modus orandi Deum*, he informs his readers: 'among the innumerable forms of prayer, the one which the Lord himself taught has always ranked first in authority with Christians.' Erasmus also recalls that the 'orthodox fathers' believed that nothing should be asked of God beyond what Jesus had prescribed in the *oratio dominica*.[4] In his catechism, the *Explanatio symboli* (1533), he refers the reader to the 'commentaries of pious and learned men, especially of Saint Cyprian.'[5] The *De dominica oratione* by Cyprian is one of the earliest expositions of the Lord's Prayer. Erasmus, whose edition of Cyprian's *Opera omnia* appeared in 1520, held the North African church father in high esteem. Cyprian was a 'great Doctor of the church' and a 'champion of Christian piety.' Upon reading Cyprian's works closely, Erasmus was so impressed by him that he found it difficult to say whom he preferred: Cyprian or his beloved Jerome.[6]

In his catechism, Erasmus teaches that the Our Father is the best prayer, prayer's 'optima formula,'[7] for it is not only found in Scripture but also originates with Jesus, the foundation of the Christocentric piety that Erasmus had been propagating since the *Enchiridion*. Léon Halkin notes that the Lord's Prayer 'occupies an eminent place in Erasmus' religious thought, for the *Pater Noster* is the only prayer which Jesus taught to his disciples.'[8] Erasmus' paraphrase of Luke 11: 1 explains why the disciples should ask Jesus to teach them how to pray: 'Lord, since we are your disciples, it is fitting that we do everything according to your directions.'[9] The Lord's Prayer enables Christians to pray as Jesus would have them pray. Erasmus took several opportunities to teach his contemporaries the meaning of Jesus' prayer.

The famous Christian editor and philologist of the Renaissance first came to grips with the prayer in his *Novum Instrumentum* of 1516 and in the accompanying *Annotations*. His translation of Matthew 6: 9–13, the version of the prayer that is longer and more familiar than that of Luke 11: 1–4, differs slightly from that of the Vulgate. Where the Vulgate reads: 'fiat voluntas tua sicut in caelo et in terra,' Erasmus translates: 'fiat uoluntas tua, quemadmodum in coelo, sic etiam in terra.'[10] In his note on this text, he points out that the Vulgate translation obscures the sense of the Greek. The passage means: 'May what you wish be so done on earth, that is, among your heavenly people, just as it is done in heaven, where no one resists your will.'[11] In the petition for our daily bread, Erasmus, following liturgical and popular practice, modifies 'panis' with 'quotidianus' instead of the Vulgate's 'supersubstantialis.'[12] He uses the verb 'remittere,' not the Vulgate's 'dimittere,' in the ensuing petition for God's forgiveness of our sins. The choice of 'remittere,' which Erasmus justifies on the grounds that the Greek verb 'aphienai' is polysemous, elicited criticism from some theologians. Among these were two Carmelites: Sebastiaan Craeys, prior of Antwerp, and Nicolaas Baechem, prior of Louvain and professor of theology at the University of Louvain. In two letters, one written in 1517 and the other in 1519, Erasmus mentions that his emendations of the Latin text of the Lord's Prayer have come under fire from the pulpit.[13] In a note of 1519, in the second edition of the *Annotations*, he defends his use of 'remittere' by appealing to the Apostles' Creed, which speaks of the remission of sins. He attacks his critics, who claim that the use of 'remittere' will bring about the downfall of Christianity, as unworthy preachers of the Gospel who ought to have their tongues cut out.[14] Although he argues that the doxology 'for yours is the kingdom, the power, and the glory, for ever and ever' (*quia tuum est regnum, & potentia & gloria, in saecula saeculorum*) was not in the earliest manuscripts of the New Testament,[15] he includes it in his translation. Erasmus renders Luke 11: 1–4 with an eye on the text in Matthew. He adds the petitions – which are not in Luke – for the doing of God's will and for our deliverance from evil, and begins the prayer: 'Pater noster qui es in coelis,' whereas Luke simply has 'Pater.'[16]

In 1517, the year after the first edition of the New Testament, Erasmus presses the Lord's Prayer into the service of his anti-war polemics in the *Querela pacis*. He shames belligerent Christians with a prayer that is common to all, is addressed to a common Father, and makes requests unsuited to brothers at war with one another. What could be more absurd and inappropriate than for a soldier to pray the Our Father at divine services? To call upon God as Father while making for a brother's throat is the height of audacity. Petition by petition Erasmus thunders against the irreconcilability between warfare and Christianity. At the fourth petition he confronts his readers: 'Do you ask daily bread from our common Father when you burn your brother's crops and would prefer them to be lost to you rather than to benefit him?'[17] Here the Lord's Prayer merely functions as one arrow in Erasmus' polemical quiver against war. Nevertheless, he establishes a link between the prayer and peace, a connection evident in his expositions of the Lord's Prayer.

Three of these were written within the space of two years. Erasmus published the *Paraphrase on Matthew* in March 1522. His treatment of the relevant passage in Matthew's Gospel begins with a paraphrase of the prayer itself followed by a recapitulation of the prayer's main points put into the mouth of Jesus. This order is reversed in the *Paraphrase on Luke*, published in September 1523. Erasmus precedes the paraphrase of the prayer with an exposition of the meaning of the prayer. Interestingly enough, the exposition touches on all seven of the Matthean petitions, despite the absence of the third and seventh petitions in Luke, whereas the paraphrased prayer leaves out the second petition –

the prayer for the coming of God's kingdom – which Luke retains.

Only weeks separated the *Paraphrase on Luke* from the publication in October of Erasmus' most substantial interpretation of the Lord's Prayer. Its full title reads *Precatio Dominica digesta in septem partes, iuxta septem dies*. Richard DeMolen states: 'Before the year [i.e. 1523] was out, the work itself proved to be immensely popular and appeared in three Latin editions.'[18] Translations were published in German (1523), English (1524), Czech (1526), Spanish (1528), Polish (1533), and Dutch (1593).[19] The English translation, *A Devout Treatise upon the Pater Noster*, which reappeared in three subsequent editions, was the work of Margaret Roper, Thomas More's daughter.[20]

Augustin Renaudet has appropriately situated the *Precatio Dominica* within the context of Erasmus' paraphrases on the Gospels.[21] (The *Paraphrase on John* had been published in February of 1523, and the *Paraphrase on Mark* went to press in the spring of 1524.) Erasmus himself referred to the *Precatio Dominica* as a paraphrase. The second edition of Erasmus' catalogue of his own writings, the *Catalogus novus omnium lucubrationum Erasmi Roterodami* (1524), lists the *Paraphrasis in Precationem dominicam*.[22]

The paraphrase is one of Erasmus' favourite literary genres. It is not a translation but a rather free form of running commentary. Unlike a commentary, its business is not to compare the opinions of various authorities on the text that formed the basis of the commentary. The paraphrase undertakes to expound the meaning of the text and the intention of the author. Erasmus also uses the paraphrase to fill in narrative gaps, smooth out abrupt transitions, impose order on disorganized passages, and explain points difficult to understand.[23] He would no doubt have been pleased if pastors consulted the paraphrases as they prepared their sermons.

Erasmus' paraphrase on the Lord's Prayer is divided, as the title indicates, into seven parts corresponding to the prayer's seven petitions. This was the format proposed by Josse Ludwig Dietz, a wealthy patron of the arts and a secretary to King Sigismund I of Poland. Dietz, to whom the humanist dedicated the work, had asked Erasmus to write a commentary on the Lord's Prayer. Erasmus conforms himself to Dietz's request and thus, as he is well aware, to the traditional approach to expounding the prayer.[24]

Erasmus' seven-part paraphrase is a collection of seven prayers, designed to be said, one a day, throughout the seven days of the week (*iuxta septem dies*). The *Precatio Dominica* thus is a short prayer-book based on the Lord's Prayer. Probably in October 1523,[25] Froben printed the *editio princeps*, a slender and very portable octavo booklet. The heading of each of the seven sections is accompanied by the day on which one may pray the section. The first part beginning with the incipit *AUDI Pater* is intended for Sunday, *Die Dominico*; the second part, entitled *Adveniat regnum tuum*, for Monday, *Die Luna*; and so on.

Eight metalcuts provide pictorial aids for praying Erasmus' paraphrase on the Lord's Prayer. The first illustration appears on the page after the dedicatory epistle and shows Jesus teaching a group of people – obviously a scene from the Sermon on the Mount. The caption is from Luke 11: 1: 'Domine doce nos orare' – 'Lord, teach us to pray'[26] (see frontispiece). Each of the seven remaining metalcuts accompanies the appropriate petition of the Lord's Prayer. For example, above the opening words of the third petition, 'Fiat uoluntas tua,' we see Christ bent under the weight of a large cross. A crowned God the Father looks down from heaven while a procession of people bearing aloft their own smaller crosses follow Christ. In metalcut we see depicted a favourite Erasmian theme: the imitation of Christ.[27] According to the engraving, to do God's will is to carry one's cross after Christ.

Recommending his *Precatio Dominica* in his catechism, Erasmus gives the rationale for his prayer-paraphrase: 'at the same time you will both pray and, by praying, you will learn a method of prayer.'[28] The same purpose most likely inspired the many other prayer-paraphrases of the sixteenth century, such as Luther's treatment of the Lord's Prayer in his *Betbüchlein* (1522) and the *Commentarius in orationem dominicam* written by Juan Luis Vives and incorporated into his prayer-book, the *Excitationes animi in Deum* (1535).[29] With his fellow paraphrasers, both Catholic and Protestant, Erasmus shared the simple pastoral insight that the act of praying makes one proficient in prayer. The *Precatio Dominica* functioned as a lesson in prayer, but more important, it nourished its readers' devotional life in the imitation of Christ by having them pray according to the formula of Jesus as interpreted by Erasmus.

Erasmus' seven prayers are all addressed to God the Father. They are of unequal length, the first being the longest and the last

Fiat uoluntas tua.

God's will being done: Christians from all walks of life imitate Christ
as they journey with him carrying the cross.
From Erasmus' *Precatio Dominica* (Basel: Froben [1523]), B3.
Courtesy of the Beinecke Rare Book and Manuscript Library,
Yale University.

being the shortest. Each prayer, except for the seventh one, ends with a Trinitarian doxology, thus evoking the liturgical practice of concluding the recitation of a psalm at the divine office with praise of the Trinity. Direct quotations from and allusions to Scripture echo throughout the *Precatio Dominica*. They point to Erasmus' humanistic propensity for explicating a text within its larger context, to his insistence on rooting theology in Scripture, and to his pastoral program of disseminating the *philosophia Christi* through the words and teachings of the New Testament.

There are three more sources for Erasmus' thinking on the Lord's Prayer: the *Modus orandi Deum* (1524/1525), the *Explanatio symboli* (1533), and the *Precationes aliquot novae* (1535). In the treatise on prayer, he briefly explains the meaning of the seven petitions of the Our Father. At the end of his catechism Erasmus highly recommends the Lord's Prayer. Besides interpreting the seven petitions, Erasmus teaches that the Our Father is the common prayer of the church. Erasmus returns to the Lord's Prayer for the last time in his prayer-book. The 'Precatio ad Patrem,' which opens the *Precationes aliquot novae* (1535), is yet another prayer-paraphrase of the Our Father, but on a much smaller scale than the *Precatio Dominica*.

Having surveyed Erasmus' various expositions of the Lord's Prayer, we can turn to the more important task of analysing the pastoral theology that underlies his undertaking to teach Latin Christendom the meaning of its greatest prayer. Using Erasmus' own categories of analysis, we shall consider the Lord's Prayer in terms of the God to whom it is addressed, the identity of those who recite it, and the sorts of things for which it asks. Of course, his expositions, especially the *Precatio Dominica*, are in themselves lessons on how to accommodate prayer to God according to the fourth category of analysis in the *Modus orandi Deum*. The best way of speaking to God is to adapt one's prayers to the seven petitions of the Lord's Prayer.

As its opening words make clear, the Lord's Prayer addresses itself to God, the heavenly Father. The seven prayers of the *Precatio Dominica* usually begin with a reference to the Father in heaven.[30] Erasmus gives his readers some insight into what is meant by saying that God the Father is in heaven. In his first note on Matthew 6: 9, he points out that in the original Greek the description of God as 'ho en tois ouranois' makes use of the definite article to distinguish the Father in the heavens from an earthly father. Erasmus expands this note in the second edition of the *Annotations* (1519) by commenting that when we pray to the Father who is in heaven, it is as if to say: 'We know no father on earth. We depend solely on you, heavenly Father, from whom we should seek all things necessary for true life.'[31]

To acknowledge that God is in heaven is to endow him with an exclusive paternity. He alone can claim to be the Father of humankind. Erasmus' philology influences his promotion of piety when, alluding to Matthew 23: 9, where Jesus says: 'And call no man your father on earth, for you have one Father, who is in heaven' (RSV), he has his readers pray to the Father in the *Precatio Dominica*: 'Your Son, through whom you bestow all things upon us, also taught us this, that after we, already being reborn in your Spirit, have in baptism renounced our father the devil and have ceased to have a father on earth, should acknowledge only a heavenly Father.'[32] Erasmus also promotes the idea of God's exclusive paternity by making him the subject of the verb *gignere*, which means to beget. Paraphrasing the fourth petition of the Our Father, he has us pray in the *Paraphrase on Matthew*: 'Father, nourish what you have begotten.' In the context of the same petition he wishes us to acknowledge in the 'Precatio ad Patrem': 'Through your word you begot us when we were nothing.'[33] By portraying the Father in heaven as a divine progenitor, Erasmus establishes God as Father in the most real sense. God, of course, is not a biological Father. Alluding to the name for God in Hebrews 12: 9, Erasmus calls God the 'Father of Spirits.' In the *Precatio Dominica*, we exclaim: 'Hear, O Father of Spirits, your spiritual children who adore you in spirit.'[34] Praying for our daily bread, we affirm: 'as spiritual children we earnestly desire from the Father of Spirits that spiritual and heavenly bread, through which we truly have life, we who are truly called your children.'[35] Since the *Enchiridion*, Erasmus' religious thought has always derived its vitality from the ontological superiority of the spiritual over the material. The heavenly Father is a spiritual Father, and as such he is the only Father of spiritual children. It is as spiritual children that Christians are only really or 'truly' children.

Not only does God's heavenly dwelling give him exclusive rights as Father, it also shows him to be a transcendent God, above and beyond earthly matters. Erasmus communicates the

Father's transcendence in the 'Precatio ad Patrem' by addressing an exalted, supreme God dwelling above all else: 'Pater, qui summus in summis habitas.'[36] No vestige of earthly conditions may be found in this God. In the *Paraphrase on Matthew*, Erasmus teaches his readers to appeal to a heavenly Father, who, although he fills all things, has nothing to do with 'the dross or the infirmity of the earth.'[37] The third prayer of the *Precatio Dominica* calls upon the Father 'dwelling in heaven and far removed from all the changeableness of creation.'[38]

The way in which Erasmus begins the *Precatio Dominica* also evokes a transcendent Father: 'Hear, O Father dwelling in the heavens, the entreaties of your children, now, indeed, on earth stuck to this mortal body, yet sighing in their souls for the heavenly fatherland and the Father's house, where, as they know, is laid up for them the treasure of eternal happiness, the inheritance of immortal life.'[39] This passage shows that being in heaven is quite a different thing from being on earth. The Father's heavenly dwelling-place, the home of eternal happiness and of eternal life, transcends in splendour and in appeal what appears to be an unhappy earthly existence in which the mortal body is an almost contemptible thing when compared to heavenly immortality. Erasmus' quite conscious and deliberate contrast between the superiority of God's heavenly status and earthly human life recurs in his various expositions of the Lord's Prayer. In the *Paraphrase on Matthew*, Erasmus has Jesus teach his readers that God is said to be in heaven, 'so that, neglecting earthly values, you may lift up your souls heavenwards.'[40] By guiding the spiritual gaze of Christians up to the heavenly and transcendent Father, Erasmus directs them to the spiritual *scopus* of prayer: eternal salvation. With sighs of great longing they desire in the Lord's Prayer to be with the Father in their heavenly home, where they will enjoy the 'treasure of eternal happiness.'

The Father may be a transcendent God, uncontaminated by the flux inherent in creation, but this does not mean that he has no relationship to the world he transcends. Erasmus uses the Lord's Prayer to call to his readers' attention that God is the Creator. The prayer teaches them that they should depend on no one else but their heavenly Father to whom they owe their creation, their redemption, and whatever virtue they may have.[41] The fourth prayer of the *Precatio Dominica* praises God's creative work as wonderful,[42] and at the outset of the first prayer Erasmus not only establishes God as Creator but also as 'Guardian (*Servator*) and Ruler (*Moderator*) of all things in heaven and on earth.'[43] The Father has not only created the heavens and the earth; he also keeps watch over his creation.

God's creation is a function of his power,[44] and power (*potentia*) along with wisdom (*sapientia*) and goodness (*bonitas*) constitute the triad of God's chief characteristics. This triad, which first appears in the *Precatio ad Virginis Filium Jesum*, emerges again in the *Precatio Dominica* and in Erasmus' paraphrase of the Lord's Prayer in the *Paraphrase on Luke*.[45]

It is by God's power that human beings, who were nothing, were created, and Erasmus in the *Precatio Dominica* has his readers pray that every creature may tremble before God's 'inescapable power.'[46] The 'all-powerful Father,' is 'the sole ruler of all things.'[47] Day and night the heavenly host praises him as King, and in the 'Precatio ad Patrem' his human subjects acknowledge him to be 'the King of kings,' longing to see him face to face in the splendour of his royal glory.[48] In the *Precatio Dominica*, the prayer for the coming of God's kingdom invokes the heavenly Father as 'author, creator, preserver, establisher, and governor of all things in heaven and on earth, from whom alone flows all authority, power, kingship, and empire to things both created and uncreated, and equally to things visible and invisible; whose throne is the sky, whose footstool is the earth, whose sceptre is an eternal and immovable will, whom no power can resist.'[49] By stressing God's irresistible power over all creation, Erasmus wishes his fellow Christians to call upon God with reverence when they pray the Our Father. Although God's power may be a source of trembling, it is also a source of hope. For the God who can do all things can certainly also answer all worthy prayers.

Just as God's 'inescapable power' demands human reverence, so too does his 'inscrutable wisdom.'[50] Christians acknowledge that God alone is wise and that they are governed and preserved by God's wisdom, and they pray that every creature will venerate it.[51] Erasmus teaches that in his wisdom God allows his children to endure strife in order to cultivate and strengthen their virtue. Putting aside their own will, they desire that the Father's will accomplish within them whatever his wisdom judges to be best for them. They pray that, even when they do not have the upper hand in the contest with evil, God's wisdom will turn this to their advantage.[52]

Although Erasmus wishes his readers to revere God, he wants them, more than anything else, to love him. Conversing with the Father in the *Precatio Dominica*, they say: 'The words "charity" and "devotion" have pleased you more than "fear." You would rather hear us call you Father than Lord. You prefer being loved by children to being feared by slaves.'[53] In the *Paraphrase on Matthew*, Erasmus, speaking through the person of Jesus, points out that God is called 'Father' so that 'you may understand that he is merciful and kind.'[54] The Father is a God of power and of wisdom, but he is supremely a God of goodness. We obtain our daily bread from a 'most generous Father,' and from his kindness we acquire a ready will to obey his commands.[55] Whether he speaks of God's 'bonitas,' 'benignitas,' 'pietas,' 'liberalitas,' 'munificentia,' 'providentia,' 'clementia,' or 'caritas'; whether he describes the Father as 'bonus,' 'optimus,' 'beneficus,' 'benignus,' 'benignissimus,' 'indulgentissimus,' or 'amans,' Erasmus' unambiguous teaching about God in his expositions of the Lord's Prayer is that God is good. His most touching expression of God's goodness comes at the end of the *Precatio Dominica*. Having stated that God is not at all like the wicked devil, God's children tell their heavenly Father: 'For you are good and kind by nature. You carry back the lost sheep to the flock, you heal the sick sheep, you call the dead sheep back to life. In your love you forestall (*praevenis*) even your enemies who blaspheme your holy name and invite them to eternal salvation.'[56]

The good Father is a God of salvation. By his power he created human beings when they were nothing; in his goodness he restored them when they were perishing.[57] At the outset of the *Precatio Dominica*, Erasmus' readers admit that they were slaves of sin and children of Satan, but they equally acknowledge that God in his mercy liberated them from the servitude of sin through his only-begotten Son Jesus and emancipated them from their old father, the devil.[58] In his catechism, Erasmus urges Christians to consider what a kind Lord and loving Father they have, who gave up his only-begotten Son to death in order to redeem them from Satan's tyranny.[59] Scholars who have accused Erasmus of reducing Christianity to a system of ethics have not appreciated the fact that he never fails to refer to the good Father as the God of redemption.

Logically enough, Erasmus identifies those who supplicate the good heavenly Father as *filii*, as God's children. By constantly referring to the *filii* in the *Precatio Dominica*, he inculcates into the minds and devotional habits of his readers the intimate relationship that exists between them and God. They begin the prayer-paraphrase by appealing to the Father as his children: 'Hear, O Father, dwelling in heaven, the entreaties of your children.' The intimate relationship between the children and the heavenly Father comes into being at birth, for God begets his children when they were nothing, but more important, the relationship begins with baptism. The Lord's Prayer is above all the prayer of the baptized faithful, the 'prayer of Christians' as Erasmus says in the *Paraphrase on Luke*.[60] In emphasizing the theme of baptism, he follows the early church's tradition of regarding the use of the prayer as a special privilege of baptized believers.[61]

Before their baptism, Christians were by nature the slaves of sin, the unhappy offspring of Adam, the children of Satan.[62] God set them free from their slavery, took them from the clutches of Satan, and adopted them as his own children. At the outset of the *Precatio Dominica*, Erasmus' readers affirm: '... you had mercy on us through your only-begotten Son Jesus, released us from the slavery of sin, freed us from our father the devil, and reclaimed us from the inheritance of eternal fire. You were pleased, moreover, to adopt us through faith and baptism as ingrafted members of the body of your Son and into the fellowship of the name and inheritance of your children.'[63] Thus Christians are God's children not by nature but by adoption,[64] and Christ's redemptive death makes this adoption a reality. He transforms them, redeemed by his death, from being the slaves of Satan into being the children of God.[65] They enjoy the benefits of the redemption as a result of their baptism in which they are reborn in the Spirit, through Christ, and for heaven.[66] In baptism not only does God forgive them all their sins, but they also, having been reborn in God's Spirit and having renounced their old father, the devil, gain God as their new and only Father.[67] To this Father the Holy Spirit within their hearts does not cease to exclaim: 'Abba Pater.'[68]

That Erasmus keeps his readers aware of their baptism within the very unambiguous context of redemption decisively contradicts Renaudet's claim that Erasmus' prayers are 'stripped of theology.'[69] The author of the *Precatio Dominica* couches his identification of those who pray with the 'renati,' God's adopted children by baptism, in the language of Saint Paul. His description of the human state before the redemption – 'We were slaves of sin' – finds its basis in Romans 6, where Paul, after proclaiming that Christians are baptized into the death of Christ (v. 4), reminds his Roman audience that they formerly were 'slaves of sin' (vv. 17, 20, RSV). Galatians 4: 4–7 serves as the source for Erasmus' juxtaposition of redemption and adoption: 'But when the time had fully come, God sent forth his Son, born of woman, born under the law, to redeem those who were under the law, so that we might receive adoption as sons. And because you are sons, God has sent the Spirit of his Son into our hearts, crying, 'Abba! Father!' So through God you are no longer a slave but a son, and if a son then an heir' (RSV). Thus, in the *Precatio Dominica*, Erasmus shares with his readers his 'Pauline preoccupation,'[70] first evident in the *Enchiridion*, in which he urges: 'Above all make Paul your special friend; him you should keep always in your pocket and "ply with nightly and with daily hand," and finally learn by heart.'[71]

Redemption involves a process of transformation from a state of slavery to a state of adopted sonship made possible through Christ's redemptive death. In the hearts of the redeemed, Christ's Spirit calls out with affection to the 'divine Daddy': 'Abba Father.'[72] God's redeemed children are 'heirs,' or, as we read in Romans 8: 17, 'fellow heirs with Christ' (RSV), a passage to which Erasmus alludes in the *Precatio Dominica* when he speaks of the 'Filii tui cohaeredes' and 'cohaeredes Jesu.'[73]

The essential point here is not so much to identify and analyse Erasmus' scriptural allusions as to discover that there is a specific scriptural and theological undercurrent in Erasmus' pastoral ministry. The first thing that Erasmus teaches his readers about themselves in the *Precatio Dominica* and in the other expositions of the Lord's Prayer is that they are God's children, born again by the blood of Christ and in the waters of baptism. By suffusing this teaching into the devotional practice of meditating upon and praying the Lord's Prayer, Erasmus has selected an effective means for instilling Christian doctrine into those who choose him as their preceptor in prayer.

The goal of Erasmus, the pastoral theologian, is to have his contemporaries live what they believe. His efforts to teach the meaning of the Lord's Prayer emphasize to his readers the importance of their baptism, since it is only by virtue of their baptism that they are truly God's children and that they can pray to God as Father. Their adoption by the Father through baptism bestows great dignity and honour upon them, for to be called God's children is the greatest honour that they can have.[74] Baptismal vows, moreover, are not only to be professed; they must also be put into action. They are not only a source of honour but a mark of great responsibility. Thus it is not enough for God's children to renounce the devil and say that they will obey God's commands. When they pray 'thy will be done,' they know they must live out their baptism by practising what they profess, by doing God's will. If they neglect God's will, they do not deserve the name of children.[75]

God's children ought to be faithful to their baptismal vows. For this reason, they must have certain spiritual qualities, since, as Erasmus writes in the *Enchiridion*, in baptism they pledged themselves 'to enter into an unending struggle with vice,' and 'to die to sin, to die to carnal desires, to die to the world.'[76] Erasmus lays down the spiritual dispositions they must have and the vices they must shun in order to be true children of their heavenly Father, to pray the Lord's Prayer worthily. As he writes in the *Paraphrase on Matthew*, Christians must distinguish themselves from pagans both in their way of life and in their prayer.[77]

First of all, Christians must be at peace with one another. In the same *Paraphrase on Matthew*, Erasmus has Jesus introduce the Lord's Prayer as a way in which 'true and sincere children, united by fraternal charity' call upon the heavenly Father, who is 'equally common to all.' Indeed, Jesus warns that the Father 'will not hear you unless you are peace with each other (*concordes*), and concord will not easily be established among you unless you forgive each other your mutual offences, without which human beings cannot lead their lives, however much they may strive for perfection.'[78]

The concord and fraternal charity that Erasmus enjoins upon those who pray the Our Father is grounded in the mutual forgiveness of sins. Charity, an essential ingredient for praying the Our Father, also demands that one ought to think of others before thinking of oneself. In his catechism, Erasmus teaches that those who pray without charity pray 'frigidly' and pray more for themselves than for others. God's children should say the Lord's Prayer as with one voice. 'All for one, and one for all' should be their motto.[79] In the *Precatio Dominica*, they recognize: 'We all depend upon the same Father; we all ask for the same things. No one asks for anything peculiar to himself, but, as members of one body quickened by the same spirit, we ask for what is necessary for all in common.'[80] The essential and common needs of God's children are expressed in the seven petitions of the Lord's Prayer.

From what Erasmus says about concord and charity it is obvious that he conceives of the Lord's Prayer as a communal Christian prayer. The praying of the Our Father does not simply establish relationships between individual children and the Father; the prayer unites those who say it. The children who pray with fraternal charity, forgiving one another and thinking of their common needs are not only *filii*; they are also *fratres*. Jesus has found them worthy to be called brothers, and the Father in his goodness has made them equal in honour. Theirs are the 'prayers of concord.' The concord that binds God's children together demands that they shun the vices of ambition, competition, hatred, and envy, anything, that is, that threatens their fraternal unity.[81]

That God's children are brothers and members of the same body immediately indicates that the Lord's Prayer is in its essence a prayer of the church. Just as whoever proclaims the Apostles' Creed declares the faith of the whole church, so whoever says the Lord's Prayer, Erasmus teaches in his catechism, 'prays with the voice of the entire church.'[82] Erasmus conceives of the church in many ways, yet his favourite image of the church is the body of Christ. At the beginning of the *Precatio Dominica*, God's baptized children remember that they are grafted onto Christ's body. In the second and third prayers, they ask that in heaven all members of the body will be joined to Christ their head.[83]

Erasmus' injection into the Lord's Prayer of his favourite themes of peace, unity, and concord thus turns the Our Father into a prayer of Christian unity, a unity that western Christendom lacked. In 1523, the year that Froben published the *Precatio Dominica*, the Edict of Worms claimed its first two victims in Hendrik Vos and Jan van der Eschen, two Augustinians who were burned for their Lutheran beliefs in Brussels on 1 July. Perhaps with the paraphrase on the Lord's Prayer Erasmus intended to come to the aid of a Christendom divided by the Reformation. In his choice of paraphrasing a prayer common to reformers and romanists alike and in his insistence on concord as an essential quality of all those who say the Lord's Prayer, one can see the irenicism of his pastoral ministry through the printing press. From this point of view the *Precatio Dominica* becomes an apt companion for the *Inquisitio de fide*, Erasmus' colloquy of 1524 that shows Lutherans and Catholics that in the Apostles' Creed they share the same set of beliefs. The Creed and the Lord's Prayer belong to all Christians, Erasmus would say.

Although Erasmus highly prizes concord and charity, he also expects other inner dispositions from the members of Christ's body. In the *Explanatio symboli*, he pairs charity with faith. The one purifies corrupt desires and concerns itself with God and neighbour; the other purifies the heart, that is, the mind and reason, and is most especially directed towards God. Faith triumphs over mistaken notions about whatever pertains to salvation. It holds all of God's sayings and promises expressed in the Scriptures as most true. Along with charity, faith is a necessary spiritual requirement to pray the Our Father worthily.[84]

The intimate relationship between the children and their Father is founded in their faith and trust in God. The source of this faith is God himself. Erasmus leads his readers to a God whose greatest name, 'Father,' is a name of love, and a God who prefers them to call him by this name than use the title 'Lord.' They approach this Father not as trembling servants but as adoring and loving children, confident that the Father will satisfy their needs. Indeed, as Erasmus teaches in the *Explanatio symboli*, they cannot really pray without faith, for their prayers would be empty, devoid of meaning. They should not doubt the words of Jesus: 'whatever you ask the Father in my name, he will give you.'[85]

This appeal to John 16: 23 also occurs in the *Precatio Dominica*. After declaring their intention to ask the Father only for those things prescribed by his Son as worthy petitions, Erasmus' readers recall Jesus' promise that 'whatever we ask in his name, we shall obtain.'[86] With God on their side nothing need frighten them. The temptations with which the devil tries to overwhelm them may give them cause for anxiety, but, relying on God's protection, they are sure to survive the 'storm of temptation.'[87] They conclude the *Precatio Dominica* by trusting that God will grant their petitions: 'These are the prayers of your children, eternal Father, and if they are pious and expressed according to the form laid down by your Son Jesus, we have every confidence that your goodness will grant what we ask for.'[88] Christians put their faith in God's great and enduring goodness, and having learned from Erasmus that God is goodness *par excellence*, they believe that their good Father in heaven will answer their prayers.

God's children must pray with faith and with concord and love. They will love each other as brothers and sisters if they avoid ambition, competition, hatred, and envy. In the *Paraphrase on Matthew*, Erasmus lists other vices incompatible with praying the Our Father sincerely. They call upon the Father in vain who neither fear nor love God, who live for themselves, who serve their own glory more than God's, who covet worldly wealth and power, who prefer to pursue what is pleasing to them instead of what is pleasing to God, who seek after earthly instead of eternal things, who esteem the gifts of the soul less than bodily pleasures, who are in conflict with a brother, who through lust and pleasure act sluggishly against the snares of Satan.[89] To be heard by the heavenly Father requires the repudiation of selfishness, vainglory, covetousness, materialism, concupiscence, strife, and lust. Yet more is at issue than the simple rejection of these vices. Erasmus denounces these vices in a context of fidelity to God and of the supremacy of spiritual values. The Lord's Prayer loses its meaningfulness if those who say it have no reverence or love for God, if they do not give priority to his glory and to his will. They who care nothing for their spiritual lives, that is, for their souls and God's eternal kingdom, renounce their calling to be spiritual children of the Father of Spirits.

Erasmus does not miss the opportunity of using the Lord's Prayer to drive home his message about the inseparable link between prayer and spiritual transformation. This transformation involves more than the mere acquisition and exercise of virtue. For Erasmus, a life of virtue is ultimately a life lived in praise of and obedience to God. The virtuous life becomes a spiritual life, founded on faith in God, nourished by love for him and for neighbour, and consolidated by the practice of virtue and the rejection of vice. The Lord's Prayer and all prayers should originate from this spiritual life and help Christians to persevere in it.

Persevering in the Christian life of virtue is no easy task. For Christians earthly life is warfare. This is the opening message of the *Enchiridion*, a theme that reappears in Erasmus' explanation of the Lord's Prayer in the *Explanatio symboli*: in the warfare of this life God's children seek no other recompense from Christ their commander than the food for body and soul necessary to perform their duties.[90]

Erasmus teaches his readers through the Lord's Prayer that the 'struggle' (*lucta, colluctatio*) with their three principal enemies – the flesh, the world, and the devil – is serious, manifold, and difficult.[91] He holds that the sixth petition is about asking protection from 'the attacks of the demons, of the flesh, and of the world.'[92] As he explains in the third prayer-paraphrase of the *Precatio Dominica*, the flesh lusts against the spirit (cf. Galatians 5: 17), the world encourages the love of transitory things, and Satan desires whatever will drag God's children down to eternal ruin.[93] These enemies thus constantly seek to prevent Christians from being true to themselves, from being spiritual children of the spiritual Father in heaven. They tempt them to value physical pleasure more than the spiritual life, to become preoccupied with the vanity of this world at the cost of devoting themselves to the attainment of our heavenly inheritance. If God's children succumb in the struggle, Satan carries them off to eternal doom.

The devil is the most terrible enemy of all. He is a very present foe, appearing in all of Erasmus' expositions of the Lord's Prayer, and again and again in the *Precatio Dominica*. It is incorrect to assume that for Erasmus the devil was nothing more than a metaphor, a metaphor 'for the vices and evil tendencies arising within the human heart,' and therefore not 'a personalized foe.'[94] On the contrary, Erasmus understands Satan to be a real individual dedicated to the triumph of evil over good and to the damnation of human beings. He is the 'malicious tempter,'[95] the 'common foe,' whose malice, depravity, and cunning are well-known.[96] Above all, Satan is a 'wicked tyrant'[97] who employs every device to subject human beings to his tyranny.

Having such a formidable opponent in the devil, God's children cannot but expect their Christian warfare to be a bitter fight. Their earthly lives will not be completely pleasant, but not simply because Satan wishes to snatch them away from their heavenly Father. Besides being a struggle, Christian life is a time of exile. In the 'Precatio ad Patrem,' God's children beseech their Father as exiles on earth.[98] As long as they live on earth, they are separated from their heavenly homeland. Thus Erasmus begins the *Precatio Dominica* with the separation of heaven and earth: his readers sigh for the Father's house where they will enjoy eternal life and happiness. In this passage, Erasmus speaks of God's children as being glued or stuck (*haerens*) to their mortal bodies. By raising this idea several times in the course of his expositions of the Lord's Prayer, he intensifies the sense of exile and of the discomfort of earthly life. He will not let his readers forget that they lug about (*circumferre*) this earthly or mortal body with them.[99] In one place, he speaks of God's children as 'burdened with a mortal body.'[100]

Although they have received from God the great honour and dignity of adoption as his children through baptism, this does not mean that Christians can afford to rest on their laurels. The devil, their exilic state, and the body that weighs them down remind them constantly that the Christian life is a life of hardship. The Our Father is a prayer not only of the community of the redeemed but also of the army of Christian soldiers who struggle in this life against the world, the flesh, and the devil. They strive to remain faithful to their baptismal vows, hoping to attain everlasting happiness in their heavenly homeland.

An analysis of Erasmus' concept of the *filii* would be incomplete without mentioning the *Filius*. Just as Erasmus' readers present themselves to the heavenly Father as *filii tui* in the *Precatio Dominica*, so they also often call to mind *Jesus Filius tuus*. God's Son, after all, gave them the Our Father.[101] Erasmus presents Jesus in many ways. He is the agent through whom the Father redeems his children, he is the splendour of the Father's glory.[102] Christians learn the Father's will through the Son, and to obey that will they must give primacy of honour to both the Father and the Son.[103] The Son promises them the coming of God's kingdom and conquers the devil.[104]

Jesus is also a teacher. Several times in the *Precatio Dominica* God's children acknowledge to the Father: 'docuit nos Filius tuus.' God's Son teaches them that they have only one Father, that God's kingdom is hidden within them, that they should hold the kingdom of this world in contempt, that they should not be solicitous for tomorrow's needs, that they should reconcile themselves to their brothers before they leave their gift at the altar.[105] All of these examples are, of course, allusions to the Gospels. Jesus' teaching is the *doctrina Evangelica*, and inasmuch as the Our Father is a Gospel text, it takes its place within this *doctrina*.

Erasmus, however, does not use the Lord's Prayer simply as an outlet for disseminating in yet another way the teachings of

Jesus as found in the Gospels. He in part gives Jesus a prominent place in the *Precatio Dominica* to make the *Filius* the great guide for being true *filii*. In calling God's adopted children *fratres*, God's Son shares his sonship with them. At the end of the third prayer, Erasmus' readers express their desire that, by doing God's will, the Father will look upon them as worthy children and that the Son will take them for genuine brothers.[106] Although they are brothers of Jesus, he is more of a Son than they are. They acknowledge to the Father: 'Your Son Jesus is the most genuine Son, for he is the most perfect image of the Father, to whom he completely corresponds and whom he completely represents.'[107] Conforming themselves to Jesus' example they try as much as possible to manifest some likeness with the Father. Jesus teaches his brothers to love the Father above everything, to love their neighbours as themselves, and to be well disposed to those who harm them in order to encourage them to imitate the Father.[108]

Erasmus' message is clear. Good children strive to resemble their Father. In loving what is good and in doing it, they imitate the Father's goodness. In following Jesus' teaching, they learn from him who knows best of all what it means to be God's Son. Erasmus' Christocentric piety pervades the *Precatio Dominica*. By adhering to the teaching and example of Jesus, whose name and whose title *Filius* is constantly on their lips as they pray, Christians become true children of the Father. They are children through the Son. The Father redeemed them through his death, from Jesus they learn to cherish concord and shun strife, under Jesus who conquers Satan they fight as Christian soldiers. They ask the Father to grant that they may constantly persevere in Jesus his Son so that they may enter the fellowship of his heavenly kingdom.[109]

The Lord's Prayer is the prayer of the church, and the common needs of the church, of God's children, find their expression in the seven petitions of this prayer. In the *Modus orandi Deum*, Erasmus concisely summarizes the meaning of each petition. The purpose of his summary is to familiarize his readers with the meanings of the seven petitions so that their own prayers may conform to the spirit of the Lord's Prayer, for it is a given that 'nothing can be asked of God which does not correspond to any of the seven parts of the Lord's Prayer.'

Any prayer that has the glory of the divine name in view pertains to the first part: 'hallowed be thy name.' To pray for the spreading and fulfilment of the Gospel is the same as saying: 'thy kingdom come.' The third petition, 'thy will be done,' is about observing God's commandments, and the fourth, 'give us this day our daily bread,' refers to whatever makes human beings strong in this life, to the 'corroboratio huius vitae.' Erasmus interprets the fifth petition, 'forgive us our trespasses as we forgive those who trespass against us,' as 'whatever pertains to the preservation of fraternal concord and of peace with God.' The mercy by which God forgives daily faults is the foundation of peace with God, while the preservation of fraternal concord implies a person's willingness to forgive the offences of his neighbour. The sixth petition, 'lead us not into temptation,' implores the protection of 'heavenly grace' against the assaults of demons, of the flesh, and of the world. Finally, a prayer for an end to all evil and for the consummation of human happiness that will only come about in the next life is the same as asking in the seventh petition: 'but deliver us from evil.'[110]

'HALLOWED BE THY NAME'

In a note of 1519 to Matthew 6: 9, Erasmus explains the meaning of the keyword of the first petition: 'sanctificetur.' He begins by saying that 'sanctus,' or holy, beyond 'pure' and 'unpolluted,' means 'venerable' and 'inviolate.' Yet, as Augustine pointed out, 'sanctificetur' does not imply that God's name needs to become holy but that his name should be declared as such.[111] This leads to the root of Erasmus' understanding of the hallowing of God's name. The first petition of the Lord's Prayer is not simply a prayer that the Father's name be glorious, but that it be glorified, and glorified exclusively. All glory belongs to God; no one should dare to 'usurp' any of God's glory.[112] Erasmus has Jesus say in the *Paraphrase on Matthew*: 'You should desire the Father's glory in such a way that no one on earth for any reason should ascribe glory to himself, for of this pride (*insolentia*) the cancer of the soul is born.'[113] As Erasmus' readers say the 'Precatio ad Patrem,' they combine the desire for the glorification of the Father's name with the wish that no one take anything away from God's glory: 'We pray that your adorable name may so shine out throughout the entire world that, just as in heaven you are the glory of all, so on earth no one will glory in himself but recognize his unworthiness and your generosity, and that all will glory in you, which alone is true glory.'[114]

Erasmus takes the opportunity to elaborate on the Father's glory in the *Precatio Dominica*. He adds a flavour of Christocentric piety as he has us recognize that 'our Lord Jesus,' while he was on earth, desired nothing more than that the Father's holy name would grow in reputation not only in Judaea but throughout all nations. Moved by his urging and example, God's children wish with burning desire that the glory of the Father's adorable name may fill heaven and earth and that every creature tremble before God's inescapable power, revere his eternal wisdom, and love his ineffable goodness. The Father's glory is boundless indeed, knowing neither beginning nor end, neither increase nor decrease.[115]

Wherever one turns, that glory is resplendent in God's creation. Day and night the angels sing his praises. The sky, the sea, the bubbling springs, the rivers, the various types of trees, plants, and all living things: what else do they declare than the glory of the Father's name? In their own way, they proclaim that the Father is the only true God, that he alone is eternal, immortal, powerful, good, merciful, just, truthful, admirable, lovable, and adorable.[116] Through his copious style, his pious *multiloquium*, Erasmus impresses his readers with this cosmic praise of God and seeks to reinforce within them the awareness of the Father's splendour and the desire for his glorification.

Erasmus' insistence upon the human desire for God's glory corresponds to the notion expressed in the 1519 edition of the *Annotations* that nothing so grieves the hearts of children as the disgrace of their parents and that nothing gives them greater joy than their parents' glory.[117] Four years later, he makes this idea a theme in the first prayer of the *Precatio Dominica*. It is a mark of 'natural piety' that children 'born according to the flesh' rejoice whenever their parents are honoured by triumphs, statues set up in the forum, or offices of state. They consider their parents' honour as their own. Yet how they groan with dejection if anyone dishonours the name of their fathers. For God's children 'divine piety' counts for more than human feelings, and thus they desire God's glory all the more and are all the more pained to see the dishonouring of the Father's name.[118]

According to Erasmus, two groups of people who have no real regard for God's glory are the *gentes*, or the heathen, and the Jews. The heathen either have no knowledge of the Creator, or they hold him in contempt. In his stead, they worship such lowly things as stones, oxen, leeks, and onions, and in these, they worship 'impure demons.' God's children feel grief on account of the heathen because the latter rob the Father of the glory that is his due and because they are perishing in their madness.[119] Perhaps by *gentes* Erasmus means the native peoples of the recently discovered and ever more explored New World. In the *Ecclesiastes*, he realizes that there are many parts of the world where the seed of the Gospel has not been planted and regrets that God had not given him the calling to go to the *barbarae nationes* in order to save souls for the Redeemer from Satan's tyranny.[120]

The heathen have not heard the Gospel, but the Jews are its enemies. Erasmus was no friend of Judaism. Heiko Oberman maintains: 'the entire body of Erasmus's thought is permeated by a virulent theological anti-Judaism.'[121] This is particularly true of his religious works. His *Paraphrases on the New Testament*, for example, are peppered with hostile remarks about Jews and their religion. He belittles the Law of Moses and disparages the Jews for their refusal to believe in Jesus as the Messiah.[122] In the *Precatio Dominica*, Erasmus claims that in their synagogues Jews constantly heap abuse upon God's only Son, and he holds that by dishonouring Jesus they dishonour the Father. The Jews supposedly ridicule Christians, declaring that it is better to be called a thief or murderer than a Christian. What is more, they reproach Christians for their glory: Jesus' cross. Erasmus bids his readers pray for the conversion of the heathen and of the Jews. May the heathen reject their idols and worship the true God, and may the Jews abandon 'the superstition of the Law' and acknowledge the Father, Son, and Holy Spirit.[123]

God's children rejoice whenever they recognize the spreading of his glory. They hear creation proclaim that glory, but Erasmus does not allow them to content themselves with that. They too must be instruments for the promotion of God's glory. Christians volunteer their services to the Father: 'through us, pure and unblemished, may your name become famous and glorious among human beings.'[124] They ask that in their teaching and life God's power, wisdom, and goodness be made ever more known to men and women.[125] Hallowing God's name therefore means being on one's best behaviour. The Father is glorified if the world sees his children living according to the teaching of Jesus by loving God above all, loving one's neighbour as oneself, and doing good in return for evil. In addition, God's children must take care not to bring disgrace to the Father's glory. Christians – and they are Christians in name only – are a disgrace to God's glory when they commit theft or adultery, quarrel, wage war, go about looking for favours (*ambiunt*), seek vengeance, cheat, swear falsely by God's name and even blaspheme it, make a god of their belly, and serve Mammon instead of God. Such false Christians give the common crowd a wrong impression of God, for the unsophisticated are prone to see God in the image and likeness of his dubious worshippers.[126]

Erasmus thus demands high moral standards of those who pray: 'hallowed be thy name.' If God is glorified in the actions of his children, they must be worthy instruments of his glory. Erasmus reminds his readers that Jesus tells his followers to let their light shine before men and women so that they may see their good works and glorify the heavenly Father (Matt. 5: 16). Yet the light and good works are not so much their own as they are God's light shining in them and God's good works working through them.[127] God will see to it that his glory will manifest itself, and Christians pray that it will manifest itself within them. Here again prayer challenges them to reform their moral and spiritual lives. God's children cannot sincerely pray the first petition of the Lord's Prayer unless they promote God's glory in their behaviour and actions.

'THY KINGDOM COME'

The second petition is, in essence, a prayer for the daily strengthening, thriving, extension, and spreading of God's kingdom on earth.[128] The *Precatio Dominica*, more than Erasmus' other expositions of the Lord's Prayer, gives us some sense of what that kingdom is. Its king, the heavenly Father, is a God of power who exercises untrammeled authority and dominion over all creation. Heaven is his throne, earth his footstool; his immovable and eternal will is his sceptre. In days gone by, the Father, through the prophets inspired by his Spirit, promised the advent of a spiritual kingdom for the salvation of the human race, a kingdom that would set free those reborn in God from the devil's tyranny. God sent his Son, whose redeeming death turned human beings from slaves of the devil into children of God, to bring this kingdom into the world.[129]

The subjects and beneficiaries of the kingdom are those who are predestined to it. The theme of predestination in Erasmus' conception of the Lord's Prayer is peculiar to the second prayer of the *Precatio Dominica*. He does not allude to it anywhere else in this work or in his other interpretations of the *Pater Noster*. God's eternal will has appointed (*destinare*) those who would be the subjects of the kingdom; his goodness has determined (*destinare*) before the creation of the world those whom he would invite into the eternal kingdom of heaven.[130]

It is not entirely clear how widely Erasmus casts his net. He does not explicitly equate the predestined with God's children. Since the children acknowledge that the members of God's kingdom are those whom he has predestined, one might conclude that the elect are a subset of the *filii*. Yet Erasmus speaks of those who are unaware of the liberty, dignity, and happiness that submission to God's kingdom entails and who prefer to be the servants of the devil instead of 'your children, fellow heirs with Jesus, partners in the kingdom of heaven.'[131] Here he places the *filii* in apposition to the *consortes regni coelestis*. In the fourth prayer of the *Precatio Dominica*, Erasmus' readers ask their Father in heaven: 'provide for us your children, chosen for the heavenly family.'[132] In the second prayer, they say in one breath that the world attacks God's children with every device, and in the next that evil spirits let loose fiery darts upon those whom God in his gratuitous goodness has chosen out of this world and has elected to his kingdom as co-heirs with his Son.[133] Did Erasmus intend an identification of the children with the elect in this passage? It remains uncertain both who the elect are – that is, whether all the *filii* are among the elect – and also why Erasmus, who in the *De libero arbitrio* (1524) opposes Luther's deterministic view of humanity with a defence of the free will in matters pertaining to salvation, introduces the idea of predestination into the *Precatio Dominica*.

Although the membership in the kingdom remains unclear, Erasmus leaves little doubt about the kingdom's essential characteristics. He equates Jesus' references to the 'kingdom of heaven' and the 'kingdom of God' with his *Evangelica doctrina*. God's kingdom consists of what Jesus taught in the Gospels. Not military power – for God is a God of peace – but modesty, chastity, gentleness, forbearance (*tolerantia*), faith, and charity combine to make up this kingdom.[134] We affirm to the Father in the *Precatio Dominica*:

Whenever, out of love for you, we spurn the kingdom of
this world and seek the promises of the kingdom of heaven;
whenever we reject mammon and embrace the unique pearl
of the Gospel; whenever we shun everything which to the
flesh seems fashionable and sweet and, moved by the hope
for eternal happiness, we bravely endure everything no
matter how difficult; whenever, for love of you, we neglect
the most ardent feelings of nature and whatever is dearest
to us such as parents, children, wives, and other relatives;
whenever we repress the hot fury of wrath by paying back
an insult with a friendly word or an evil deed with an act of
kindness out of respect for you; you wage war in us against
the kingdom of Satan and manifest the power of your kingdom.[135]

God's kingdom becomes present in the lives of his children when
they put the values of the Gospel, the *Evangelica doctrina*, into
practice. As with the first, so also the second petition of the
Lord's Prayer obliges them to reform themselves spiritually.
Christians do not merely pledge to reject the pursuit of worldly
wealth or the passions of flesh. They do not merely promise to be
friendly instead of furious or to respond to wicked deeds with
kindness. Their repudiation of vice and dedication to virtue has a
spiritual orientation. They are motivated to make God's kingdom
present in their lives by their 'hope for eternal happiness,' their
scopus, and by their love for God that exceeds their love for their
dearest ones.

The above passage from the *Precatio Dominica* assumes two
other desires in the second petition: the destruction of Satan's
kingdom and the exercise of God's rule within his children. Erasmus also refers to the former as the abolition of Satan's tyranny,
the casting down of Satan's kingdom, and the expulsion of the
tyranny of sin.[136] The devil is indeed a formidable foe of God's
kingdom, a foe against whom one needs to be on guard. God's
children pray that the almighty Father, who by his kindness liberated from the tyranny of sin those whom he chose for his kingdom, will by the same kindness grant that they may persist in
their freedom, lest anyone abandon him and his Son and relapse
into the devil's tyranny.[137]

Jesus, who brought God's kingdom with him, also routed
Satan. Through Jesus, the Father has wondrously fought and

conquered; through Jesus he triumphs and rules.[138] Erasmus explains that when fathers receive honours, their children rule in their shadow and consider themselves to accede to whatever dignity and authority their fathers possess.[139] Thus, Christians pray that through Jesus they may rule in God, yet they ask not only for this but also that God will rule in them for the glory of his name.[140] The Father rules in them whenever they conform their lives to the teachings of his Son.

Although God's kingdom dwells within his children, it is not yet complete. Jesus must still present to the Father the kingdom complete and intact when all the evil spirits who rebel against the Father's majesty have been subdued.[141] Even within the church may be found those who plot with the devil. Erasmus has his readers pray for the coming of the future kingdom at the end of time when God's angels will purge the church, uprooting the weeds and separating them from the wheat (cf. Matthew 13: 30). After the resurrection of the dead, God will separate the sheep from the goats and invite into his kingdom all of those who embraced the kingdom of the Gospel to the best of their ability (cf. Matthew 25: 31–46). As exiles weighed down by their earthly bodies, groaning on account of the many hardships they suffer and their separation from God's fellowship, Christians long for the day of judgment, the day, promised by Jesus, of the coming of God's heavenly kingdom, when they shall see their King and Father face to face. They long for the kingdom that knows neither hunger, nor poverty, nor nakedness, nor disease, nor death, nor persecutor, nor any evil at all, nor any fear of evil, but in which the members of Christ's body will be joined to their head. In order that God's children may have some share in their Father's kingdom, they pray that he will grant that they may constantly persevere in his Son Jesus.[142]

The desire to be included in God's heavenly kingdom indicates that, although the kingdom has come, it still has not come in all its fullness. Erasmus also sees the kingdom as an eschatological reality. He shares the eschatological interpretation of the kingdom with Augustine, who understands the second petition in terms of Christ's second coming to judge the living and the dead, to separate the just from the unjust, and of the perfection of the blessed life in the saints for eternity.[143] The Protestant reformers, like Erasmus, interpret the coming of God's kingdom as its spreading throughout the world in our obedience to God's will and as the destruction of Satan's power.[144] Unlike Erasmus, however, they tend not to teach their followers to pray for the coming of the future kingdom in their exposition of the second petition. According to Karl Barth, the reformers 'have not discerned here or elsewhere the eschatological character of the reality of God's Kingdom.'[145]

'THY WILL BE DONE ON EARTH AS IT IS IN HEAVEN'

The meaning of the third petition is simple. It asks that God's children obey and do the Father's will. Yet Erasmus wants not only Christians but all people on earth to do the Father's will. Erasmus' readers pray that God's children, who already in many lands obey God's will and pay heed to the Gospel of his Son, may do the same throughout the entire world 'so that all people may understand that you are the sole ruler of all things and willingly and with pleasure obey your divine laws on earth, just as there is no one in heaven who rebels against your will.'[146] Just as rebellion in God's holy and heavenly palace is an impossibility, all mortals should abandon every human pleasure and obey God's commands in good times and in bad, in life as well as in death.[147]

Erasmus takes care to emphasize heaven as an exemplar of peace for those on earth. To be sure, heaven is the place where God's will is done perfectly, but Erasmus expresses this negatively, asserting that in heaven no one 'fights against' the Father's will.[148] 'Rebellion' against God does not and cannot exist in heaven,[149] for everything there is peaceful.[150]

The celestial city of peace is both reward and example; in conforming their actions to the will of their Father, God's children strive to remain faithful to its peaceful image.[151] When they pray that God's will be done, they understand that this requires them to live on earth the future life of heaven as far as is humanly possible. They all want to enter the heavenly kingdom, but they will not be received into its tranquillity unless they piously practise in this life what they will do in heaven.[152] Erasmus takes the opportunity to use the third petition of the Lord's Prayer as a means of teaching the importance and necessity of peace. If Christians genuinely seek to do God's will, they must be advocates and practitioners of concord.[153]

Peace is not the only lesson of the third petition. Erasmus

teaches that God's will, revealed by Jesus in Scripture, is always for the best. True and obedient children of the Father refrain from arguing about why God has willed such and such. It is enough for them to know God's will, trusting that he could only will what is best.[154]

The goodness of God's will stands opposed to the flesh with its lusting against the spirit, to the world with its fascination with the transitory, and especially to the devil with his desire for the doom of all humankind. Those who do Satan's will sacrifice to idols, revile God's adorable Son Jesus – perhaps another reference to the *gentes* and to the Jews – put no trust in Jesus' promises, plan to rebel against the Gospel, with envy seek the downfall of their neighbours, stop at nothing to become wealthy in this world, and defile themselves with foul pleasures. God's will, however, is to keep body and soul chaste and pure of all the filth of this age; to honour Jesus above everyone else; to subject no one to wrath, envy, or revenge, but to return good for evil; to suffer hunger, exile, imprisonment, torture, and even death rather than dissent from the Father's holy will.[155]

To pray that God's will be done Christians must trust in the perfect goodness of God's will. In faithfulness to their baptismal vows, they should dedicate themselves to goodness and virtue, to a life worthy of God's children and of Jesus' followers. Through the exercise of virtue and the repudiation of vice they show that God, and not the devil, is their true Father. Contrasting the wicked ways of Satan with the goodwill of the Father, Erasmus champions the superiority of the latter by making obedience to the Father well worth any hardship, no matter how painful or life-threatening. In Jesus, who was obedient unto death and who prayed: 'Father, if possible let this cup pass me by, but nevertheless let your will, not mine, be done' (Matthew 26: 39), God's children find an example of unwavering obedience to the Father's will and a challenge not to prefer human desires to his will.[156]

Yet they cannot by their own efforts show such obedience. Without divine assistance no one can will what God wills or observe his commandments.[157] In order that they may never allow any hardship to deter them from doing God's will, Christians ask the heavenly Father for daily help so that the flesh will strive less with the spirit and so that the human spirit may become increasingly one with God's Spirit. Just as God's children trust that God's will is always best, they also are confident that he will be so gracious as to endow them with a ready and firm will that they may not neglect his commandments, but that, mortifying their flesh and being led by his Spirit, they may do everything that is pious and pleasing in his sight. Then the Father will take them for worthy children, and the Son will recognize them as true brothers.[158]

'GIVE US THIS DAY OUR DAILY BREAD'

Over the centuries Christian thinkers have understood the daily bread of the fourth petition in two ways. As spiritual bread it signifies spiritual nourishment, food for the soul, that is, the Eucharist and the Word of God. As material bread it refers not only to bread made from wheat, but also to whatever is necessary for a healthy physical life, such as food, clothing, and shelter. With Origen at their head, the Greek church fathers tended to emphasize a spiritual interpretation of the daily bread, while the Latin fathers usually favoured a combination of the spiritual and material interpretations. Western medieval theologians adopted the Latin fathers' understanding of the bread.[159] Thomas Aquinas, for example, explained that the daily bread meant both the necessities of life as well as the Eucharist and the Word of God.[160]

With some exceptions, the Protestant reformers generally opted for an exclusively material meaning. Although in his early expositions of the Lord's Prayer Luther stressed the spiritual bread, by the time of his Large and Small Catechisms (1529), he spoke of the daily bread only in a material sense.[161] In the Small Catechism, Luther teaches that the daily bread refers to 'everything that belongs to the nourishment and needs of the body, such as food, drink, clothes, shoes, house, home, fields, cattle, money, property, a devoted spouse, obedient children, faithful servants, pious and trustworthy lords, good government, good weather, peace, health, discipline, honour, good friends, trustworthy neighbours, and similar things.'[162] Melanchthon, Brenz, Bucer, Osiander, Calvin, and Beza followed in Luther's footsteps. Catholics continued the tradition of the Latin fathers.[163] The Roman Catechism taught that in the Scriptures bread meant many things, but it especially signified 'first whatever we use in terms of food and of other things for the provision of the body and of life, [and] then whatever has been given to us by God's gift for the spirit, for the life of the soul, and for salvation.' Catholics were to understand the spiritual bread (*animae cibus*) as referring to the Word of God and to the Eucharist.[164]

Erasmus' conception of the daily bread does not square with that of Luther and the Protestant reformers. Nor does it always fit in precisely with Catholic tradition. Erasmus conforms more or less to the view of the Greek fathers, whom he prized above their Latin counterparts as the best interpreters of Scripture. In the *Annotations*, the *Paraphrases* on Matthew and on Luke, the *Precatio Dominica*, and the 'Precatio ad Patrem,' he emphasizes the spiritual interpretation, excluding the material sense or at least relegating it to an inferior status.

The *Modus orandi Deum* and the *Explanatio symboli* present a more balanced approach, for the spiritual and material senses are on an even footing. In the treatise on prayer, Erasmus first gives a rather vague explanation of the fourth petition: 'Quicquid ad corrobationem huius vitae [pertinet].' If by 'this life' he means this bodily and earthly life, he seems to be suggesting an exclusively material explanation. Yet a little further on he interprets the bread in both a material and spiritual sense: 'Nam vt panis nomine comprehenditur, quicquid ad huius vitae corporalem necessitatem pertinet, ita quicquid animum corroborat, panis est, sed praecipue sermo Domini.' Our daily bread refers to our bodily needs and to the Word of the Lord, the food of the soul. Interestingly enough, the verb 'corrobare' takes 'animus' as its object, and not 'corporalis necessitas.'[165] Erasmus points out in his catechism that the daily bread consists not of honours, wealth, treasures, and the pleasures of this age but of what is necessary for the life of the body and for the salvation of the soul.[166]

In the *Annotations*, Erasmus adheres to an exclusively spiritual interpretation. He invokes the authority of Augustine, who interprets the fourth petition as a prayer to the heavenly Father, the Father of Spirits, to provide us with 'the heavenly bread, the food for the soul.' Erasmus also believes that Christ in such a heavenly prayer could not be referring to the bread that even the heathen receive from their parents.[167] Martin Bucer, who interpreted the bread of the petition as food and the other needs of earthly life, criticized Erasmus, although not by name, for this statement. He disagreed with those who took the daily bread to mean 'the bread of the soul, because they deem it unworthy with such a heavenly prayer to request that bread that even the heathen receive from their parents.'[168] Perhaps Bucer did not mention

Erasmus by name because of the esteem he had for him. The Strassburg reform leader openly acknowledged Erasmus' influence, but the two obviously did not agree on everything.[169] Calvin was more explicit and blunt than Bucer his mentor: 'Indeed, the explanation (*ratio*) that Erasmus advances is not only trifling, but it is incompatible with piety. It does not seem likely to him that, when we go into God's presence, Christ should bid us to speak of food.'[170]

In the *Paraphrases* on Matthew and Luke, our daily bread is the Father's bread of 'heavenly teaching' or 'the bread of heavenly teaching and grace.'[171] Erasmus' readers ask God to provide them with 'spiritual and heavenly nourishment' in the *Precatio Dominica*.[172] It is no great accomplishment for the Father to supply with bread the weak human body (*corpusculum*) that will eventually die. God's spiritual children earnestly entreat the Father of Spirits for that spiritual and heavenly bread that gives them all life.[173] God's heavenly bread is his Word (*sermo*) Jesus, and it is the sacrament of the Eucharist inasmuch as it is the body of God's only-begotten Son, the bread of all the members of the church.[174] Our daily bread is also the 'sermo Evangelicus,' the message of the Gospel: 'Whoever teaches the message of the Gospel sets this bread before us.'[175] Erasmus' conception of the spiritual bread as word and sacrament harmonizes well with the teaching of the Roman Catechism.

The metalcut in the *Precatio Dominica* aptly depicts Erasmus' interpretation. In the right-hand corner of the foreground, we see a cleric preaching from a pulpit to a group of men and women sitting below. Off to the left in front of an altar supporting two long, lit candles stands a priest who is administering the host to a person who is most likely kneeling. Both scenes are set in what seems to be the nave of a church. In the background, outside of the church proper, a party of four men sit at table.[176] The engraving that illustrates 'Panem nostrum' gives us to understand that our daily bread is primarily spiritual: the Word of God and the Eucharist. Less important is the material bread of physical nourishment.

In the 'Precatio ad Patrem,' Erasmus' readers ask the most bountiful Father: 'give us today what, in your judgment, the needs of this life demand.' Yet most of all, since God is the Father of Spirits, they ask him to feed their souls with spiritual nourishment, milk for the weak and solid food for adults. This food comprises the knowledge of God through the Scriptures, the grace of

Panem noſtrum.

Our daily bread: food for the soul in the Word and the Eucharist,
and, in the background, food for the body.
From Erasmus' *Precatio Dominica* (Basel: Froben [1523]), B5.
Courtesy of the Beinecke Rare Book and Manuscript Library,
Yale University.

God's Spirit, and Jesus Christ himself who, in an allusion to the Eucharist, is the heavenly bread and the new wine.[177]

Predicating the verbs *pascere* and *alere* of God, Erasmus shows that the Father feeds and nourishes Christians and that they depend on him and his providence for their sustenance. They can trust that the Father will provide for them. Since, owing to the kindness of their fathers, the children of this world have no anxiety about getting food, it is fitting that, in accordance with Jesus' teaching (Matthew 6: 34), God's children should be even less anxious for the needs of tomorrow.[178] Jesus left them with an image of a heavenly Father who is so bounteous, kind, and loving that the God who feeds the sparrows and clothes the lilies of the field will not allow his children to lack clothing or food. Since they desire spiritual and heavenly nourishment, they nevertheless neglect all else in order to seek God's kingdom and his justice (cf. Matthew 6: 33), which is a spiritual justice.[179]

The spiritual bread with which the Father nourishes his children helps them to keep his commandments.[180] This bread refreshes the afflicted, raises up those who have fallen down, gives strength to the weak, lifts up the diffident, and confers eternal life.[181] In making us grow daily in virtue 'until we, according to the measure of our nature, reach the perfect strength of fullness, which is in Christ Jesus,'[182] it also brings about our spiritual transformation. Erasmus' readers tell the Father: 'If daily you will be pleased to bestow on your children their share of this bread, day by day the hunger and thirst for worldly things will decrease in us.'[183] Not all people will find this bread 'sweet,' for it is bitter to those whose souls are infected by the fever of evil desires.[184]

God makes the spiritual bread efficacious, for it does not bring life unless God, adding 'the seasoning of heavenly grace,' provides it every day. If God does not provide it, preachers offer in vain the bread that is the Gospel. Many eat Christ's body and hear the Gospel, but they are by no means invigorated by the spiritual bread since they did not deserve that the Father invisibly give it to them. Therefore, Christians ask their most kind Father to impart this bread to his children every day until they eat of it in heaven.[185]

'FORGIVE US OUR TRESPASSES AS WE FORGIVE THOSE WHO TRESPASS AGAINST US'

Explaining the fifth petition of the Lord's Prayer, Erasmus points out the obvious: sin is an inescapable fact of human life. It is impossible to live in this world without human wrongdoing.[186] As long as we lug about our mortal flesh, we sin every day.[187] Erasmus treats sinful human nature gently. Human beings, as Cornelis Augustijn has observed in Erasmus' defence of the free will, are not so much evil as they are weak.[188] Sins are not the product of a corrupt and thoroughly vitiated nature. Human beings sin every day on account of their human weakness, which Erasmus calls *imbecillitas* or *infirmitas*. In the *Paraphrase on Mark*, he contrasts the malice of Judas with the disciples who desert Jesus 'through the weakness of their nature' and with Peter who denies Jesus 'through human weakness.'[189] Erasmus often refers to human weakness, usually in connection with human sinfulness and especially in his interpretation of the fifth petition of the Lord's Prayer.[190]

Since Christians sin every day, they are daily in need of God's mercy.[191] Erasmus fashions the prayer for God's mercy and forgiveness as a prayer for peace with God. Invoking God's *clementia*, readers of the *Paraphrase on Matthew* implore the Father: 'When you are offended by our faults, do not take away your spirit from us, but, according to your clemency, forgive us our faults, which we have committed against you through weakness, so that we may have peace with you.' Yet it is not only peace with God that they desire. They pray that he forgive them their offences as they forgive those who offend them. Erasmus uses the fifth petition to remind his readers that they also need to be at peace with their neighbour, a peace without which they cannot pray the Lord's Prayer worthily as members of Christ's body, the church. Resuming the request for mercy quoted above, they ask God to forgive their faults so that they may have peace with him, 'just as we foster mutual concord by forgiving each other if anyone has offended another.' Enjoying God's favour and mutual concord, they fight with greater strength against the devil, the common enemy.[192]

Perhaps Cyprian inspired Erasmus to present the fifth petition as a prayer for peace. Peace is a conspicuous theme in the *De dominica oratione*. God is 'the teacher of peace and the master of unity' who instructs us to 'maintain peace with our brothers.' Discussing the fifth petition, Cyprian explains that God teaches us to be peacemakers, to be of the same heart (*concordes*) and of the same mind (*unanimes*). We, who through our second birth have begun to become the children of God, ought to remain in God's peace. God does not receive the sacrifice of someone at odds with a brother but commands him to leave the altar and first be reconciled to his brother (Matthew 5: 23–4) 'so that with peaceful prayers God too may be appeased.' 'The greater sacrifice to God,' Cyprian maintains, 'is our peace and fraternal concord and a people joined together in the unity of the Father, and of the Son, and of the Holy Spirit.'[193]

As with Cyprian before him, it seems at times that Erasmus accords greater priority to encouraging human concord than to praying for peace with God. Perhaps this is because God forgives more easily than human beings. In the *Modus orandi Deum*, Erasmus writes that the fifth petition 'pertains to the preservation of fraternal concord and of peace with God.'[194] The order here is significant: peace with one's neighbour precedes peace with God. Although in the *Precatio Dominica* God's children ask their Father to correct their faults,[195] the fifth prayer emphasizes their sins against each other and the consequent need for human harmony. Calling upon the 'heavenly Father, author of peace, and lover of concord,' they recollect the many ways in which his goodness unites them with 'so many bonds of harmony.' He quickens them with the same Spirit, cleanses them with the same baptism, brings them together in the same house, which is the church, supports them with the sacraments common to the church, and calls them in equal measure to the same heavenly inheritance. It is his will that his children live harmoniously within his family so that, united by mutual charity, they might live at peace with each other in his family and not allow any strife among the members of the same body. Yet, owing to the weakness of human nature, they do sin, and their sins would 'cloud over,' if not extinguish, the 'serenity of fraternal concord' if God in his mercy did not daily forgive them. Whenever Christians offend their brothers, they offend the Father, who commanded them to love their neighbour as themselves.[196]

Erasmus' insistence on the need to preserve love and harmony among God's children shows that the second part of the petition, 'as we forgive our debtors,' takes on in his thought at least as much importance as the request for God's forgiveness. In the first edition of the *Annotations*, he holds that the clause added to this request represents a resemblance or comparison (*similitudo*) between our forgiveness and God's, not a condition for receiving

God's mercy.[197] He expresses the comparison with the word 'quemadmodum' in the *Paraphrases* on Matthew and Luke and in the 'Precatio ad Patrem.' Christians pray that God may forgive their sins just as they forgive those who sin against them.

Despite his judgment in the *Annotations*, Erasmus also understands the fifth petition to impose on Christians the condition of mutual forgiveness for receiving God's mercy. Having explained the Our Father, Jesus challenges the readers of the *Paraphrase on Matthew* to consider whether they are worthy to say the prayer he has taught them. He first prefaces his explanation of the prayer by demanding of his readers peace and charity through their forgiveness of one another's sins. He concludes with another exhortation to concord. To determine their worthiness in praying the Our Father, they must especially consider if they are peace with their neighbours. Erasmus makes Jesus admonish his audience: 'The Father will treat you in the same way you treat your neighbour. He does not recognize anyone to be his son who is not at peace with his brother. If you forgive those people who offend you, your heavenly Father will forgive your offences against them. And if you will be severe and unrelenting towards other people, your Father will not forgive you your sins.'[198] In this paraphrase of Matthew 6: 14–15,[199] the verses which immediately follow upon the Lord's Prayer and reinforce the fifth petition, Erasmus completes his treatment of the Lord's Prayer in the *Paraphrase on Matthew*.

Although in the *Paraphrase on Luke* Erasmus at first compares human forgiveness with God's forgiveness, in recapitulating his paraphrase in the form of a prayer he makes it sound as if our mutual pardoning *causes* the bestowal of God's mercy: 'forgive according to your clemency because (*quandoquidem*) we forgive each other.'[200] This notion of causation appears also in his enumeration of Christian commonplaces in the preface to the *Paraphrase on James* (1520). Mutual forgiveness takes its place among these. Erasmus believes: 'The virtuous action which most inclines God to forgive our sins is that we should forgive our brother when he sins against us and that when he wanders we should lovingly recall him to the right way.'[201] In his catechism, Erasmus asserts that God's children pray that God may pardon their faults but they are not really willing to obtain this request unless they have called down God's mercy on themselves by forgiving one another.[202] His most explicit expression of the conditional nature of God's forgiveness occurs in the *Precatio Dominica*. Here the pardoning of one's neighbour from the heart is the 'aequissima impetrandae veniae conditio,' the most equitable condition of obtaining God's mercy.[203]

This condition is a 'remedy' for sins and a 'sure hope' that God will forgive them. It rests both upon the authority of Jesus' command to forgive and upon his teaching to leave one's offering at the altar in order first to reconcile oneself with one's brother.[204] With some rhetoric of righteous indignation, Erasmus in the *Precatio Dominica* reinforces the condition that Jesus lays down. How can someone who is prepared to take revenge on his brother for a minor fault be so bold as to beseech God to stay his vengeance; or how can anyone who continues to be angry with a neighbour demand of the Father to abate his wrath? With what sort of self-confidence does a sinner, refusing to forgive a brother whom he repeatedly wrongs, boast of being a member of Jesus, who was innocent of any wrongdoing and who on the cross asked the Father to forgive his executioners?[205] Erasmus makes it very clear that it is rash and unworthy of Christians to pray for God's mercy and at the same time obstinately to refuse to forgive the faults of their neighbour, faults that are, according to the 'Precatio ad Patrem,' mere 'offensiunculae' or peccadilloes compared with their more serious offences against the Father.[206] Christians must fulfil the condition to forgive in order to be forgiven. Since this may be difficult to do, Erasmus includes in the *Precatio Dominica* and the 'Precatio ad Patrem' a prayer that God help his children to forgive their neighbours so that they might all live in peace with one another.[207] In making this prayer, Erasmus' readers acknowledge that they cannot pray with any sincerity unless they are inwardly disposed to pardon others. As people who pray, God's children are obliged to be at peace with their neighbours, a peace that is grounded in their desire and ability to forgive.

Erasmus' insistence on mutual forgiveness as a necessary condition for obtaining God's pardon harmonizes well with patristic, medieval, and Tridentine thought. Cyprian teaches that Jesus imposed upon us a 'definite condition and stipulation that we should ask our debts to be forgiven us only in so far as we ourselves also forgive our debtors, knowing that we cannot obtain what we seek for our sins unless we ourselves also do likewise for those who sin against us.'[208] Augustine singles out for special attention the fifth petition of the Lord's Prayer. In no other request do we pray in such a way as if to enter into a sort of contract with God. If we violate this contract, the entire prayer is of no advantage to us.[209] In harmony with Augustine, Thomas Aquinas states that only in the fifth petition 'is a condition laid down when it says "As we forgive those, etc." If, therefore, you do not forgive, you will not be forgiven.'[210] The Roman Catechism teaches that these words have both 'the force of a comparison' and 'the mark of a condition.'[211]

It would seem that the Protestant reformers, with their theology of God's unmerited forgiveness, could not countenance imposing any condition on the bestowal of what God gives at his pleasure and of what human beings undeservingly receive. Yet Jean Carmignac's assessment that the Reformation regarded the second part of the fifth petition as a 'simple similitude' is inadequate.[212] Luther and Calvin regarded our forgiveness of those who sin against us as a condition for obtaining God's mercy. As Erasmus in the *Precatio Dominica* called forgiveness a 'sure hope' for obtaining God's mercy, so Luther in the Large Catechism writes that God, in order to assure us, has promised that everything will be forgiven us inasmuch as we also forgive our neighbour.[213] Calvin admonishes that 'we should not seek of God the forgiveness of sins unless even we ourselves forgive the offences against us of all those who harm us or who have harmed us.' If we continue to hate these people, we are in effect praying that God should not forgive us.[214] Both theologians, however, take care to point out that human forgiveness does not merit God's forgiveness; it is simply a sign to assure Christians that God has forgiven them.[215]

That Luther and Calvin relegate the condition to the status of a sign shows that they are uncomfortable with the condition. Erasmus, who does not bring up the subject of merit in his treatment of the fifth petition, is much more resolute in asserting the condition of forgiving our neighbour as a means to obtaining God's forgiveness. This is not to say that the concept of merit is foreign to his expositions of the Lord's Prayer. At the end of the second prayer of the *Precatio Dominica*, Erasmus points out that it is the Father's kindness, expressed in the giving of his Son and of his Spirit, and not our merits, which amount to nothing, that gives us confidence that we will see the Father face to face in his heavenly kingdom.[216] Although Erasmus discounts human merit, he nevertheless believes, as he holds in the *De libero arbitrio*, that human beings freely can make some minimal contribution to the accomplishment of their salvation. His insistence that God's forgiveness of sins depends on mutual forgiveness among Christians accords well with his belief about the free will. It is for Christians to choose whether they sincerely desire God's mercy. If they do desire it, they know what they must do.

'LEAD US NOT INTO TEMPTATION, BUT DELIVER US FROM EVIL/THE EVIL ONE'

The church fathers were not overly concerned with the enumeration of the petitions of the Lord's Prayer. Tertullian and Cyprian treated the last two petitions as two separate requests, whereas Gregory of Nyssa, Ambrose, and John Chrysostom joined them into one. Expounding the Sermon on the Mount, Augustine, who attached great significance to the symbolic value of the number seven, kept the petitions separate. Influenced by Augustine in so many ways, western Christian thinkers perpetuated the tradition of seven petitions as distinct from six. This was the case before and after the Reformation with the notable exceptions of Bucer and Calvin, who both understood the petition for deliverance to be an appendage to the petition about temptation and therefore taught that the Lord's Prayer comprised six petitions.[217]

Erasmus accepts the established tradition, dividing the *Precatio Dominica* into seven and giving the sense of the seven petitions in the *Modus orandi Deum*. Nevertheless, he thinks the last two petitions could be considered as one. As he points out in the dedication to the *Precatio Dominica*, the sixth and seventh petitions, 'Et ne nos inducas in tentationem, sed libera nos a malo,' should no more rightly be separated than the fifth petition, 'Et remitte nobis debita nostra, sicut et nos remittimus debitoribus nostris,' should be split into two.[218] Consequently, he usually explains the last two petitions as though they were of one piece. The concluding sentence of the exposition of the Lord's Prayer in his catechism gives the sense of the sixth and seventh petitions (in reverse order) in rapid succession: 'Finally, when they [i.e. God's children] consider what a kind Lord they have [and] what a loving

Father, who gave up his only-begotten Son to death in order to redeem them from the tyranny of Satan, they pray that they not fall back by the Father's permission into the power of that wicked one and thus be drawn into temptation so that they deserve to be disinherited by a good Father.'[219] Since Erasmus sees fit to consider the last two petitions together, so shall we.

Erasmus believes that temptations are an inescapable part of this earthly life. His readers learn from him that the Christian life is a warfare against vice and against their inclinations to sin, and he constantly encourages them to choose virtue over vice. He begins the *Enchiridion* by pointing out that 'we are ceaselessly under attack by the armour-clad forces of vice, ensnared by so many wiles, beleaguered by so many treacheries.'[220] His readers acknowledge in the *Precatio Dominica* that to the very end of their lives a thousand means of destruction threaten them. The devil's snares confront them everywhere. No one can hope for immunity from temptation, not even those who enjoy God's favour in a special way. Job, David, Solomon, and Peter, the prince of the apostles, all experienced temptation, and the last three succumbed. When God's children consider their temptations and their sins, they cannot but take fright at the dangers of temptation. Dangers beset them not only when they are threatened by adversity: the plundering of their property, exile, insults, imprisonment, physical torture, and horrifying death. For they are no less at risk from the blandishments of prosperity.[221]

Erasmus advises in the *Enchiridion*: 'For we must expect one temptation after another and must never put down our arms, never desert our post, never relax our guard, while we are in the garrison of this body.'[222] The readers of the *Precatio Dominica* learn that they stand on guard when they arm themselves with sobriety, vigilance, and prayer against the constant attacks of Satan, the tempter.[223] All the same, in the battle against temptation Christians cannot rely on their own strength. Consequently, they pray for the Father's protection so that he might keep them safe from the devil's machinations and so that they might conquer temptation.[224] When they pray 'lead us not into temptation,' they do not so much ask the Father to spare them from the experience of temptation as to protect them in time of trial.

Satan, of course, is the one who tempts God's children. Yet if Satan tempts them, why do they ask the Father not to lead them into temptation? How could a good God possibly be responsible for tempting his children? Expositors of the Lord's Prayer have traditionally sought to shift away from God the responsibility for the enticing suggestion to sin by giving God a passive, not an active, role in temptation. Thus the request 'lead us not into temptation' does not mean that God should not tempt Christians or cause them to be tempted. They pray rather that he should not allow, permit, or suffer them to enter into temptation.[225] Hence Cyprian, in conformity with the widespread usage in the North Africa of his day, reads the relevant passage from Matthew as 'Et ne patiaris nos induci in temptationem.'[226] A few writers, however, departed from the traditional passive understanding of the petition. Among these were Hugh of St Victor, Albert the Great, and in the sixteenth century, Bucer and Calvin, who thought that God actively caused temptation.[227] Bucer speaks of God leading into temptation both those who sin but do not persevere in sin and those who are 'perpetually inured to impiety.'[228] Calvin holds that God not only surrenders human beings to the lust of Satan, but also, by using the devil as the minister of his wrath, God himself in his own way leads them into temptation whenever he wishes to drive them headlong to their doom. Nothing stands in the way of God's selling them off to Satan, his thrusting upon them a reprobate mind and foul desires, and thus his leading them into temptation by a just but inscrutable judgment.[229]

Erasmus, who could not have agreed with this aspect of Calvin's conception of God, never states categorically in his expositions of the Lord's Prayer whether God tempts human beings or not. Nevertheless, he obviously conforms to the traditional interpretation when in the *Paraphrase on Luke*, the *Precatio Dominica* and the *Explanatio symboli* he speaks of God's permitting or allowing his children to be afflicted by or to enter into temptation or to fall back into the devil's power.[230] In the *Paraphrase on Matthew* and in the 'Precatio ad Patrem,' however, he has his readers pray that God should not hand them over to be tempted by the devil or should not deliver them into the devil's hands.[231] Erasmus is inconsistent. On the one hand he absolves God of responsibility, for it is human beings who enter temptation, and on the other he suggests that God is an instrumental cause of temptation by 'turning us over to Satan' as Calvin says. The inconsistency becomes even more complex when one observes that the request in the *Paraphrase on Matthew* that God should not hand us over to be tempted by the devil reappears two sentences later in passive form when we ask the Father, if he should allow us to enter into temptation, to deliver us from the devil.[232] Given Erasmus' emphasis on God's goodness and his adamant refusal in the *De libero arbitrio* to accept God as the author of human evil,[233] it is safe to say that, despite the inconsistency in his exposition, he sides with the consensus in interpreting the relationship between God and our susceptibility to temptation. He adheres to the consensus in his paraphrase of the warning of James 1: 13 that no one should say that anyone is tempted by God. God is not at fault if someone should choose to be taken in by the allurements of this age or to depart from true piety when afflicted by hardships. God does not present human beings with opportunities for sinning. The truth of the matter is that they turn what God in his goodness bestows on them for the sake of piety into an opportunity for destruction. God blesses them with prosperity to elicit their gratitude, and on occasion he allows them to suffer adversity to put their piety to the proof and increase our reward. If things turn out differently, the blame falls on them, not on God. Since he is good by nature, he cannot be tempted (*sollicitari*) by any evils, nor does he incite (*sollicitat*) anyone to do evil.[234]

The Father does not tempt us, but he allows us to be tempted in order to 'test (*explorare*) the firmness of our souls' or to prove our patience and to chasten and correct our faults.[235] Accepting this from the Father, his children pray that the devil's attacks will turn out for their good, that the Father will see to it that the final result of their temptations will be a happy one and give them the strength to match the evils that confront them.[236] Just as they rely on God's protection to uphold them in the 'storm of temptation,' so they also are sure that their adversary the devil can do nothing against them without God's permission.[237] Erasmus thus would agree with Cyprian, who teaches that the petition that God not allow us to be brought into temptation shows that 'the enemy can do nothing against us unless God first permitted it, so all our fear and devotion and observation may be turned towards God since in temptations nothing is allowed the evil one unless the power be given him from God.'[238]

The devil has no autonomous power to ensnare human

beings; he is subject and subordinate to God. Christians need not worry that the Father has given up his government of the world or has abandoned them in their warfare against temptation. When they are the weaker party in the confrontation with temptation, they look to God's wisdom to arrange things for their good. For his Son conquered Satan, the flesh, and the world in such a way that he triumphed most of all when he seemed to be in the greatest distress. 'And what is more,' Erasmus' readers tell the Father in the sixth prayer of the *Precatio Dominica*, 'for us he has fought, for us he has conquered, for us he has triumphed. May we also conquer by his example and by your protection through the Holy Spirit proceeding from both of you for all ages. Amen.'[239]

The Satan whom Christians wish to conquer with God's protection is a frightful enemy. With Chrysostom Erasmus takes the Greek word *ponerou*, the genitive of either *poneros* or *poneron*, to be masculine instead of neuter and thus prefers to seek deliverance from 'the evil one' more than from 'malice.'[240] Erasmus portrays this evil one in all his wickedness. In the seventh prayer of the *Precatio Dominica*, we call to mind 'what a foul father we had ... and what an unkind lord we served' in our former unredeemed state.[241] God did not create the devil a malicious being, yet this he became by rebelling against God's majesty. Envying our first parents' happy state in paradise, he enticed them into death, and now he is inflamed with even fiercer envy because the Father opens heaven to those who were initially excluded from paradise and because he invites those destined for death to blessed immortality through faith in his Son Jesus. Thus Satan never sleeps, never ceases to prowl about like a hungry, roaring lion, looking for someone to devour (1 Peter 5: 8). With, as it were, a thousand tricks up his sleeve he tries to bring about our doom.[242]

No one can be more unlike God the 'kind Lord' and 'loving Father,'[243] who cares for his lost and sick sheep,[244] than Satan the tyrant, our former foul father and unkind lord. In the *Paraphrase on Matthew*, we ask our 'best Father' to deliver us from this the worst of creatures: '... tu, Pater optime, libera nos ab illo pessimo.'[245] Finally, as exiles on earth, Erasmus' readers end the 'Precatio ad Patrem,' requesting the heavenly Father that they, persevering through faith and charity in the church, in the company of his most kind Son, may attain eternal life which knows no wrongdoing or danger from Satan.[246]

This final petition from the 'Precatio ad Patrem' reminds us again of the *scopus* of prayer. In the *Explanatio symboli*, Erasmus explains that the Lord's Prayer lacks a petition for attaining eternal life because good children, solely interested in enjoying the favour of their father, do not worry about their inheritance.[247] The obvious inference is that God's children should not be anxious about their eternal destiny. Nevertheless, the desire for heaven as well as the love of God's glory pervade Erasmus' interpretation of the Lord's Prayer. Whether Erasmus' readers call upon the Father in whose heavenly house they hope to enjoy eternal happiness; pray for the glorification of his name; long for the manifestation of his kingdom; seek to do his will so that they will increasingly become one with his Spirit; desire that he give them in word and sacrament his Son Jesus, the spiritual bread which confers upon them eternal life; or cry out for liberation from Satan's tyranny, Erasmus constantly keeps the desire for eternal life and for whatever pertains to God's glory at the centre of the prayer to the heavenly Father. In pursuit of their spiritual goal, Erasmus' Christian soldiers stand ready to transform themselves and to allow themselves to be transformed by saying the Lord's Prayer. Their hope for eternal happiness moves them to endure everything. Their love for the Father and his heavenly kingdom encourages them to conform their lives to the *Evangelica doctrina* that Christ preached when he spoke of God's kingdom. Wishing to attain that kingdom of concord, they commit themselves to do God's will and to promote peace by forgiving those who offend them.

Erasmus' image of God in his expositions of the Lord's Prayer certainly inspires reverence in those who invoke the all-powerful and most wise heavenly Father. In his wisdom, God knows what is best for them, what they really need; in his power he can grant their petitions. God's goodness crowns his power and wisdom. That the Father in heaven is good by nature and that he lovingly carries his children like a kind shepherd disproves the claim that in Erasmus' religion the Father's role is 'abstract and distant.'[248] In keeping with his pastoral accommodation to his readers, Erasmus makes God very accessible and portrays him as lovable. By emphasizing God's goodness he wishes his readers above all to love God, who not only *can* answer their prayers, but who in his kindness *will* answer them. Their good Father is the God of salvation. Encouraged by Erasmus to love his kindness, they cannot but fervently desire the object of all their prayers: to be with God for ever in his heavenly kingdom and their heavenly home.

FOUR

Erasmus' Prayer-Book:
The *Precationes aliquot novae*

༄

In the *Precatio Dominica*, Erasmus paraphrased the Lord's Prayer in the form of seven prayers so that his readers could learn about prayer by praying. In 1535, Froben published another collection of prayers by Erasmus, the *Precationes aliquot novae*. This prayer-book was one of many new sixteenth-century devotional manuals, both Catholic and Protestant, that competed with the popular late medieval Books of Hours, celebrated for the beautiful illuminations that many of them contain. Erasmus' 'new prayers' bear witness to his fundamental concepts of the 'certain principal part of piety.'

A brief survey of the history of Christian prayer-books will help to put the *Precationes aliquot novae* into context. The first Christian prayer-book, the Psalter, was not Christian but Jewish. Throughout the centuries, the psalms have served as the basic staple of monastic prayer, but they have also been the prayers of all Christians. Paul's command to 'sing psalms and hymns and spiritual songs with thankfulness in your hearts to God' (Colossians 3: 16, RSV) had universal application. Since the beginnings of Christianity, the Psalter served as the prayer-book both in the public liturgy and in the private sphere. It 'became the Christian's earliest book of private devotion and source of fresh devotional creation.'[1] Eusebius of Caesarea (d. c.339) recorded that among the Greeks and 'barbarians' the psalms were not only sung in churches but also in the alleys and streets and upon the fields.[2]

In the forward to his *De psalmorum usu*, Alcuin (d. 804) establishes nine themes or categories into which the psalms can be divided. Not surprisingly, the first of these themes is penance, for

Alcuin's prayer life was dominated by 'the prayer of petition, petition for forgiveness of sin.'[3] The *Officia per ferias*, attributed to Alcuin, supplies psalm texts for each day of the week as well as a lengthy confession of sins, the *Te Deum*, a litany of the saints, and prayers attributed to, among others, Augustine, Ambrose, and Gregory the Great.[4] This prayer-book is one of the so-called *libelli precum*, books of devotion intended in the first place for Carolingian emperors and kings.[5] Characteristic of these *libelli precum* are prayers for the forgiveness of one's sins and prayers addressed to the Trinity or to the Father, the Son, and the Holy Spirit individually. The strong Trinitarian element of these prayers together with an emphasis on the divinity of Christ functioned as a bulwark against adoptionism, a heresy that denied Christ's divinity and that had surfaced again in eighth-century Spain.[6]

The Carolingian *libelli precum* served as supplements to the Psalter,[7] whose prestige remained unchallenged until the thirteenth century. Over the centuries, prayer texts other than the psalms found their way into the Psalters. The Utrecht Psalter, dating from the early ninth century, contains the *Te Deum*, the *Gloria in excelsis Deo*, the *Pater Noster*, and the *Credo*. By the thirteenth century, many Psalters incorporated the church's liturgical calendar, the litany of the saints, prayers to individual saints and in honour of the Holy Cross or Blessed Sacrament, and votive offices to the Trinity, to the Holy Spirit, to the Virgin Mother, and for the dead.[8]

One of these offices, the Little Office of the Blessed Virgin Mary, became the 'basic text of Books of Hours'[9] or, to use Roger Wieck's metaphor, 'the main altar as it were, around which was constructed an elaborate Gothic cathedral of prayers and pictures.'[10] The Books of Hours, the Latin prayer-books for laypeople from kings and queens to wealthy burghers, take their name from their most common incipit: 'Incipiunt hore beate Marie Virginis.'[11] Except for those produced by the printing press, no two Books of Hours are exactly alike. Their popularity may be measured by the fact that 'they form the largest single category of illuminated manuscripts which now exists ... So many were made, so many still exist, that nobody can hope to see or record them all.'[12]

Through its various votive offices, which comprised all or some of the eight liturgical hours of matins, lauds, prime, terce, sext, none, vespers, and compline, a Book of Hours allowed the laity to imitate the liturgical piety of monks and clerics. The Hours of the Virgin, the Marian prayers *Obsecro te* and *O intemerata*, the hymn *Stabat mater*, and the prayer recalling the Fifteen Joys of the Virgin bear witness to the late medieval cult of Mary. Devotion to the other saints manifested itself in the litany of the saints and in the suffrages, consisting usually of an antiphon, a versicle, a response, and an oration. The antiphon commonly addressed one or more saints, whereas the oration invoked God.[13] A typical Book of Hours also included, among other things, a liturgical calendar, a lesson from each of the four Gospels, the seven penitential psalms, and the Office for the Dead. The *Hortulus animae* first appeared in the last decade of the fifteenth century and was soon translated into German. To the texts commonly found in the Books of Hours it adds various occasional prayers, such as morning and evening prayers, prayers to be said upon leaving one's house, upon entering a church, and upon receiving Communion.[14]

In England, the Book of Hours, called the Primer, survived the first waves of Protestantism, but not without undergoing in the 1530s several experiments at reform. Primers began to appear in English. The liturgical calendar was simplified by the reduction of the number of saints' feast-days. The commemoration of Gregory the Great was retained, but he was listed as the bishop of Rome and not as the pope. Some primers shortened or suppressed the litany, while another offered a litany accompanied by an admonition about superstitious prayers to the saints. The cult of Mary was weakened by replacing antiphons and hymns addressed to her in the Office of the Virgin with texts addressed to Christ. A reduced Office for the Dead used psalms whose themes were praise and thanksgiving as distinguished from petition and penance.[15] So significant was the reform begun in the 1530s that the Primer edited in 1539 by John Hilsey, the bishop of Rochester, at the order of Thomas Cromwell, and the official King's Primer, which appeared under the patronage of Henry VIII in 1545, were essentially Protestant books.[16]

Unlike the English Reformation, which initially retained the Primer, the German Reformation had little use for the *Hortulus animae*. Luther did not reform the *Hortulus animae* but produced an alternative to it. The first edition of his *Betbüchlein*, published perhaps in the beginning of June 1522,[17] provides a list of the various ways one can violate and fulfil the Ten Commandments, an explanation of the Apostles' Creed, a paraphrase of the Lord's Prayer in the form of seven prayers to match its seven petitions, an exposition of the *Ave Maria*, a German translation of eight psalms, and the Epistle to Titus.[18]

Early Protestant prayer-books supplied prayers taken directly or adapted from the Scriptures. The most notable example is Otto Brunfels' *Precationes Biblicae Sanctorum Patrum, Illustrium Virorum et Mulierum utriusque Testamenti*, published in Strassburg in 1528 and appearing in the same year in German translation as the *Biblisch Bettbüchlein der Altvätter und herrlichen Weibern, beyd Alts und Newes Testaments*.[19] This book went through many editions and was translated into several languages. In England, Robert Redman published it in 1535 under the title of *Prayers of the Byble*. Another example of what appears to be an English version of Brunfels' compilation is the *Praiers of holi fathers, Patryarches, Prophetes, Iudges, Kynges, and renowmed men and women of eyther testamente*, published by Richard Grafton in the 1540s.[20]

As books of prayers taken from Scripture appeared in print, Protestants and Catholics also published their own collections of prayers. These prayers were occasional in nature, intended to be said at certain times and in particular circumstances. The new prayer-books also provided prayers to be said by or for people of different ages, of various walks of life, and of specific standing in family and society. Thus, Paul Althaus argues that these books show signs of 'an increasing individualization of prayers' that marks a significant turning-point in the development of Protestant prayer-books in the middle of the sixteenth century.[21] Convinced of the impossibility of writing a history of Protestant devotional literature without taking Catholic writings into account,[22] Althaus looks for the origins of this turning-point in Catholic prayer-books. He begins his search with Erasmus' *Precationes aliquot novae*, which clearly belongs to the genre of the books of occasional prayers.

First published by Froben in Basel in August 1535, the *Precationes aliquot novae, ac rursus novis adauctae, quibus adolescentes assuescant cum Deo colloqui*, as the full title of the *editio princeps* went, consisted of the *Precationes* proper, a collection of twenty-seven prayers to which Erasmus appended the *Eiaculationes*, a series of thirty-five short prayers. Also included in the volume were three previously published texts: the *Precatio ad Virginis Filium Jesum*, which first appeared in the *Lucubratiunculae* of 1503, the *Precatio ad Dominum Jesum pro pace ecclesiae* (1532), and the *Precatio Dominica* (1523). The title of the prayer-book is misleading, therefore. The first series of twenty-seven prayers are 'new,' but the texts that supplement these prayers do not constitute entirely new material. Even the last thirteen texts from the *Eiaculationes* are, as the running heads on the pages in question indicate, 'precationes e scriptis Erasmi,' from which we can infer that they predated the prayer-book. J. Trapman has called attention to this and has located the sources of the thirteen prayers. One of them reproduces the *secreta* of the *Virginis Matris apud Lauretum cultae liturgia*; the rest come from the *Colloquies*.[23] Erasmus took two of the texts that appear in the *Convivium religiosum* from a hymn recited by monks after meals and quoted in John Chrysostom's *Homilies on Matthew*.[24] Trapman surmises that the title of the book with its 'new' prayers 'was devised by the publisher to arouse the interest of the public.'[25]

Some posthumous editions of the prayer-book added other material. In 1551, Jerome Frobenius and Nicolaus Episcopius of Basel put out a version that concluded with Erasmus' *Rhythmus iambicus in laudem Annae, aviae Iesu Christi*.[26] That a press of Protestant Basel should print a poem in praise of Saint Anne is quite peculiar. In 1563, Erasmus' poem appeared in an edition of his prayer-book published by Arnold Birckmann's Sons in Catholic Cologne.[27] Given that all of Erasmus' works were prohibited by Pope Paul IV's Index of 1559, the printing of the *Precationes aliquot novae* in Cologne is remarkable. The 1563 edition becomes all the more fascinating when one considers the *Simplex et succinctus orandi modus* that the Birckmanns appended to Erasmus' prayer-book.[28] The author, whose name is not given, is Martin Luther, and the work is a Latin translation of *Ein einfelige weise zu Beten fur einen guten freund*,[29] first published in the same year as the *editio princeps* of the *Precationes aliquot novae*. A similar combination of the two Latin works was published by Sébastien Gryphe of Lyon in 1542 and by Jean Frellon of the same city in 1556.[30] Although adversaries in life, Erasmus and Luther, once dead, appeared together as preceptors of piety.

Erasmus, as was evident from the title, intended his prayer-book for youths so that they could accustom themselves 'to converse with God.' Except for the students' prayers 'Pro docilitate' and 'Euntis ad ludum litterarium' as well as for the prayer 'Pro parentibus,' Erasmus' prayers are appropriate for young and old alike. Indeed, Erasmus sent a copy of the prayer-book to his friend and fellow humanist, Julius Pflug.[31]

In keeping with his desire to shape the piety of adolescents, Erasmus dedicated the book to David Paumgartner, a lad fourteen years of age and the youngest son of Johann Paumgartner. The father, a prosperous merchant of Augsburg – Erasmus described him as 'amplissime diues'[32] – was chiefly engaged in the sale of silver from the mines in which the Paumgartner family firm owned significant shares. Johann was an 'ardent Catholic,' who did not share the enthusiasm for Protestantism of his fellow Augsburgers. Unlike many Catholics, he obviously did not associate Erasmus with Luther, for he gladly became one of the humanist's patrons.[33] Erasmus admired his patron. In the dedication to David, he praises his father for ensuring that his children be instructed in piety, a possession that he deemed more blessed than all his wealth, popularity, and honours. Owing to the kind regard in which he holds Johann, Erasmus comes to the assistance of the father's requests and of the boy's efforts by sending David the prayer-book so that he might accustom himself to converse with God (*cum Deo colloqui*).[34]

The *Precationes* begin with a prayer to each person of the Trinity. The tradition begun by the Carolingian *libelli precum* thus still held sway in the sixteenth century. Prayers to the Father, the Son, and the Holy Spirit were eventually incorporated into Luther's *Betbüchlein* and may also be found, for example, in Thomas Becon's *Flower of Godly Prayers* and *Pomander of Prayer*.[35] After an extended salutation to the Virgin Mother Erasmus provides a morning and an evening prayer, and a prayer to be said in each of the four seasons of the year. Then follow a prayer for *docilitas*, that is, for the aptness to be taught, a prayer against temptation, a thanksgiving for victory, and prayers in time of affliction and of serious illness. Five prayers are intended to be said by specific types of people: by a penitent, and by persons about to receive Communion, to go on a journey, to set sail, and to enter battle. A prayer for the preservation of purity precedes a prayer for a happy marriage and another to be said on the eve of one's wedding. Erasmus continues with a prayer in time of plague, another for spiritual joy, and yet another for the preservation of a good reputation. He completes the *Precationes* with a prayer for one's parents.

To the *Precationes* Erasmus adds, as he informs David Paumgartner, several prayers taken from Scripture, 'since in these very
words, proceeding from the Holy Spirit, lies hidden a certain
mysterious spiritual energy.' These short prayers or *Eiaculationes*
burst forth from an ardent feeling of the mind, and thus they
penetrate into heaven all the more quickly. Saint Augustine
approved of these ejaculatory prayers either because the human
heart in its weakness cannot endure sustained concentration for a
long time, or because they are the sort of prayers that can be said
in any place and in the midst of carrying out one's affairs. Erasmus intended his selections simply as specimens and examples,
'for everywhere Scripture supplies countless similar [prayers].'[36]

To be exact, twenty-two of the thirty-five prayers are taken
from Scripture, and thus the *Eiaculationes* demonstrate a solidar-
ity with books such as Brunfels' *Precationes Biblicae*. The scriptural
prayers include a prayer for the pious fear of God, another
against despair, two prayers to be said in danger of death, two
prayers for the ability to be taught piety, one prayer each for the
forgiveness of sins, for purity of heart, and in time of affliction,
two prayers to be said once a temptation has been overcome, and
one prayer each against the railings of the wicked, for innocence
and uprightness of life, at the time of death, a prayer to be said by
a person recovering from illness, two prayers for a person repent-
ing of his sins, a short petition to be said for clerics, two prayers
for a young prince, a prayer against pride and extravagant desire,
and a prayer against avarice.

Erasmus completes the *Eiaculationes* with eleven prayers of his
own composition and two prayers before meals recorded by John
Chrysostom.[37] A morning prayer precedes a prayer to be said by a
student going to school, and a prayer to be said at the recitation of
1 Corinthians 5: 7: 'Cleanse out the old leaven that you may be a
new lump, as you really are unleavened' (RSV), at the reading of
the parable of the sower (Matthew 13: 1–9 and parallel texts), and
of the story of the wedding feast at Cana (John 2: 1–11). Erasmus
then provides a prayer to be said by someone about to receive the
Eucharist; a prayer to Christ for true piety; a prayer for a consensus in doctrines that, except for the mention of Reuchlin, is the
same as the collect composed by Brassicanus in the colloquy *Apotheosis Capnionis* (1522);[38] three graces in the form of two *consecra-
tiones mensae* and of one thanksgiving; and finally the two graces
that together make up the hymn related by Chrysostom.

Most of the scriptural prayers are taken from the psalms. Erasmus uses the Vulgate translation of the psalms according to the Septuagint. Psalm 24 (25): 5 is the text for the second prayer for the docility of piety: 'Lord, show me your ways and teach me your paths. Guide me in your truth and teach me, for you are God, my saviour.' The prayer 'Pro statu ecclesiastico,' the shortest of the *Eiaculationes*, is adapted from Psalm 131 (132): 9: 'May your priests put on justice, and may your saints rejoice.'[39] Erasmus sometimes stitches together his scriptural prayers from more than one source. The petition 'Pro innocentia et rectitudine vitae' begins with Psalm 85 (86): 11 and ends with Psalm 118 (119): 105: 'Lead me, Lord, in your way, and I will walk in your truth. Let my heart rejoice so that it may fear your name. May your word be a lamp for my feet and a light for my paths.'[40]

Erasmus quarries other books from the Old Testament for the *Eiaculationes*. He combines Psalm 117 (118): 18 and Isaiah 12: 1 for the prayer 'Revalescentis.' Jeremiah 31: 18–19 establishes the text for the second prayer to be said by a penitent person. The first prayer for a young prince comes from Solomon: 3 Kings 3: 7–9 (=1 Kings 3: 7–9, RSV) and Wisdom 9: 6, while Wisdom 9: 10 comprises the second prayer. The prayer 'Adversus superbiam et luxum' consists of Sirach 23: 4, of an adaptation of Isaiah 2: 22, of Psalm 35 (36): 12, of an adaptation of Sirach 23: 5, and of the text of Sirach 23: 6.[41]

The scriptural prayers indicate that Erasmus was well-versed in the Old Testament. He must have known many of the psalm texts by heart, probably having absorbed them from reciting the breviary. The twenty-two scriptural prayers can be understood as a remedy for what Erasmus criticized as a perfunctory mumbling of the psalms, most likely the mumbling of the offices in the Books of Hours. The *Eiaculationes* are short and are based on a particular theme, and thus they are quite different in spirit from what Erasmus must have felt to be a mechanical recitation of prescribed psalms.

In compiling prayers from Scripture, Erasmus puts into effect the advice he gives his readers in the *Modus orandi Deum*, namely that, if possible, they should pray with the words of Scripture.[42] Of course, they need not restrict themselves to quoting scriptural passages. They can also let such passages inspire their own discourse with God. The prayers of Erasmus' own composition manifest scriptural inspiration either through direct quotations from or allusions to Holy Writ. Into the prayer 'Pro victoria gratiarum actio' Erasmus incorporates two Pauline sayings: 'If God is for us, who can be against us?' (Romans 8: 31) and 'I can do all things in him who strengthens me' (Philippians 4: 13).[43] By putting the words of Paul into the mouths and hearts of his contemporaries Erasmus reminds them of the source of their strength in time of temptation. God is on their side, and they can do all things in Christ who strengthens them.

The student's prayer of the *Eiaculationes* quotes the divine words heard at Christ's transfiguration: 'This is my beloved Son, in whom I am well pleased; listen to him' (Matthew 17: 5).[44] Erasmus attached great importance to this text. In the *Paraclesis* (1516), this passage supports his contention that Christians should learn the philosophy of Christ, the essentials of their Christian faith, not from the scholastic doctors, but from Christ, who is their sole teacher. Erasmus insists: 'hic unicus est doctor.'[45] Youths attending school who wish to learn from Erasmus how to converse with God recall the passage from Matthew as they make their prayer to Jesus.

In the same prayer, Erasmus alludes to Luke 2: 46 when he invokes Christ, who as a boy of twelve taught the teachers in the Temple.[46] Erasmus takes liberties with this passage, for it merely says that Jesus listened to and questioned the doctors in the Temple. He does the same with John 17: 3 in the prayer 'Ad Filium.' The passage reads: 'And this is eternal life, that they know thee the only true God, and Jesus Christ whom thou hast sent' (RSV). Erasmus, however, wants to infuse the doctrine of the unity of the three persons of the Trinity into the piety of his readers. He writes: 'For eternal life is to know that the Father, and the Son, and the Holy Spirit are the one true God.'[47] His allusion to the story of the finding of Rebekah as a wife for Isaac (Genesis 24: 1–61) seems apt for someone who prays for a happy marriage. In the story, Abraham sends his servant to find a wife for his son Isaac. Sitting at a well, the servant prays that the woman who gives him some water to drink will be the woman whom God has destined to marry Isaac. Erasmus points out that the 'faithful servant of faithful Abraham ... asked of the Lord, and what he asked for he obtained.' The lesson is that Christians will find a suitable spouse by relying not on their own efforts but on God's goodness.[48]

Published scriptural prayers were not likely to arouse contro-

versy in the midst of the theological contest between Protestantism and Catholicism. One might think, however, that prayers for
the dead and to the Virgin Mary did not enjoy a firm consensus
in a doctrinally divided Christendom. Both in private prayer and
in the liturgy of the Eucharist, Christians had been praying for
deceased colleagues, friends, and family members long before
'the birth of purgatory' in the second half of the twelfth century.[49]
Once the idea of purgatory was born, the notion became current
that one could cut short the suffering of the poor souls by praying
for them. Although Reformation theology discarded purgatory,
the Reformation did not immediately abolish praying for the salvation of the dead. A Swedish burial prayer of 1529 asked God to
be gracious to a departed brother, albeit with the proviso that he
be 'in such a state that we may pray for him.' The burial ceremony in the first edition of the *Book of Common Prayer* (1549)
included petitions for the person who had died. These petitions
did not appear in the second, 1552 edition, however.[50] The various new editions of Luther's *Betbüchlein* never added a prayer for
the dead, but in two sermons of 1522 and again in 1528 in a treatise on the Eucharist, Luther allowed that one could, once or
twice, privately pray that God be gracious and merciful unto a
departed soul. Nevertheless, he condemned celebrating Masses
for the dead. Ironically, the same Luther who denounced the
invocation of the saints because Scripture did not sanction this
saw no sin in praying for the dead since Scripture was silent on
the matter.[51] Calvin was more consistent. The lack of scriptural
support led him to oppose both prayers for the dead and to the
saints.[52]

Protestant prayer-books usually did not contain prayers for
the dead, whereas Catholic prayer-books generally did. Juan Luis
Vives, the Spanish Catholic humanist, included a prayer entitled
'Pro fratribus vita functis' in his *Excitationes animi in Deum*
(1535).[53] The fact that Erasmus' *Precationes aliquot novae* provides
no similar prayer does not indicate that Erasmus disdained the
practice of praying for the dead. Amused by a rumour about his
death, he wrote to Paul Volz: 'Many thanks for the prayers you
offer for my late self, which I will gladly reciprocate when you
too are so good as to die.'[54] Death was no laughing matter for
Erasmus, however. When his friend William Warham died in
1532, he was deeply upset. In his sorrow, he was confident that
'that heavenly soul' was with Christ, and he expressed the wish

that the mercy of Christ would allow him soon to embrace his friend in that place where they will never again be separated.[55] He assured Bishop John Longland of Lincoln that he had always considered praying and offering Masses for the dead as pious.[56] Before Ulrich von Hutten died in 1523, he wrote his polemical *Expostulatio* against Erasmus. Nevertheless, when the latter heard of Hutten's demise, he 'prayed in a Christian spirit for God's mercy on his soul.' In 1531 he also commended the recently deceased Nicolò Leonico Tomeo, an Italian Greek scholar with an international reputation, to the mercy of the Lord.[57] Since Erasmus himself prayed for the dead, we cannot attribute the lack of a prayer 'pro defunctis' in his prayer-book to his personal piety or to an objection of principle. He may have omitted a prayer for the dead in the *Precationes aliquot novae* in order to make the book acceptable in the eyes of those who had broken with Rome. Trapman speculates: 'I suppose that this book of *Precationes* was read by Protestants too, and it seems likely that it was compiled with an eye to this particular readership as well. In this connection it should be noted that the *Precationes* include prayers for the sick and dying, but not for the dead.'[58]

Erasmus' *De sarcienda ecclesiae concordia*, his peace plan for a divided Christendom, proposes a *modus vivendi* for Catholics and Protestants over the issue of what one may do, if anything at all, for the departed. He begins by affirming that it is pious to believe that one can help the dead with prayers and good works. Those, however, who see to the funeral procession and make arrangements for Masses to be said should beware lest they do so for their own glory. At the same time, those who are not yet of the same opinion about helping the dead should refrain from carping at the simple nature of those with whom they disagree. Instead, with good works they should come to the assistance of the poor to weaken the belief that the dead are helped by human benefactions.[59] Although Erasmus thinks that one's money is more wisely spent on the needs of the living than on the dead, he says nothing that would undermine the practice of praying for those who have died. Here his attitude would be similar to his position in the controversy over the invocation of the saints. Those who pray for the dead should be able to do so without harassment, while those who object to such prayers should be free not to say them.

Just as the Reformation did not immediately suppress prayers for the dead, it also retained a measure of devotion to Mary. The Reformers, particularly Luther and to a lesser extent Zwingli and Calvin, honoured Mary as the ever Virgin Mother of God and as an important exemplar of Christian discipleship.[60] Lutheran Germany remembered Mary in its hymns and retained within its liturgical calendar the feasts of the Purification of Mary (Candlemas, 2 February), the Annunciation (25 March), and the Visitation (2 July), feasts on which Luther continued to preach.[61] The English Primer of 1539 contained several prayers addressed to Mary in the form of memories and anthems for the offices of lauds, prime, terce, sext, none, and evensong. At lauds, the hymn *Laudetur Deus* includes the petition: 'O Virgin Mary most gracious, / O mother of God incomparable, / To thy Son pray for us, / That he after death be favourable.'[62] The Primer of 1545 retains the invocation of the 'Holy Virgin Mary, mother of God our Saviour Jesu Christ' in the litany.[63] The *Ave Maria* appears in the above two Primers as well as the Byddell-Marshall Primer of 1535, which translates Luther's explanation of the prayer.[64]

From the twelfth century, when it became popular, until the beginning of the sixteenth century, the *Ave Maria* consisted only of the angelic greeting (Luke 1: 28) and of Elizabeth's blessing (Luke 1: 42): 'Ave Maria, gratia plena Dominus tecum. Benedicta tu in mulieribus et benedictus fructus ventris tui.' To this salutation a petition was eventually added: 'Sancta Maria, Mater Dei, ora pro nobis peccatoribus nunc et in hora mortis nostrae.' It seems that Saint Bernardino of Siena (d. 1444) was the first to use the petition, although he stopped at 'peccatoribus.' The entire prayer, as we know it today, received official sanction from Pope Pius V, who made it part of the divine office in his reform of the Roman Breviary in 1568. Yet the greeting and petition together entered into general usage only in the middle of the seventeenth century.[65]

The *Betbüchlein* and the Primers, in keeping with the medieval tradition, provide the shorter text of the *Ave Maria*. In the *Betbüchlein*, Luther warns against putting one's trust and confidence in the Mother of God or in her merits, for such confidence is due to God alone. Through Mary and through the grace given to her Christians praise and thank God, and they honour and love her as one who has received grace without earning it. As with every other part of creation, she becomes a means for reminding them to pray to God with thanksgiving. The words of the *Ave Maria* consist only of praise and honour; they do not express a petition to or invocation of Mary. The prayer provides an opportunity to recall the graces that God has bestowed. Luther suggests that if one wants to add a wish to the prayer, one ought to pray for all those who curse Christ, the fruit of the Mary's womb, namely for the Jews and papists who persecute and curse Christ's word, the Gospel.[66]

Erasmus' prayer 'Ad Virginem Matrem' is the fourth of the *Precationes*, following the prayers to the three persons of the Trinity. Beginning with the words 'Ave Maria,' it loosely paraphrases the angelic greeting. The 'Dominus tecum' of Gabriel's salutation may have inspired the statement: '... inasmuch as the Lord was with you in a unique way, so through you he also has begun to be with us in a special way.'[67] The veneration of the names of Jesus and of Mary[68] suggests a parallel with the blessing pronounced upon the Virgin and upon the fruit of her womb. Erasmus' prayer furthermore makes no petition, and in this important point he is in harmony with Luther but not with Vives. The latter composed two prayers 'Ad divam Virginem Matrem' for the *Excitationes animi in Deum*. The first of these asks Mary to obtain for us from her son that we may experience the happiness that she had when Christ was on earth; the second beseeches her to bring it about that, through the imitation of her virtues, we may belong to Christ, who belongs to her in soul and in body.[69]

In Vives' first prayer, we acknowledge that Mary ranks first in favour and in grace.[70] Erasmus' prayer avoids the theme of grace; it does not salute Mary as a woman 'full of grace.' Erasmus departed from the Vulgate at Luke 1: 28 by translating the Greek word *kecharitōmenē* as *gratiosa*, not as *gratia plena*. As Erika Rummel points out, in the 1519 edition of the *Annotations*, he 'denied that *gratia* was used here in the technical sense and cited Origen, who had described it as a common form of affectionate greeting.'[71] The text of the *Ave Maria* in Luther's *Betbüchlein* still described Mary as 'full of grace' (*voll gnaden*),[72] but in his translation of the New Testament published in September 1522 Luther followed Erasmus' lead. The relevant passage reads: 'Hail, O gracious one' (*Gegrusset seystu holdselige*).[73]

Although he passes over Mary's possession of grace in silence, Erasmus does not fail to shower praise upon the Virgin. Because of this praise, Hans Düfel claims that the Mariology inherent in Erasmus' prayer conforms to the 'exaggerated form of devotion to Mary' that was common at the end of the fifteenth century.[74] By asserting that Mary, 'the Queen of prudent virgins,' turned the curse upon Eve into a blessing, Erasmus plays on a theme whose origins lie in Justin Martyr, Tertullian, and especially Irenaeus[75] and that helped to shape medieval Marian devotion. Mary is the new Eve and the antithesis of the old Eve. The woman of the Ave undoes the wrongdoing of Eva. Mary's perfect chastity and her role in the history of salvation are the basis for her praise. Erasmus' readers salute the 'ornament of chaste mothers, who gave birth to the salvation of all.' They bid her rejoice, she, the 'glory of angels and of human beings, who brought forth the fountain of heavenly joys without the loss of virginity.' God took pleasure in her 'most modest chastity,' and out of so many thousands of virgins he judged her alone to be worthy to bear the Son of God, born for the redemption of the world. The Father loved her as a spouse; the Spirit filled her completely; the Son, both Son of God and Son of the Virgin, took on a human body from her.[76]

Christians, Erasmus believes, should not praise Mary apart from God or apart from God's plan to save the world. Erasmus evokes love for the mother of the Redeemer without indulging in sentimentality. Vives, however, recalls that Mary received the gurgling of her child with laughter and joy.[77] Compared to Vives' prayers, Erasmus' salutation of the Virgin is far from paying exaggerated devotion to Mary. Vives, not Erasmus, invokes the Virgin as a heroine and as a demigoddess: 'O vere germaneque heroina ac semidea.'[78]

The Spanish humanist alludes to Luke 2: 51 when he writes that Jesus was subject to Mary and served her: 'subditus fuit tibi, tibi inservivit.'[79] When the boy Jesus returned from the temple, he was subject to Mary and Joseph: 'et erat subditus illis,' as the Vulgate says. In 1527, Erasmus commented on this passage in the *Annotations*. He intensely disliked prayers that attributed more power to Mary than to Christ and rejected any notion that Christ, even as a man, was inferior to his mother. To be under someone means in this passage to comply (*obsecundare*) with him or her, and the person who complies is not necessarily inferior. The Lord was not in need of his mother's commands. He complied with Mary and even with Joseph, who was not his father, in order to give an example of supreme obedience, and yet Erasmus recoiled at the idea that Christ owed obedience to anyone.[80] In the *Para-*

phrase on Luke, Erasmus explains that Jesus obeyed Mary and Joseph 'not because he owed them any obedience in the business of the Gospel, but out of his goodness he submitted for a time to their weakness.' Jesus, who owed obedience to no one other than his heavenly Father, provided an example to children with what eagerness and reverence they should obey their parents. In his paraphrase of Luke 2: 51, Erasmus even adds that Mary 'in turn complied (*obsecundavit*) with her son, sensing that a certain divine power gleamed forth in him.'[81]

Not the slightest hint of the passage from Luke can be detected in the prayer 'Ad Virginem Matrem.' Mary is certainly worthy of praise, but she has from God the honour that she possesses. Erasmus' readers tell the Virgin that the 'whole world acknowledges with what honour God has distinguished you.' Mary, moreover, does not impugn the primacy of her son. Christ is clearly more important, and upon him does his mother's exalted position depend. When Erasmus' readers venerate their names, they first venerate the name of the son, at which every knee bends in heaven, on earth, and in the underworld (Philippians 2: 10), and then they honour that of Mary, in which every soul that loves the name of Jesus finds joy. As they speak to the Virgin, they compare Christ to the sun, who with his brightness outshines the glory of all the saints. The implication seems to be that Mary, although the greatest of the saints, cannot exceed her son in glory. Among all praiseworthy women she shines like the moon in the midst of lesser stars.[82] The moon may seem brighter than the other stars in the sky, but it only reflects the light of the sun. Erasmus' use of the metaphors of the sun and of the moon appropriately conveys the relationship between Jesus and Mary. The Virgin is *subdita Christo*, subordinate to her son, and not the other way around. She derives her significance from him. The prayerful greeting concludes: 'Indeed, the splendour of your name is so bound up with the glory of [your] son, that however often the adorable name of Jesus is heard, the memory of his blessed mother Mary presents itself. Once you shared in the sorrow of your son who suffered for us; now you sit beside the one who reigns in heaven, a partner in his dignity and joy. Amen.'[83]

Given what Erasmus says and does not say in his prayer, especially when we compare it with the prayers composed by Vives, one cannot agree with Düfel. The prayer's praise of Mary is generous but not excessive. By subordinating Mary to Christ

Erasmus incorporates Marian devotion within the framework of a Christocentric piety. His respect for the Virgin is modest, circumscribed by the mystery of the redemption, but still genuine. Erasmus' Greek votive poem, the liturgy in honour of the Virgin of Loreto, and the two prayers to Mary included in the colloquy *Peregrinatio religionis ergo* corroborate this assessment. Luther's admonition about saying the *Ave Maria* introduces an element of uneasiness about devotion to the Virgin Mother that is not imparted by Erasmus' prayer.

Althaus claims that the communal 'we' of the earliest Protestant prayers eventually gave way to the subjective 'I' in the new books of occasional prayers, to the individual concerned with his own needs and experiences.[84] The majority of Erasmus' prayers, seventeen of the *Precationes* and four of the *Eiaculationes*, are made in the first person singular, but some of these keep the wider Christian community in mind. The person who says the prayer 'Ad Filium' introduces a petition with 'I pray' (*oro*) yet in the same breath remembers that Christ gave himself to save 'us' and a few phrases later affirms that from him 'we have learned the sure and ready way to true salvation.'[85] The Communion prayer 'Sumturi Corpus Dominicum,' which makes its request in the first person singular, begins by recalling Christ's 'ineffable charity towards us.'[86] Erasmus' construction of the petition to God 'Pro parentibus' in a rather puzzling way mixes the first persons plural and singular: 'Preserve, we ask, my parents with all my family first of all in the love of your religion, [and] then safe from disturbance in body and in mind.'[87]

Not counting the prayer for one's parents, nine of the *Precationes* are addressed in the first person plural to God, while two prayers are similarly expressed in the *Eiaculationes*. A single individual offers the requests in the prayer 'Ad Christum pro vera pietate' and in the second of the Erasmian prayers at table, but the requests are made for 'us': that, in the first instance, Christ draw us to himself and, in the second, that he be pleased to be in our midst as we eat.[88] The first grace by Erasmus is a wish in the third person singular: 'May he who nourishes all things with his kindness bid whatever has been and will be set before [us] to be fruitful and sacred. Amen.'[89]

Fifteen of the *Precationes* and one of the *Eiaculationes* end with a Trinitarian doxology. For example, the prayer 'Diluculo ad Christum' concludes: 'You who live and reign for all ages with the Father and the Holy Spirit.'[90] In the *Precationes*, ten prayers are addressed to God the Father, fourteen to the Son, two to the Holy Spirit, and one, as we have seen, to the Virgin Mother. Two of the Erasmian *Eiaculationes* are addressed to the Father and seven to the Son, while two other prayers do not invoke a particular person of the Trinity. The many prayers to the Son infuse a Christocentric piety into Erasmus' readers. They greet Christ in the morning and in the evening, and they appeal to him for the gifts of teachableness (*docilitas*) and spiritual joy, for the ability to withstand temptation, and for support in time of affliction and of serious illness.

In the *Modus orandi Deum*, Erasmus invokes liturgical tradition and the early interpretation of the New Testament to show that the early church prayed to the Father in the Son but not to the Son or to the Holy Spirit. Most of the ancient collects were addressed to the Father, some to the Son, but none to the Holy Spirit, although in every collect all three persons of the Trinity are mentioned. The first Christians, the *veteres*, did not even have prayers to the Spirit in the octave of Pentecost.[91] Furthermore, such was the character of their devotion that the *veteres* dared not do what was not expressed in Scripture. The early church read how the apostles taught the faithful to pray to the heavenly Father, but in the Son, and how the Son prayed to the Father and promised the Spirit but did not pray to the Spirit. Only in John's Gospel (14: 14) does Jesus say: 'if you ask me anything in my name, I will do it,' yet the pronoun 'me' appears neither in most Greek manuscripts nor is it found in every Latin codex.[92]

Erasmus concedes that Stephen, before he died, had no qualms about praying: 'Lord Jesus, receive my spirit' (Acts 7: 59), and recognizes that Christians overcame their inhibition about praying to Christ as true God. They did not believe that the Son could grant something that the Father could not, but they persuaded themselves that the Son wills and can do what the Father wills and can do, although the Father is the source of all things.[93] Prayer, like doctrine, develops, and Erasmus obviously agreed with and approved of the way prayer had evolved. Further on in the *Modus orandi Deum* he says, as I have noted in chapter 1, that it makes little difference to which person of the Trinity one prays, although it is more fitting to ask the almighty Father for protection from enemies and demons, the Son for reconciliation with the Father, and the Spirit for an increase of divine grace.[94] He begins the *Enchiridion* by beseeching the 'Lord's gracious Spirit' to give him good counsel and ends his *De utilitate colloquiorum* (1526), the apology for his *Colloquies*, with a prayer that 'the Spirit, the pacifier of all things,' would 'make us of one heart and mind in sound doctrine and holy morals so that it might come about that we may attain in equal measure the fellowship of the heavenly Jerusalem, which knows no strife.'[95]

Although the Father and the Son clearly dominate his prayers, Erasmus does not discount the role of the Spirit in prayer. 'Father' and 'Son' are names of love that no one could pronounce if it were not for the kindness of the Holy Spirit.[96] In Romans 8: 26–7, Paul writes that 'we do not know how to pray as we ought, but the Spirit himself intercedes for us with sighs too deep for words' and that 'the Spirit intercedes for the saints according to the will of God' (RSV). Erasmus' paraphrase of the passage adds that 'God does listen to the prayers of those who belong to him if only they pray not according to the desires of the flesh but according to the wish of the Spirit acting in us in hidden ways.' The human spirit may sometimes be preoccupied with trivial matters, but the 'heavenly Spirit which is incorporated into the hearts of the pious demands things which, if they are absent, are to be desired with unspeakable groans; if they are present, they bring true and perfect beatitude.' We often 'pray for pernicious rather than health-giving things'; the Spirit, however, 'desires only what contributes toward our eternal salvation, it desires only what contributes toward the glory of God.'[97]

In the *Precationes*, the Spirit is often mentioned, even if only two prayers directly invoke him. Erasmus portrays the third person of the Trinity as a Spirit of life and of strength, and as an agent of spiritual transformation. Christ through the consolation of his Spirit restores human strength, and this same consolation of his Spirit alleviates the troubles of the soul much more efficaciously than sleep.[98] Erasmus' readers pray that they might flourish in perpetual innocence through the inspiration of Christ's Spirit and that through the grace of the Father's Spirit the desire for piety might grow and be perfected within their souls.[99] The penitent person beseeches the Father through the death of his only-begotten Son: 'impart to me your Spirit so that he may purify my heart and confirm me in his grace so that I through my thoughtlessness may not fall back into the place from which I was called back by your clemency.'[100] The person who prays for spiritual joy asks Christ 'that the anointing of your Spirit may often shake off from me the weariness of evil things and gladden my mind with the joy of salvation (*salutari gaudio*).'[101]

The prayer for the preservation of purity acknowledges that the 'divine Spirit' spurns all defilement and delights in dwelling in chaste and pure minds. Erasmus' readers beseech the Spirit that they may so preserve the distinguished treasure of purity that they carry within them that, pleasing him with increasing purity of heart and body, they may at last attain that life that knows no corruption.[102] The prayer 'Ad Spiritum Sanctum' calls upon the 'Adorande Spiritus,' proceeding from the Father and the Son. Mindful that all things depend on the Spirit for life and that he takes delight in remaining in the hearts of the simple, Erasmus' readers ask that the Spirit preserve the gifts of his kindness within them and daily increase what he has been pleased to bestow so that under his direction the desires of the flesh may increasingly die within them while the longing for celestial life may grow. With the Spirit as their guide or ruler (*gubernator*) they also seek to be free of the darkness of this world so that they will neither be defiled by the vices of Satan, nor be enveloped in any errors that conflict with the inviolable truth that the Catholic church under the prompting of the Spirit has handed down to them.[103] For Elizabethan England, this last petition must have smacked of loyalty to Rome. The version of Erasmus' prayer that appears in Richard Daye's *Booke of Christian Prayers* (1578), often called Queen Elizabeth's Prayer-book, translates 'Ecclesia Catholica' as 'the true catholic church.'[104]

Erasmus fosters a devotion to the three persons of the Trinity by conveying a clear sense of the nature of the triune God. The 'Gratiarum actio' of the *Eiaculationes* recalls the familiar triad: the heavenly Father has created all things by his ineffable power, governs all things by his inscrutable wisdom, and nourishes all things with his inexhaustible goodness.[105] The man who prays for a happy marriage calls upon the Father as 'almighty God.'[106] He is the Creator, a title he shares with his Son.[107] The prayer to be said in springtime praises the Lord Jesus, 'the almighty renewer of all things,' for creating 'this most beautiful world for our sake.' He has adorned the heavens with so many lights for the day and the night, and in the wake of his resurrection the earth revives.[108] Each person of the Trinity receives the title of 'ruler' (*gubernator*).[109] Erasmus combines wisdom and power when he describes the Father and Jesus Christ as 'most wise' rulers, and he appeals to divine wisdom on its own when he has students invoke Christ as the 'eternal wisdom of the Father,' or the 'eternal wisdom of the Father most high.'[110]

As we might expect, the accent falls on God's goodness. The heavenly Father is 'most gentle' (*indulgentissime*), 'most merciful' (*clementissime*), and 'most kind' (*benignissime*).[111] The repentant sinner regrets having forsaken a 'kind and generous Father' and a 'most loving parent.' Although the prayer in time of plague begins by addressing the 'most just Father,' it does not fail to present him also as the 'Father of mercies.' Hearing the Gospel lesson about the wedding feast of Cana makes one think of Jesus as 'the fountain of all good things.' The person who prays for purity remembers that he owes the treasure of our purity to the kindness of the Holy Spirit.[112] Erasmus' prayers are replete with references to the divine kindness, goodness, mercy, charity, and providence.

In Erasmus' night prayer 'Sub noctem,' we acknowledge before Christ that in nothing else does anyone 'rest more safely or more sweetly than in your mercy, Redeemer most excellent (*Redemtor optime*).'[113] God in his goodness not only created human beings; he also redeemed them. The person afflicted with illness appeals to Christ: 'Most merciful Redeemer, you who are ever merciful, you who are ever the Saviour, whether you send us sad or happy times.' The person awaiting his wedding day invokes the most kind Father as the 'Creator, Redeemer, and Propagator of the human race.'[114] In the *Eiaculationes*, the Communion prayer 'Accedentis ad sacram synaxim' thanks Christ for his ineffable charity because he was pleased to redeem the human race by his death.[115] The person who prepares himself for Communion with the 'Sumturi Corpus Dominicum' of the *Precationes* considers:

> What tongue or what mind can worthily give thanks to you, Lord Jesus, for your ineffable charity towards us? You, who in order to redeem lost humanity, were pleased to become a human being and to take upon yourself all the iniquity of our condition. Then on the altar of the cross, as the spotless lamb, you endured to become the sacrifice for us, paying the penalty owed by our sins, so that you might reconcile us

with the Father. Both living and dying, you entirely expended, gave, and dedicated yourself for us.[116]

In this passage, Erasmus obviously seeks to plant within his readers a love for Christ, their loving Redeemer. The Christocentric piety that his prayer-book promotes does not portray Christ as a moral preceptor, whose lesson and example Christians should respect and follow. Erasmus exalts Christ as the provident Son of God, the merciful Redeemer to whom heartfelt love and devotion are due at all times and in all circumstances.

Those who seek Christ's help against temptation begin their prayer with a fanfare of titles in his praise: 'sole protection of our mortality, our only hope, our salvation, our victory, our glory, and our triumph.'[117] The person about to go on a journey hails Jesus as the 'most faithful guardian of human beings ... under whose protection there is no danger [and] without whose protection nothing is ever safe.' He asks for a safe departure and return so that he may give thanks to Christ's goodness. Similarly, the person ready to set sail asks Christ to be the guiding star of the voyage 'so that in every element we may give thanks to your mercy, to whom be honour and rule in every age.'[118]

Erasmus also celebrates Christ through the use of light imagery. He is the 'singular light that shines on all through the desert of this age.' The prayer in summertime petitions Christ, 'our true sun,' to shine the rays of his grace 'upon the earth of our mind, so that each day it may glow more and more with the fire of your charity and bring forth various fruits of good works.' Erasmus' morning prayer greets Jesus as 'the true sun of the world, always rising, never setting,' or as the 'eternal sun, giving life to, nourishing, and gladdening all things.' His night prayer recalls that Jesus by the grace of faith exposes to light the deeds of piety more brightly than the sun shines on the world.[119]

The prayer 'Ad Filium,' only slightly shorter than the 'Precatio ad Patrem,' the longest of the Erasmian prayers, provides the most sustained inculcation of Christocentric piety. The text of John 14: 6, in which Jesus refers to himself as the way, the truth, and the life, lends thematic unity to the prayer. He is the way by virtue of his teaching, precepts, and examples; the truth on account of his promises; the life because of the reward he offers. Invoking his 'ineffable charity,' we open our prayer by asking that we may never stray from him, nor distrust his promises, nor find rest in anything other than him, who is eternal life. Towards the end, we beseech 'the most merciful Saviour' to grant us greater faith so that we may never waver in his heavenly teaching, greater obedience so that we may never turn away from his precepts, and greater steadfastness so that we may not be seduced by Satan's blandishments, nor be cast down by terrors, but persevere unto death in Christ, who alone is 'true life.' Increase our trust in your promises, we beg him, so that our zeal for piety may never stagnate. Increase within us your grace so that more and more we will be able to die to ourselves and live by your Spirit, 'fearing nothing besides you, than whom nothing is greater or more powerful; loving nothing other than you, than whom nothing is more lovable; glorying in no one except in you, who are the true glory of the saints; seeking nothing save you, than whom nothing is better; desiring nothing beyond you, who are complete and perfect happiness with the Father and Holy Spirit throughout all the ages. Amen.'[120]

Erasmus' readers must acquire or already be possessed of an intense devotion to Christ, therefore, if they use his prayer-book to accustom themselves to speak with God. Through prayer they seek spiritual growth and transformation. They ask Christ for an increase in faith, obedience, steadfastness, trust, and grace. In the prayer 'In aestate,' they make this petition: 'Increase, Lord Jesus, what you have given, perfect what you have begun until we grow up into the perfect man, into the measure of your fullness.'[121] Before Communion, they ask Christ to purify their hearts so that they may not approach the altar unworthily but grow in him with whom their minds have become diffused.[122] Their growth will be complete, their transformation fulfilled, when in heaven they become as Christ is. They profess in the prayer 'Ad Filium' that now they see God 'through faith as in a mirror and in a riddle, but then, gazing upon the glory of the Lord face to face, we will be transformed into his image' (cf. 1 Corinthians 3: 12).[123]

The process of transformation has already begun, however. In his ineffable kindness, God the Father has honoured Christians with the name of 'children' (filii) and bestowed his Spirit upon them that they might dare to exclaim: 'Abba Pater.'[124] They were unhappily born of the first Adam, expelled from paradise, and sent into exile, yet they were reborn in Christ through baptism.[125] In this life, they fight as Christ's soldiers, seeking strength from him against the devil and hoping that with spiritual weapons they may stand battle-ready for the attacks of the enemy.[126] Erasmus has his readers approach God in humility as sinners and mindful of their human weakness. The person in affliction wishes to submit to Christ's will, asking that he might patiently and obediently drink of the chalice of suffering, as if it were given to him by Christ. He tells Christ: 'You nevertheless know the frailty of the human condition, and for that reason, just like the merciful Samaritan, you pour wine into our wounds, stinging our vices.' If Christ, instead of increasing his pain, is content with a mild reproof, the afflicted person prays: 'may calm follow upon this storm so that I might thank you on two accounts: both because you have mercifully corrected your unprofitable servant, and because you have taken away the bitterness of affliction with the sweetness of consolation; on the one hand taking account of necessity, on the other being not unmindful of our weakness.'[127] The person who says Erasmus' night prayer appeals to Christ's 'wonted goodness,' asking forgiveness for the sins he has committed through human carelessness during the day.[128] The penitent person regards himself as unworthy to raise his eyes to God or call him 'Father.' Taking the part of a prodigal son, he sighs: 'A slave worthy of every punishment, I do not seek an embrace and a kiss, nor do I demand a cloak and ring, the insignia of the original dignity which I cast away.' He does not pray that the Father should treat him as a son, but he will be content to share the lot of the lowest slave so that he can at least have some share in the inheritance of the Father's children.[129]

The repentant sinner not only humbly confesses his sinfulness but also puts his faith in God's mercy. When he contemplates God's boundless mercy, 'a certain aura of hope,' he tells God, 'restores my soul.' Why should he despair of God's forgiveness when in the Scriptures God so often calls sinners to repentance? God does not desire the death of the sinner but that he convert and live (Ezekiel 33: 11).[130] Faith and trust in God are necessary spiritual qualities for those who pray. In the winter, Erasmus' readers keep in mind that the 'hope of the resurrection' (*spes reviviscentiae*) soothes the fear of death. They believe that this is a most certain hope because God's Son, the eternal truth, who can neither be deceived nor deceive, promised it to them.[131]

In the *De praeparatione ad mortem* (1534), Erasmus advises that those caring for a dying person should have at hand various passages from Scripture and appropriately composed little prayers to shore up his wavering faith and hope.[132] Erasmus' own prayers for the dying cultivate their faith. The first prayer 'In mortis periculo' of the *Eiaculationes* ends by quoting from Psalm 15 (16): 8–9: 'I will always keep the Lord before my eyes; since he is at my right hand, I will not be moved. On account of this my heart is gladdened and my tongue rejoices, and, moreover, my flesh rests in hope.'[133] The second prayer closes by quoting Psalm 22 (23): 4: 'And if I walk in the midst of the shadow of death, I will not fear for myself, for you are with me.'[134]

Erasmus' *ars moriendi* attempts to replace the fear of death with faith in Christ. Christians must believe that we will be saved through their trust in and love for Jesus. Their most efficacious consolation is 'never to move the eye of faith from Christ.'[135] The prayer 'In gravi morbo,' which in the estimation of Peter Bietenholz is 'nothing less than the essence of the *De preparatione ad mortem* condensed into thirty lines,'[136] also engenders faith in Christ's mercy in the dying person. After saluting the Lord Jesus as the 'only hope of the living, eternal life of the dying,' the dying person humbly submits and yields to Christ's most holy will. Whether he remains alive longer to serve Christ or departs from this world, he is certain that whatever has been entrusted to Christ's mercy cannot perish. Thus with a calm heart he lays down his fragile and unhappy flesh in the hope of the resurrection.[137]

The *artes moriendi* traditionally prescribed remedies against temptations of the devil. In the *De praeparatione ad mortem*, Erasmus wards off the temptation to despair by imagining a dialogue between the devil and the dying person, in which the latter holds fast to God's mercy. When Satan charges that his faith is wavering, the dying person responds: 'I will pray the Lord that he may increase my faith.'[138] In his prayer, Erasmus bids the dying person to petition Christ: 'I ask that your grace may strengthen me against all temptations. And against all the attacks of Satan gird me with the shield of your mercy, by which you made your martyrs invincible against horrible tortures and the cruelest deaths.'[139] The dying person knows that he cannot defend himself and that he has neither merits nor good works to bring before Christ, but, as he says, 'through your justice do I have confidence that I will be numbered among the just.' He also puts his faith in all that Christ has done for him: 'For my sake you were born, for my sake you thirsted, for my sake you went hungry, for my sake you taught, for my sake you prayed, for my sake you fasted, for my sake you performed such good works in this life, for my sake you suffered such bitterness, for my sake on the cross you surrendered your precious soul to death.'[140] This passage echoes Erasmus' reminder in the *De praeparatione ad mortem* that for us Christ was born, taught, healed the sick, cast out demons, was hungry and thirsty, was treated to insults, was overwhelmed with anguish and weariness of life at the time of death, sweat blood, was put in chains and scourged, died and rose, and now sits at the right hand of the Father.[141]

'May what you have given me of your own accord,' the dying person in Erasmus' prayer asks Christ, 'now be profitable to me, you who gave yourself completely for me.' He desires that Christ's blood wash away his sins, that Christ's justice cover his injustice, that Christ's merits commend him to the supreme judge. Afflicted with illness, he prays for an increase in Christ's grace, 'so that faith will not waver in me, nor hope totter, nor charity grow cold, nor human weakness be cast down by the fear of death.' The dying person asks that at the very end his mind will not turn away from Christ and that, although he no longer may be able to speak, his heart may constantly cry out: 'Into your hands, Lord, I commend my spirit.'[142] In the *De praeparatione ad mortem*, Erasmus recommends that the dying person should 'with religious faith' say these dying words of Christ (Luke 23: 46) in order to imitate him.[143]

Concord is another important element of Erasmian piety that finds expression in the *Precationes aliquot novae*. All of Erasmus' Christian soldiers are bound to be at peace with each other, and this rule of Christian life applies even to men going into battle. Ross Dealy argues: 'Erasmus claims that Christ's teachings deny war absolutely, but Erasmus the person never denies war absolutely.'[144] The Erasmian pacifism that pervades the soldier's prayer 'Inituri praelium' grudgingly accepts war as a necessary evil, yet an evil urgently in need of the remedy of peace. This prayer invokes the God of power. He is the 'almighty King Sabaoth,' the Lord of hosts who through his angels administers both war and peace, the God who gave to David, defenceless and unskilled in war, the strength to defeat Goliath. Erasmus' praying soldier is no friend of warfare. He offers his prayer in such a way that it depends on the justice of the cause for fighting and on the unavoidable necessity of undertaking a military campaign. Given these provisions, he prays that the minds of the enemy be converted to the zeal for peace so that no Christian blood need be shed. Alternatively, he asks that God may cause panic to come upon them. If hostilities do begin, may victory come with a minimum of the loss of life and with the least hardship to the side whose cause God favours the most. Once the fighting ceases, and that as quickly as possible, 'may we sing,' hopes the peace-loving soldier, 'hymns of triumph to you with concordant hearts.'[145] Thus, as Rudolf Padberg rightly points out: 'What is at stake in this prayer is not the victory of one's own faction, but the triumph of God and of justice.'[146]

Erasmus never praised the military profession, but he did esteem marriage. He published in 1518 an *Encomium matrimonii* and in 1526 the lengthy treatise, *Christiani matrimonii institutio*. In his catechism, the *Explanatio symboli* (1533), of the seven sacraments he lists marriage first.[147] John Payne remarks that Erasmus does not stress the union of bodies in marriage; rather, 'the essence of marriage' for him inheres in 'the indivisible conjunction of souls which is the primary sign of this union.'[148] This union of souls accomplishes concord between husband and wife. Without concord they cannot truly pray. 'Prayer is the sacrificial offering (*oblatio*) of Christians,' Erasmus tells married people in *Christiani matrimonii institutio*, but God will not accept it even if a wife has a just reason for quarrelling with her husband or vice versa. The wife must be reconciled to her husband before she can make her offering. Erasmus concludes: 'The prayers, moreover, which wife and husband pour out together with concordant hearts are most pleasing to God.'[149]

The theme of concord is always present in the prayers he composed for those who are married or who intend to marry. In his treatise on marriage, he inserts a prayer for a married couple to say on their wedding night. They ask God: 'May all impurity and all discord be banished from our home. Give us that true peace which the world cannot give.'[150] In the prayer 'Pro felici conjugio' of the *Precationes aliquot novae*, a man prays that through God's kind providence he may find a wife 'with whom, living in concord and in joy, I may serve you with oneness of heart (*unanimiter*).' He recalls that God gave Adam a wife to end his solitude and to be his helpmate. God made her from Adam's rib to point out to married people the intimacy and indissoluble partnership required of them.[151] 'Sub nuptias' is the title of the prayer Erasmus writes for a person on the eve of his or her wedding. The bride or groom to be beseeches God the Father: 'I pray that you may be pleased to bring good fortune to this marriage, entered upon with your blessing (*tuis auspiciis*), so that, by loving and worshipping you above everything, two hearts may become one.' A 'chaste, mutual, and perpetual love' should cement the married couple's physical union, and their children make their 'most intimate charity' (*arctissimam caritatem*) even more intimate.[152] Erasmus gives his readers to understand that the harmonious marriage for which they pray is a sacrament. Saying the prayer in the *Christiani matrimonii institutio*, the married couple recognizes that Christ 'recommended this sacrament to us in many ways': by being born into a marriage, by taking the church as his spouse, by performing the miracle of changing water into wine at Cana, and by wishing that this sacred covenant should not be dissolved.[153]

In 'Sub nuptias' Erasmus alludes to the famous passage from the fifth chapter of Ephesians. After enjoining wives to be subject to their husbands and husbands to love their wives (vv. 21–8), Paul writes: 'This mystery is a profound one, and I am saying that it refers to Christ and the church' (v. 32, RSV). The Vulgate translated this passage: 'Sacramentum hoc magnum est; ego autem dico in Christo et in ecclesia.' In his own Latin translation of the New Testament, Erasmus preferred to render the Greek word *mysterion* as *mysterium* and not as *sacramentum*. Interpreting Erasmus' translation and note on this passage, Emile Telle unjustly criticizes him for rejecting marriage as a sacrament.[154] Erasmus did disagree with many medieval exegetes that the text from Ephesians proved that marriage was a sacrament, but, as he made clear in the *Annotations*, he did not therefore deny the sacramental nature of marriage.[155] The person who says the prayer 'Sub nuptias,' however, acknowledges to the Father: 'through [your] chosen vessel Paul you taught that this union was a great sacrament (*magnum sacramentum*) in Christ and in the church.'[156] Erasmus thus employs in his prayer the passage from Ephesians in order to remind Christians that marriage is a sacrament. In so doing, he departs from his exegetical judgment for the sake of promoting piety. By writing of marriage as a 'great sacrament' he reinforces with sacred purpose the petition for a union of hearts.

In his colloquy *Inquisitio de fide* (1524), Erasmus calls the church, the Christian community of peace and concord, 'a participation in the same sacraments.'[157] Willi Hentze argues that in

Erasmus' thought the sacraments are not only 'means to salvation'; they are at the same time 'means and signs of the unity of
the church.'[158] As Otto Schottenloher maintains, for Erasmus the
Eucharist is the 'central sacrament of the church' and, according
to Hentze, it serves as the 'guarantee and bond of unity' for the
church.[159] Not only does the partaking of Christ's flesh and blood
make Christians one with Christ; in receiving Christ in this sacrament, Erasmus points out, they also become one with each
other.[160] In the *Modus orandi Deum* and in the *Explanatio symboli*,
he refers to the Eucharist by the Greek term *synaxis*, a bringing
together (*conciliatio*) or a communion (*communio*), which symbolizes a 'covenant of charity among all the members of Christ' and
establishes 'a most intimate union (*arctissima coniunctio*) of the
mystical body with the head and with all who truly profess the
name of Christ.'[161]

The body of Christ signifies both the church and its great sacrament of concord. The person preparing to receive Christ's body
prays that he may grow up into Christ so that 'I may persevere in
the blessed society of your mystical body, which you wanted to be
one with you in the way in which you are one with the Father,
joined together by the Holy Spirit.'[162] In the *Eiaculationes*, the
prayer intended for the person approaching Holy Communion (*ad
sacram synaxim*) also links the receiving of the sacrament to a prayer
for lasting personal union with the church. Nourished by the body
and blood of Christ, the communicant prays: 'may I be prove to be
a fitting member of your mystical body, which is the church, and
may I never depart from that most holy covenant which, when the
bread had been shared and the cup offered, you made with your
chosen disciples at the last supper and through these with all who
are grafted into your company through baptism.'[163] The Eucharis-
tic piety that Erasmus promotes in his prayer-book inculcates the
importance of Christian concord. He does not want his readers to
receive the sacrament without desiring to be one with their fellow
members of the body of Christ, the church.

Erasmus not only wanted people to pray for unity among the individual members of the body of Christ; he wanted them to pray for
the peace of the body as a collective whole. That is why he wrote
the *Precatio ad Dominum Jesum pro pace ecclesiae*. In his opinion, the
strife that grew out of the controversy over Luther's Ninety-five
Theses urgently demanded prayers for reconciliation.

It is well-known that Erasmus preferred not to become entangled in the conflict between Wittenberg and Rome until he yielded to the pressure from the pope and Catholic princes and published the *De libero arbitrio* in 1524. His hesitation to take a public stand against Luther has commonly been seen in the light of his attempt to reconcile Lutherans and Catholics. Johan Huizinga understood Erasmus' irenicism as a result of 'his fear and lack of character,' of 'his inveterate dislike of siding with a person or a cause,' and of 'his deep and fervent conviction' that neither side of an argument can completely possess the truth.[164] Other scholars have variously attributed the humanist's neutrality to his desire to protect Luther either as an innocent man or as a proponent of shared theological convictions,[165] to his aversion to disputing dogma,[166] to his commitment both to 'bonae litterae' and to 'libertas,' which is associated with 'his critique of ceremonies' and 'a spontaneous ethical piety,'[167] or to his belief that the truth of doctrine could only be pursued in an environment of consensus and concord.[168]

Although this is not the place to validate or refute these interpretations, I should like to suggest another reason why Erasmus was reluctant to enter the fray. He did not wish to intervene precisely because he did not see how he could resolve the theological quarrel that was tearing western Christendom apart. Only Christ could restore peace to the church, and the best remedy for the crisis was prayer.

Writing in October 1520 to Albert of Brandenburg, the cardinal of Mainz, Erasmus had nothing to suggest 'except to pray that the whole affair may tend towards the glory of Christ, whatever it may mean for us.'[169] He told George Spalatin, chaplain and private secretary to Frederick the Wise, Luther's prince: 'We must pray that Christ himself will defend his spouse, and put into the minds of princes counsels that may save the day.'[170] With the burning of the papal decretals and with the publication of both his attack on the sacramental system of the church, the *De captivitate babylonica ecclesiae*, and of the *Assertio omnium articulorum*, his response to the papal bull *Exsurge Domine*, Luther 'has made the evil to all appearances incurable.' 'One thing remains,' Erasmus confided to his friend Ludwig Baer in May 1521: 'I pray that Christ the almighty may turn all things to good effect, for he alone can do so.'[171]

Erasmus saw no way out for western Christendom 'unless

Christ himself, like some god from the machine, give this lamentable play a happy ending.'[172] Although he complained about the schism that afflicted the church, Erasmus never lost hope that Christ, moved by prayer, would intervene. One must not despair, he wrote in August 1530 to the prince bishop of Würzburg, Konrad von Thüngen: 'Long ago in the time of Saint Jerome, [the church] endured more serious tumults, and even now Christ lives, who with a word calms the sea, however much it roars and threatens destruction. Only let us rouse him with our prayers and pluck at him until he awakes and bids this storm to grow still. He wants this glory to be attributed to himself, not to our prudence.'[173] The turmoil in the church was like the storm (*tempestas*) that Christ pacified in the Gospels (Matthew 8: 23–7 and parallel passages). In June 1530, Erasmus assured Christoph von Stadion, the bishop of Augsburg: 'Every day with the most ardent prayers I pray God that by his Spirit he may be pleased to suggest plans for the health of the Christian republic to the minds of the Emperor and the princes; and that he may be pleased, through the Emperor's supreme power and a piety equal to his power, to turn to tranquillity this fatal storm, which human defences cannot stay.'[174]

With his *Precatio ad Dominum Jesum pro pace ecclesiae* Erasmus invited Christendom to pray for an end to the storm. He first published the prayer in 1532 and dedicated it to Johann Rinck, a professor of law at the University of Cologne who also sat on the Cologne city council.[175] Rinck's own pious prayers for the removal of 'the calamities threatening Germany' had inspired Erasmus to write the *Precatio*.[176] He sent a copy of his prayer to Bernhard von Cles, the bishop of Trent. Owing to the bishop's request and to the requests of many of his correspondents, Erasmus thought it was fitting 'to write the formula of a prayer with which we, who love the beauty of the house of God, might all pray at the same time.' Having read and reread it, von Cles judged that it was most appropriate for the times in which they were living.[177] In 1533, Erasmus appended the *Precatio* to his commentary on Psalm 83 (84), the *De sarcienda ecclesiae concordia*. In the latter work, he interrupts his exposition with a prayer to the Lord of hosts 'to open the eyes of us all, so that, seeing how lovable, how beautiful, how peaceful, how safe, how happy are your tabernacles [and] on the other hand how unlike these are the tabernacles of impiety, we may, once the conflicts of opinions and feelings have been put aside, dwell in harmony with the same mind and purpose in that blessed company of all the saints, so that it may be truly said of us: Behold how good and how pleasant it is for brothers to live in unity' [Psalm 132 (133): 1].[178] In every subsequent edition of the *De sarcienda*, the *Precatio* appeared along with it.[179] In 1535, Erasmus included the prayer in the *Precationes aliquot novae*.

Erasmus begins the urgent appeal to Christ for the peace of the church by calling to mind the almighty power by which he created all things visible and invisible, the divine wisdom by which he governs and arranges the universe with the most beautiful order, and the ineffable goodness with which he preserves, beholds, and quickens everything. To the three customary divine attributes Erasmus adds mercy. He has his readers beseech Christ: '... you who according to your boundless mercy have restored what has fallen apart, refashioned what has collapsed, brought back to life that which has died: be pleased, we ask, to turn at last your face to your bride the church, chosen especially for you, but that gentle and gracious face with which you brighten everything in heaven, on earth, above the heavens, and beneath the earth.' They ask that Christ may look upon the church with the same merciful eyes both with which he gazed at Peter, who eventually repented of his denial, and with which he beheld the crowd that wandered about like scattered sheep for want of a shepherd.[180]

The *Precatio* is essentially a pressing cry for Christ's mercy. Those who recite it call upon him as the 'most merciful Jesus,' and twice they implore him to have mercy on them.[181] They have good reason to be in need of Christ's mercy in the church's time of crisis. In the *De sarcienda*, Erasmus explains that the divisions among Christians are a consequence of an excessive fault-finding that prevents one from recognizing the virtues of others.[182] He also writes that 'the principal source of this tumult is the impious way of life of human beings.' Christians who have provoked the Lord's wrath must turn back to him with sincere hearts, and he, who is moved by prayer (*exorabilis*), will turn to them and pacify the disturbance.[183] The *Precatio* admits: 'We realize and confess that our sins (*scelera nostra*) have brought this storm upon us. We acknowledge your justice, and we deplore our injustice, but we call upon your mercy, which according to the prophetic Psalm (144 [145]: 9), is above all your works.' We have already suffered so much punishment, so many wars, expulsions, diseases, plagues, and floods. We have been frightened by so many heavenly portents, and yet it seems that matters will only become worse. We have, no doubt, deserved the many terrible evils that have befallen us; nevertheless, 'we do not complain about your severity, most gentle Saviour, but we acknowledge here also your mercy, even if we have deserved far more terrible things. But do not, most merciful Jesus, consider what we deserve (*quid nostris meritis debeatur*), but what befits your mercy.'[184]

Interestingly enough, just as Erasmus in the *De sarcienda* does not mention God's wrath without describing him as *exorabilis*, so too in the *Precatio* he juxtaposes Christ's severity with his title as most gentle Saviour. Christ's anger yields to his desire to hear the prayers of Christians, for he is the 'Redemtor exorabilis.'[185] His severity gives way to his gentleness. For plunging the church into the depths of discord Christians deserve all the bitter fruits of strife, but Erasmus directs their sight beyond their sins, beyond the divine punishment that is their due, to the mercy of Jesus. His merciful goodness knows no limits.

Erasmus of course realizes that the church's troubles stem not only from moral and spiritual decay but also from doctrinal dispute. That is why he converts the collect commemorating Reuchlin into a prayer 'Pro consensu dogmatum' and includes a petition in the prayer 'Ad Spiritum Sanctum' against becoming entangled in any errors that break with the truth that the Catholic church teaches. In the prayer for the peace of the church, Erasmus points out that the primeval chaos out of which Christ brought forth the world is not as bad as the chaos of the absence of charity, of faith, of trust, of law, of respect for superiors, and of the 'dogmatum consensus,' the consensus in matters of doctrine.[186] The prayer asks Christ: 'grant that inasmuch as for all who dwell in your house there is one law, one baptism, one God, one hope, [and] one spirit, so also may there be one voice among those who profess the Catholic truth.'[187] Erasmus' readers exclaim: 'You see, good Shepherd, how many types of wolves have broken into your sheepfold, each of them crying: 'Here is Christ! Here is Christ!' so that even the perfect might be, if possible, dragged into error. You see with what winds, with what waves, with what gales your little ship (*navicula*) is tossed, outside of which you wish no one to be saved.'[188] The storm caused by human sins is the very tempest of doctrinal error in which the 'navicula' that is the church finds itself. Once at the cry of a few disciples Christ awoke in the boat to calm the waves and silence the winds with his almighty voice. Now in this far more perilous storm his sixteenth-century followers call upon him: 'at the clamour of your entire church in danger we ask that you rouse yourself. So many thousands of people cry: "Lord, save us, we are perishing"' (Matthew 8: 25). Since human efforts are useless, 'Your voice is necessary, Lord Jesus. Say only the word, silence the storm, and may that wished-for tranquillity shine out right away.'[189] Indeed, only Christ can help the church and restore peace: 'For your mercy is accustomed then to be especially present when in a particularly hopeless situation neither human strength or prudence can be of assistance. You alone, the sole author and guardian of peace, can return affairs, however discordant, to concord.'[190]

Christ's agent of concord is the Holy Spirit. Through this Spirit he has reconciled earthly and heavenly things and joined together so many languages, nations, and different types of people into the one body of the church, which adheres to him as its head through the same Spirit.[191] Erasmus has his readers ask Jesus to send out his Spirit to drive out from every heart the impious spirits of extravagance, greed, ambition, and lust, the masters of vengeance and discord.[192] Peace obviously cannot be restored unless Christians become spiritually transformed. It is not enough for them to wish their strife to cease. They must desire that the Holy Spirit rid them of impiety, the root of this strife.

After Christ ascended into heaven, he bestowed on humankind the different gifts of the Spirit. The *Precatio* asks him, in accordance with the generosity he demonstrated of old, to grant to his church, now heading for disaster, what he gave her when she was born.[193] The subsequent petitions in the *Precatio* conform to the principle that Erasmus enunciates in the *De sarcienda* for the restoration of peace: let everyone perform his allotted task. Bishops should look after Christ's flock with sincere hearts, princes should act as ministers of divine justice, and the laypeople should pay heed to their priests and faithfully obey the laws of their princes.[194] The peace of the church thus rests on what Augustine would call a tranquillity of order[195] in which everyone fulfils the function of his or her station in the Christian commonwealth.

For the princes the *Precatio* asks that Christ may give them the fear of him so that they might so look after the state as if they soon had to give account of every single matter to the King of kings. Erasmus adds a petition that Christ give wisdom to the princes, to those who constantly attend his throne, so that they might perceive what is best and put it into effect. From the princes we move to the priests: 'Give to the pastors, with whom you have been pleased to delegate your authority, the gift of prophecy, so that they might interpret the Scriptures not according to human judgment but according to your inspiration. Grant the threefold charity, which you required of Peter, as you were about to entrust to him the care of [your] sheep. Give to your priests the love of sobriety and chastity.' Erasmus completes his consideration of the Christian republic with a prayer that Christ give to the people the goodwill to obey his commands and the readiness to yield to those through whom he has desired to govern human affairs. His wish is that, if the princes command and the pastors teach things worthy of Christ, the people will obey their rulers and teachers, and the church will return to its original dignity and peace.[196] Having invoked Jesus as Creator, Redeemer, Saviour, Lord, Head, King, Prince of Peace, and God, the *Precatio* petitions him to have mercy on his supplicants and to be 'all things for all people, according to Paul's saying, so that the whole chorus of the church with concordant hearts and harmonious voices may, for the mercy she has obtained, give thanks to the Father and to the Son and to the Holy Spirit, who as an absolute example of concord are distinct in the property of persons, [but] one in nature, to whom be glory for ever. Amen.'[197]

In our analysis of Erasmus' prayer-book, we have encountered familiar features of his understanding of prayer. The contents of the *Precationes aliquot novae* are either prayers taken directly from Scripture or demonstrate scriptural inspiration. Erasmus instils in his readers a devotion to a good God and to Christ, the loving and merciful Redeemer. The devout approach God with humility but also with the confidence that he hears their prayers. As they prepare themselves for the sacraments of the altar and of matrimony and as they lament the sad state of the church, Erasmus' Christian soldiers commit themselves to concord.

The spiritual orientation of their prayers is quite evident. They hardly ever ask for material benefits, and when they do, as when they petition Christ for a safe journey or for his guidance while at sea, they make their requests so that they can thank him for his goodness and mercy. Whereas the first 'Consecratio mensae' asks God's blessing upon what has been put on the table, the focus of the second one is not on food or drink but a petition for Christ's presence during the meal. The third Erasmian prayer at table beseeches the Father: 'grant to your children that they may at last drink with you in your kingdom that nectar of immortality, which you have promised to and prepared for those who truly love you, through Jesus Christ. Amen.'[198]

This petition for eternal life complies with the spiritual *scopus* of Erasmian prayer. This *scopus* recurs when Erasmus' readers pray to Christ that they find rest in nothing other than in him, who is eternal life, and when they ask the Holy Spirit that the desire for the life of heaven grow within them. In time of plague, they recognize the Father's discipline by which he calls them away from putting their trust in this world and by which he draws them to the desire for eternal life.[199] Students seek Christ's help in their studies so that they may apply what they learn to his glory.[200] Upon waking, the person who says the morning prayer in the *Eiaculationes* combines the two elements of the *scopus*: the desire for Christ's glory and for everlasting life. First, he prays that Christ may bless for him the entire day unto his glory, and then, he asks the eternal sun to shed his light upon his mind so that he might avoid sin and attain eternal life under his guidance.[201] The prayer 'Ad Christum pro vera pietate' requests: 'may you lead us through the truth of the Gospel to eternal life, that is, may you draw us unto you, you who alone are blessed immortality.'[202]

When this prayer was printed in the *Precationes aliquot novae* in August 1535, Erasmus' thoughts were already on the hereafter. In a letter of 18 August to Damião de Goes, formerly an envoy of the Portuguese crown, he expressed his wish that 'the Lord be pleased to call me out of this age of fury into his rest; so far am I from desiring the long life for which you pray for me.'[203] Sickness seemed to plague his feeble frame throughout his career, and he knew no relief from pain in his final year of life. He believed, as he told the humanist Bartholomaeus Latomus on 24 August, that it was only right 'for us to bear patiently whatever the supreme Lord should send upon us, whose will no one can resist and who alone knows what is good for us.'[204] In the *De praeparatione ad mortem*, he had urged that in the most painful of afflictions we should say with Samuel: 'It is the Lord, may he do what seems good in his eyes' (1 Samuel 3: 18).[205] In December 1535, Erasmus wrote to Goes that he did not fear death but was more interested in pleasing the Lord.

Wishing that his suffering were more bearable, Erasmus concludes his letter: 'But it is the Lord; let him cut and burn here, provided that he spare [me] for eternity.'[206] His dying words, spoken on the night of 11–12 July 1536, appealed to his merciful Lord and dear God: 'O Iesu misericordia; Domine libera me; Domine fac finem; Domine miserere mei, Lieuer Got!'[207]

Erasmus' teaching on prayer in the *Modus orandi Deum* and the prayers he published in the *Precationes aliquot novae* put Christ at the centre of his readers' piety and encouraged them to put their faith in Christ's mercy and to direct their prayers towards the attainment of salvation, who is Christ, the fulfilment of eternal life, of blessed immortality. The deterioration of his health at the end of his life and the final moments upon his deathbed provide us with a rare opportunity to see Erasmus' own piety in action. Erasmus practised the piety he preached as he submitted to and trusted in God's will. The claim that Erasmus 'wrote copiously about piety, but no evidence shows that he was especially pious himself'[208] lacks any justification.

Yet the theme of this study has not so much been Erasmus at prayer as Erasmus as a teacher of prayer. At the end of the *Precatio ad Dominum Jesum pro pace ecclesiae,* he has his readers ask Christ to be *omnia in omnibus,* to be all things to all people, in order to bring peace to Christendom. In the prayer 'Ad Filium,' they acknowledge that in heaven 'Christ will be for us all things to all people.'[209] Perhaps it was in imitation of Christ that Erasmus sought to accommodate himself to his contemporaries in the *Precationes aliquot novae.* He responded to the needs of a Christendom in the crisis of doctrinal conflict, but he also addressed himself to the young, to married couples, to travellers, to repentant sinners, to the sick and the dying, and to all his Christian soldiers, engaged in the struggle against temptation and sin and devoted to their triune God at the various times of the day and the various seasons of the year. With his prayer-book he helps them to adapt their speech and their lives to God by providing them with prayers, taken directly from or inspired by Scripture, that express their trust in God, their desire for mercy and concord, and their yearning for spiritual transformation. The *Precationes aliquot novae* bears witness to Erasmus' determination and pastoral enterprise to teach Christendom how to pray.

Conclusion

The Roman Catechism, *Catechismus ex decreto Concilii Tridentini ad parochos*, was first published in 1566. Its fourth and last part discusses prayer in general and the Lord's Prayer in particular. It begins: 'In the pastoral office, instruction in Christian prayer is an especially necessary duty for the salvation of the faithful, and the importance of and reason for prayer would of necessity be lost on many, if it were not handed down by the pious and faithful diligence of the pastor. That is why the principal care of the parish priest should concern itself with this, namely that pious listeners understand what one should ask of God and how one should pray.'[1] Teaching people to pray is one of the most important tasks of pastoral ministry. The reference to the 'pious listeners' indicates, it seems, that this task should be carried out from the pulpit of every parish.

Marjorie O'Rourke Boyle believes: 'If Erasmus had wished, he could have mounted the pulpits of Europe. He was no preacher, however, but a teacher of teachers. The printing press could straddle the continent more effectively than any sermon, and it served him well.'[2] Manfred Hoffmann has observed in Erasmus an analogue between accommodation as a scriptural hermeneutic and accommodation as a pedagogical principle, for 'Erasmus believed that it is incumbent on the pedagogue to adjust to the student's natural disposition, mental capacity, and level of learning.'[3] Erasmus was certainly a dedicated pedagogue, an 'educator of educators' and a 'professor of professors.'[4] Yet any view of Erasmus as educator would be incomplete if it did not understand that accommodation was a pastoral as well as a pedagogical and hermeneutical principle, if it did not recognize the link between teaching and preaching, and if it did not see teaching as a part of ministry. To be sure, Erasmus did not preach from a pulpit, but through the printing press he had an effect on sixteenth-century Christians – potentially on every parish in western Christendom – far beyond the influence of any single parish priest. Decades before the publication of the Roman Catechism Erasmus was devoting himself, among other things, to the important pastoral duty of 'instruction in Christian prayer,' of teaching others how to pray.

Erasmus wrote in an age of pastoral renewal and reform that had its beginnings in the fifteenth century in Italy and Spain. Italian confraternities busied themselves with caring for the sick, providing for orphans, and performing other works of charity. Although by 1425 Nicolò Albergati, the bishop of Bologna, had set up a lay confraternity to teach catechism to children, only in the first half of the sixteenth century did confraternities in various Italian cities set up the Schools of Christian Doctrine, 'a movement devoted exclusively to religious instruction of the poor.'[5] The Theatines, an order recognized by the papacy in 1524, provided an example of what good priests should be, and in Verona, Gian Matteo Giberti became a model bishop of the Catholic Reform movement. The best-known reforming prelate of the Spanish Renaissance was Cardinal Franciso Ximenes de Cisneros, the archbishop of Toledo.[6] Another Spaniard, Ignatius of Loyola, founded the Society of Jesus in 1540 not to fight Protestantism but to take up the work of pastoral ministry, or 'to help souls' as the first Jesuits would say.[7]

In March 1536, four months before Erasmus' death, Hermann von Wied, the archbishop of Cologne, presided over a synod that issued a series of constitutions intended for the reform of ministry in the ecclesiastical province of Cologne. Even if von Wied did not trouble himself to enforce the synod's decisions, its 'pastoral program,' printed numerous times, 'circulated widely in the Catholic world as a pastoral model.' In Verona, Giberti had the synod's constitutions published in 1541 and again in 1543.[8] A draft of proposed amendments to what would become the final and official text of the constitutions prescribed Erasmus' recently published *Ecclesiastes* as required reading for pastors.[9] Although the synod did not adopt this specific proposal, it was still in many respects an Erasmian council. Suffused with abundant quotations from Scripture, the constitutions placed special

emphasis on the selection of worthy candidates for the priesthood, on high moral standards for the clergy, and on the ministry
of preaching, which, according to the synod, the Apostle Paul
'preferred by far to all others.' Erasmus would have supported
this decree: 'Organ music will be performed in the churches in
such a way that it does not stir up titillation more than devotion,
nor resound with and call to mind anything but sacred hymns
and spiritual canticles.'[10] He would also have welcomed the
demand that priests be constantly engaged in reading the Bible
and that preachers should accord greater importance to explaining the Gospel and Epistles than to recalling the stories of the
saints and of their miracles.[11] Although the synod of Cologne
required parish priests to teach the faithful the meaning of the
sacraments,[12] it made no mention of teaching the rudiments of
prayer.

Erasmus' contemporaries applauded his pastoral efforts. In
1519, Jan Becker of Borssele, a priest, was the first of several of
Erasmus' correspondents to urge him to write a treatise on
preaching. Becker was a devoted Erasmian. He admired the *Paraphrase on 1 and 2 Corinthians* and had perused the *Ratio verae theologiae*. After calling to mind the *Enchiridion*, the *Institutio principis
christiani*, and Erasmus' many pedagogical works, Becker maintains: 'It remains for you to lay down the right principles for a
preacher of the Gospel, which will in fact be a benefit to a far
larger public, not only to those who have imbibed your instruction and thereafter will preach better and with better results, but
also to the public who in this way will listen to preachers more
effectively and with much greater profit. Such a thing will be the
greatest joy to me on behalf of us all and privately for my own
use.' Becker urges Erasmus to agree to his request 'for two reasons: the very great and widespread benefits that will accrue and
your own passionate devotion to the religion of Christ. On promoting that religion you have spent so much energy and toil,
with enormous expense and to the unquestioned prejudice of
your health.'[13]

With the publication sixteen years later of the *Ecclesiastes*
Becker's request was fulfilled. In this long-awaited book, Erasmus fondly remembers the recently departed archbishop William
Warham (d. 1532) in the context of insisting that bishops should
take their ministry seriously. He recalls that Warham once conferred upon him a benefice. This was the rectorship of the parish

of Aldington in Kent, which he received in 1512 and held for only
a few months before resigning it. Warham then allowed him to
draw a pension from the living. Erasmus protested that it was not
fair for him to collect money from people to whom he was not
being of any use. But the archbishop tried to console his conscience. The money was well spent on him, Warham believed, for
with his books Erasmus was teaching all pastors to their great
advantage.[14]

I will add one more voice, this time that of a layman, Thomas
More. In 1526, More was praying for Erasmus' health. For the
sake of Christendom he hoped that the discomfort caused by a
recent bout with a painful kidney stone would not disturb 'your
most famous works with which you promote Christian piety.'[15]
More, Warham, and Becker recognized what must have been
very obvious to many among Erasmus' reading audience,
namely that Erasmus was using the medium of print to promote
piety. He may have deftly manipulated print to create and con-
solidate for himself an international reputation as a consummate
man of humane letters,[16] yet this was not his only use for the
printing press. Through his pastoral publications he sought to
shape the piety of Europe. The printing press became his pulpit,
his medium for exercising a literary cure of souls throughout
Europe. With his books he was able to teach the pastors of Christendom and to accommodate himself and the philosophy of
Christ to men and women at the various stages of their Christian
soldiering.

Erasmus taught that prayer is the human 'colloquium cum Deo.'
Towards the end of his monumental study of Erasmus' rhetoric,
Jacques Chomarat notes: 'If rhetoric naturally plays an essential
role in preaching, it will come as a greater surprise to see that it
finds its way into prayer as well.'[17] Of course, the Modus orandi
Deum is not a book like the Ecclesiastes. Erasmus' application of
the rules of rhetoric to prayer is not as thorough and demanding
as his rhetorical analysis of preaching. Nevertheless, accommodation, a fundamental principle in hermeneutics, rhetoric, and
pastoral ministry, is at work in Erasmus' teaching on prayer. The
sacred rhetoric of prayer must be adapted to its divine audience,
to the person praying, to the object of one's petitions, and to the
mode in which one expresses these petitions.

The Modus orandi Deum, Precatio Dominica, and Precationes ali-

quot novae, to say nothing of Erasmus' other religious writings, make it evident that goodness is the most outstanding quality of God's nature. In his goodness God created human beings; in his goodness he redeemed them through the death of his Son, adopting them as his children. The heavenly Father cares for the lost sheep and welcomes all to eternal salvation. Erasmus' prayers seek to instil within his readers a special love for Christ, who in Scripture teaches them how to pray by word and example, and whose kindness and mercy they always call to mind when they converse with him. By emphasizing God's kindness, generosity, and goodness as Creator and Redeemer, Erasmus presents his fellow Christians with a God who does not frighten them away from prayer but invites them to speak to him.

Christians enjoy the great unmerited dignity of being God's redeemed children. This dignity does not spare them from their earthly state of exile, from their constant struggle against the world, the flesh, and the devil. Sin is an inescapable reality in their lives of exile and struggle, and thus they approach God as sinners unworthy of his goodness. They therefore must pray to him with humility, yet they must also have faith that in his kindness he will hear them. Their prayers, however, will never pierce the heavens if they turn a deaf ear to the needs of their neighbours and if they withhold forgiveness from them. Christians cannot pray to God in a state of impiety. In order to pray, they must be spiritually transformed; they must be loyal soldiers and imitators of Christ. Their spiritual transformation is not only a prerequisite for praying but also its consequence. When they speak with their good God, they should become more like him. Prayer may be called a *pie vivendi studium* a zeal for leading a pious life. The piety that Christians practise is not the acquisition of virtue for virtue's sake. Their piety is not merely moral but also spiritual, for it is centred on imitating Christ and on doing the Father's will.

That Erasmian prayer is a matter of a spiritual, and not only a moral, transformation is evident from its spiritual *scopus* or focus. At the very beginning of the *Precatio Dominica,* Erasmus casts his readers as God's children, longing to be with the Father in their heavenly homeland. He wishes young people to dedicate their studies to Christ's glory when they ask for his help in learning letters. One may certainly pray for earthly needs, such as for a safe journey by land or a secure voyage by sea, but these needs must be subordinated to higher ends, the attainment of eternal life and the praise of God.

The fundamental rule of the *Enchiridion* operates in Erasmus' prayers and in his treatise on prayer. One must pass from the visible to the invisible, from the material to the spiritual, from the earthly to the heavenly. This does not mean that Erasmus espouses a spiritualized piety, a form of devotion liberated from any external manifestations. Erasmus did not promote a purely spiritual religion but a religion of a pure spirit in which people would bring the right attitude to their devotions. Men and women should not mechanically mumble the psalms; they should mean what they pray. Human beings were not made for the Sabbath, nor were they made for ceremonies. Ceremonies do not exist for their own sake but for the sake of fostering love for God and for one's neighbour. If Erasmus had wanted to abolish liturgical prayer, he would never have proposed the celebration of the Mass in the vernacular; nor would he have composed a liturgy in honour of the Virgin of Loreto in which he adopts the voice of father and pastor.

One need only read Erasmus' prayers to see that the claim that they are 'stripped of theology' is also a mistaken judgment. It is inconceivable to speak of and with God without engaging in theology. To emphasize goodness as the chief characteristic of God, to call God Creator and Christ Saviour, and to direct the devout to the goal of salvation demonstrate the theological nature of Erasmus' prayers. Yet there is more theology in them than that of creation and salvation. Erasmus incorporates the sacraments into prayerful devotion. The theme of baptism is conspicuous in the beginning of the *Precatio Dominica*, and marriage and the Eucharist form the basis of four prayers in the *Precationes aliquot novae*. Important also is Erasmus' irenic ecclesiology, which manifests itself in his belief that people pray as members of Christ's body who are at peace with one another. This ecclesiological motif is evident in the *Precatio Dominica*, in Erasmus' two Communion prayers, and, of course, in the *Precatio ad Dominum Jesum pro pace ecclesiae*.

Ultimately, it does not matter how one prays to God – that is, with which words one speaks to God – provided that these words, silent or spoken, come from a pious heart. The Lord's Prayer, however, is the most appropriate form of human conversation with God. All other good prayers take their inspiration from the prayer that Jesus taught, from Scripture in general, or from the tradition of the church verbalized in the liturgical collects. In accommodating human hearts, desires, and words to God, Erasmus is performing the same ministry as the parish priest required by the Roman Catechism to help his flock 'understand what one should ask of God and how one should pray.'

Erasmus nowhere views prayer as a vehicle for achieving a momentary rapturous union with God. He is not an heir of the late medieval mystical tradition of Mechtilde of Magdeburg, Eckhart, Tauler, Suso, and Ruysbroeck.[18] Erasmus' relationship to the medieval mystics has not engaged scholars as much as the question whether Erasmian spirituality is directly indebted to the Devotio Moderna. Albert Hyma maintained that Erasmus was a 'child of the Devotio Moderna,' who owed his theological notions and his humanism to the teaching of the Brothers of the Common Life.[19] More recently, Richard DeMolen has drawn parallels between Erasmus' religious thought and the Devotio Moderna and between the *Enchiridion* and the *Imitation of Christ*, the work most closely associated with the religious movement that has its origins in Geert Grote.[20] R.R. Post believes, however, that in Erasmus one 'can detect few characteristic traits of the Modern Devotion' and cautions against taking it for granted 'that everyone who showed any signs of piety at the end of the Middle Ages, or who was assumed to be devout, belonged to the Modern Devotion, or that any pupil from the schools of Deventer or Zwolle who achieved something in later life was a product of the Brothers.'[21] Indeed, a comparison of the concept of prayer in the writings of the Brothers and Sisters of the Common Life with that of Erasmus may contribute to show that there is no concrete evidence for a decisive influence on the humanist by the Devotio Moderna. The prayer of the New Devout was an ordered prayer, practised through the recitation of the liturgical hours and within the context of spiritual exercises.[22] Erasmus, although he had nothing in principle against praying the divine office, feared that this form of devotion could deteriorate into a mechanical mumbling of psalms. He preferred a freer type or prayer, springing *of* from an individual's *pius affectus*. Unlike Gerhart Zerbolt of Zutphen (d. 1398), whose *Spiritual Ascensions* 'was the one devotional work probably common to nearly every house of the Modern

Devout,'[23] he did not make prayer a part of a series of three spiritual ascents.

As important as investigating the potential influences on Erasmus is the task of placing him within the context of devotion in the sixteenth century. One notable difference between Erasmus and the Protestant Reformation is his position on the cult of the saints. Erasmus sought to reform the cult of the saints in order to preserve it. His *Colloquies* attacked the superstitions associated with it. He wanted devotees of the saints to stop considering the saints as so many gods with powers to heal diseases, provide protection from injury or death, and guarantee prosperity. God, not the saints, was the source of every gift and blessing. True devotion to the saints had to be Christocentric. It consisted of imitating their virtues, which they had received from Christ, but it also included praying to the saints, especially in order to acquire their Christian virtues. Invoking the saints for an increase in chastity or generosity was the same as praying to Christ, but in a different way.

Myron Gilmore maintains that 'Erasmus gave wide publicity to the ideas and even to the very language which formed the basis for the Tridentine decree on images.'[24] The Council's pronouncement on images concluded the broader decree 'De invocatione, veneratione et reliquiis sanctorum, et de sacris imaginibus.' One may detect Erasmian influence on or at least an Erasmian resonance in the text of the decree, since it justifies the invocation of the saints on the basis of the consensus of the church and not on the basis of Scripture.

By the middle of the sixteenth century, Erasmus came to be seen as a threat to the Catholic church. Pope Paul IV's Index of 1559 prohibited all of the humanist's works in their various genres, whether they discussed religious topics or not. The Tridentine Index of 1564 was less severe but still forbade, among other works, the *Colloquies*, the *Praise of Folly*, the *Christiani matrimonii institutio*, and an Italian edition of the *Paraphrases*. Other religious writings by Erasmus were forbidden until they had been scrutinized and purged of error by the theologians at Paris or Louvain.[25] According to Silvana Seidel Menchi, the enforcement of the Tridentine Index in Italy 'signified the expulsion of Erasmus from Italian cultural life.'[26] Although by 1550 it was rare for Erasmus to be praised openly and without qualification in Catholic Christendom and although he was considered a *persona non grata* at the Council of Trent, this does not mean that Catholics in general or the Council fathers were impervious to his ideas.

We know, for example, that in April 1546, six months after the opening of the Council, his *Enchiridion* was proposed at Trent as a possible model for a new Catholic catechism.[27] Moreover, the Roman Catechism bears remarkable resemblances to Erasmus' religious thought, although it is impossible to prove direct Erasmian influence. The catechism begins its discussion of faith in God by distinguishing 'the wisdom of this world' from 'Christian philosophy,'[28] a term reminiscent of Erasmus' philosophy of Christ. The concept of God in the catechism could be shared by Erasmus. The parish priest was to remind the faithful that God's goodness and mercy surpassed his justice.[29] Wherever we look, we see 'the wonderful light of divine generosity (*beneficentia*) and kindness (*benignitas*).' When we appeal to God's generosity in prayer, we should eventually arrive at the contemplation of his power, kindness, and wisdom.[30] While explaining the meaning of 'Father' in the Lord's Prayer, the parish priest should preach especially about 'the riches of God's kindness towards the human race.' For God still loves us despite our many sins.[31] He is the 'most generously merciful God' (*liberalissime misericors Deus*) who hears the prayers of the penitent.[32] God's creating and governing of the world indicate how much he loves and cares for human beings, but the greatest proof of our Father's kindness toward them is the fact that he redeemed them. The parish priest should emphasize to his spiritual children God's most excellent charity towards them so that they may understand that, being redeemed, they have in a wondrous way become God's children.[33]

The reprinting of Erasmus' prayers in Catholic prayer-books is another indication of his influence on sixteenth-century Catholic devotion. In 1538, Friedrich Nausea, who would become bishop of Vienna three years later, published his *Christlich Bettbüchlein.* Nausea was a zealous Erasmian who regarded his hero as a saint: 'Sanctus enim erat Erasmus.'[34] His prayer-book included twelve prayers by his humanist saint.[35] Erasmus' prayers also appeared in Timmanus Borckensis' *Enchiridion precationum illustrium virorum* (1551) and in Johann Wild's *Christlichs und sonder schöns betbüchlein* (1551).[36] In his *Euchologium Ecclesiasticum* (1561), Georg Witzel reprints Erasmus' 'Precatio ad Patrem,' praising it as the best exposition of the Lord's Prayer, but shrouds the prayer's author in anonymity. The heading simply reads: 'Enarratio Dominicae orationis per N. omnium optima.'[37]

Marcel Bataillon has noted the influence on Catholic Spain of Erasmus' teaching on prayer. A Spanish translation of the *Modus orandi Deum* was published in 1546 in Seville. The translation, however, made the invocation of the saints a matter of necessity, and not of one's free choice as Erasmus had originally suggested. A treatise on prayer written by Antonio de Porras and published in 1552 seems to owe much to the *Modus orandi Deum*. Bataillon also sees Erasmian ideas in Luis de Granada's *Libro de la oración* (1544) and *Guía de peccadores* (1566).[38]

The Spanish humanist Juan Luis Vives is another figure who should be mentioned in connection with Erasmus. Like Erasmus, he understood prayer as a 'sacred colloquy' (*sacrum colloquium*) and stated this definition: 'Prayer is a conversation (*collocutio*) with God.'[39] His prayers frequently refer to God's goodness and kindness. In a prayer asking for God's forgiveness, Vives reminds his readers that without due consideration of God's goodness their many sins would cause them to despair and directs them to appeal to a 'most gentle and most placable Father.' Vives addresses another prayer for mercy to the 'most merciful Jesus Christ.' A morning prayer invokes Christ as the 'most kind patron of the human race,' while a prayer for the love of God refers to Christ as one's best friend (*amicissime*). In an excursus after a prayer for the imitation of God's Son, Vives extolls the goodness, the kindness, and the generosity of God towards us.[40] God's goodness is a recurring theme in Vives' commentary on the Lord's Prayer, which at the outset applies the triad of *potentia*, *sapientia*, and *bonitas* to the heavenly Father.[41]

Like Erasmus, Vives prays for the peace of the church. A prayer for the holy Catholic church asks Christ, the 'author and advocate of charity, peace and good will' to soften our hardened hearts 'so that we might each wish the other well.' In this way, everyone will 'acknowledge us to be your disciples, and we will now already begin to express that life of heaven in which there is no discord, no hatred, but peace and mutual love.' Another prayer for the peace and unity of the Christian people beseeches Christ to grant that all the baptized might come together into one body worthy of his headship. 'Wake up, Christ Jesus, save us,' exhorts Vives, for 'only a look from you can calm and pacify this most savage storm.'[42]

The constant emphasis on God's goodness in the prayers of Vives and Erasmus may very well point to a significant element common to humanist piety. Charles Trinkaus in his study of 'humanity and divinity in Italian humanist thought' has elucidated various conceptions of human nature and dignity held in the fourteenth and fifteenth centuries.[43] What Trinkaus has done for humanity still needs to be done for divinity. How did the humanists of the sixteenth century both north and south of the Alps understand God? The relationship between God and human beings should be studied not only in terms of philosophical anthropology but also in terms of humanist theology and devotion.

Erasmus' apology for the invocation of the saints was, so he said, directed against Luther, and he and the Protestant theologians diverged at certain points in their interpretation of the Lord's Prayer. The divergences between Erasmus and Protestant piety should not overshadow the points of contact, however. His prayers were printed not only in Catholic but also in Protestant prayer-books. Wolfang Capito included thirteen of these prayers in his *Precationes Christianae* (1536), while Ludwig Rabe incorporated twenty into his voluminous two-part *Christlichs Bettbüchlins* (1565–8).[44]

Erasmus' devotional writings were particularly popular in England. James McConica has called attention to their translation into English under Cromwell's sponsorship as a means of enlisting humanist support for the Henrician reform of the English church.[45] A few of Erasmus' prayers appeared in Henrician prayer-books. Bishop Hilsey's Primer of 1539 includes two of Erasmus' graces as well as the two that Erasmus took from Chrysostom.[46] The official Primer of 1545 provides translations of Erasmus' morning prayer 'Diluculo ad Christum,' his prayer for the peace of the church, for the keeping of a good name, and for a dying person.[47] The anthology of prayers collected by Katherine Parr, Henry VIII's last queen, contains 'A prayer for men to say entering into battayle,' Erasmus' 'Inituri praelium.'[48] Craig Thompson has noted that Erasmus' prayers lived on in various Elizabethan prayer-books.[49] To identify them all would demonstrate how much Erasmus influenced English devotion.[50]

Bataillon's statement in 1937 that devotional literature, 'la littérature d'oraison,' represents a 'domaine vaste, fort peu exploré,'[51] still holds true today. Both the intellectual and social history of the Reformation would benefit from an examination of the rhetoric and the religious themes of the prayers that became part of the daily lives of countless Christians in the sixteenth century. A study of sixteenth-century prayer-books and catechesis on prayer will no doubt discover a considerable measure of devotional cross-fertilization between Protestantism and Catholicism. As Helen White has suggested: 'Perhaps there is less controversy anyhow when men pray to their Maker rather than talk about him.'[52] We should not be surprised if scholarship attributes a good deal of the common ground between Protestants and Catholics to the great humanist scholar who wished all Christians to pray for the peace of the church. Nor need we hesitate to see Erasmus as a sincerely religious thinker, who, through his literary cure of souls, helped to shape the piety of early modern Europe.

Notes

✻

ABBREVIATIONS

Allen   *Opus epistolorum Des. Erasmi Roterodami,* 12 vols., ed. P.S. Allen, H.M. Allen, and H.W. Garrod (Oxford: Clarendon Press, 1906–58).

ASD   *Opera Omnia Desiderii Erasmi Roterodami,* ed. C. Reedijk et al. (Amsterdam: North-Holland Publishing Company, 1969–).

CCSL   *Corpus Christianorum: Series Latina* (Turnhout: Brepols, 1954–).

CEBR   *Contemporaries of Erasmus: A Biographical Register of the Renaissance and Reformation,* 3 vols., ed. Peter G. Bietenholz and Thomas B. Deutscher (Toronto: University of Toronto Press, 1985–7).

CWE   *Collected Works of Erasmus* (Toronto: University of Toronto Press, 1974–).

Holborn   *Desiderius Erasmus Roterodamus: Ausgewählte Werke,* ed. Hajo Holborn and Annemarie Holborn (Munich: C.H. Beck'sche Verlagsbuchhandlung, 1933).

LB   *Desiderii Erasmi Roterodami opera omnia,* 10 vols., ed. J. Leclerc (Leiden: 1703–6).

OC   *Corpus Reformatorum: Ioannis Calvini opera quae supersunt omnia,* 57 vols., ed. Wilhelm Baum, Eduard Cunitz, and Eduard Reuss (Braunschweig: C.A. Schwetschke et Filium [M. Bruhn], 1863–97).

PG   *Patrologiae cursus completus ... series graeca,* 161 vols., ed. J.-P. Migne (Paris: 1857–77).

PL   *Patrologiae cursus completus ... series latina,* 221 vols., ed. J.-P. Migne (Paris: 1878–90).

RSV   *The Holy Bible,* Revised Standard Version.

WA   Martin Luther, *D. Martin Luthers Werke: Kritische Gesamtaus-*

gabe, 61 vols. (Weimar: Hermann Böhlaus Nachfolger, 1883–
1983).

WABr.   Martin Luther, D. *Martin Luthers Werke: Briefwechsel*, 15 vols.
(Weimar: Hermann Böhlaus Nachfolger, 1930–78).

INTRODUCTION

1 Lee Daniel Snyder, 'Erasmus on Prayer'; J. Trapman, 'Erasmus's *Precationes*'; Alice Tobriner, 'The Private Prayers of Erasmus and Vives.'
2 CWE 8: 263, Ep. 1219, lines 145–6.
3 For posterity's judgments upon Erasmus, see Andreas Flitner, *Erasmus im Urteil seiner Nachwelt;* and Bruce Mansfield, *Phoenix of His Age: Interpretations of Erasmus, c. 1550–1750,* and *Interpretations of Erasmus, c. 1750–1920: Man on His Own.*
4 WABr. 1: 90, Ep. 35, lines 15–20; WABr. 2: 387, Ep. 429, lines 5–6.
5 Allen 11: 134, Ep. 3019, lines 53–4.
6 Johan Huizinga, *Erasmus and the Age of Reformation*; Augustin Renaudet, *Etudes Erasmiennes (1521–1529)* Joseph Lortz, 'Erasmus – Kirchengeschichtlich,' in *Aus Theologie und Philosophie*, ed. T. Steinbüchel and T. Müncker.
7 Lortz, 'Erasmus – Kirchengeschichtlich,' 305.
8 Renaudet, *Etudes Erasmiennes*, xviii, xx, 174–6, 181, 189.
9 Ibid, xxi.
10 Alfons Auer, *Die vollkommene Frömmigkeit des Christen*, 56, 95.
11 Joseph A. Jungmann, *Christian Prayer through the Centuries*, 138.
12 Roland Bainton, *Erasmus of Christendom*, 67, 165.
13 Richard Marius, *Thomas More*, 83.
14 Jacques Chomarat, *Grammaire et rhétorique chez Erasme*, 1: 16–20, 654, 698.
15 Ibid, 1: 663, 699. For an extensive review of Chomarat's book, see Manfred Hoffmann's assessment in *Erasmus of Rotterdam Society Yearbook* 5 (1985): 65–83.
16 *Dictionnaire de Spiritualité*, s.v. 'Humanisme et spiritualité chez Erasme,' by Jean-Pierre Massaut, vol. 7/1, 1006.
17 Ibid, 1025–7.
18 Léon-E. Halkin, *Erasme et l'humanisme chrétien*, 9; Georges Chantraine, 'Théologie et vie spirituelle,' 809–10.
19 John W. O'Malley, introduction to CWE 66: xv.
20 C. Augustijn, 'The Ecclesiology of Erasmus,' in *Scrinium Erasmianum*, 2: 135.
21 Georg Gebhardt, *Die Stellung des Erasmus von Rotterdam zur römischen Kirche;* Willi Hentze, *Kirche und kirchliche Einheit bei Desiderius Erasmus von Rotterdam.*
22 James McConica, *Erasmus*, 45.

23 Léon-E. Halkin, 'Erasme et le célibat sacerdotal,' 'La Mariologie d'Erasme,' and *Erasme parmi nous*, 401, 426. Halkin's advocacy is at times excessive. It is hard to believe that the touchstone of Erasmus' piety was his Mariology, and it is at least anachronistic to call his theology of peace 'a theology of liberation' and to regard him as a supporter of women's emancipation. See *Erasme parmi nous*, 330, 418, 430.

24 Halkin, *Erasme et l'humanisme chrétien*, 111; *Erasme parmi nous*, 421; 'La piété d'Erasme.'

25 *Modus orandi Deum*, ASD V–1: 128.

26 Ernst-Wilhelm Kohls, *Die Theologie des Erasmus;* Manfred Hoffmann, *Erkenntnis und Verwirklichung der wahren Theologie.*

27 CWE 66, xxx.

28 Ibid, xxi.

29 Rudolf Padberg, *Erasmus als Katechet;* Jean-Pierre Massaut, 'La position "oecuménique" d'Erasme sur la pénitence,' See also Padberg, 'Personale Seelsorge bei Erasmus von Rotterdam'; Manfred Hoffmann, 'Erasmus on Church and Ministry'; and Hilmar M. Pabel, 'Promoting the Business of the Gospel.'

30 CWE 66, xv.

31 ASD V–4: 132.

32 Emile Telle, *Erasme de Rotterdam et le septième sacrement*, 176.

33 Halkin, 'Erasme et le célibat sacerdotal,' 497–8; and 'La piété d'Erasme,' 674–5. For another positive evaluation of Erasmus' priesthood, see Germain Marc'hadour, 'Erasmus as Priest.'

34 Allen 7: 454, Ep. 2033, lines 47–8.

35 John W. O'Malley, 'Grammar and Rhetoric in the *Pietas* of Erasmus,' 87.

36 CWE 3: 204, 205, Ep. 373, lines 218, 219–20, 228–31.

37 Allen 4: 123–4, Ep. 1043, lines 1–7, 36–7.

38 ASD V–1: 99.

39 James Michael Weiss, '*Ecclesiastes* and Erasmus,' 89. For other studies of the *Ecclesiastes*, see Robert G. Kleinhans, 'Erasmus' Doctrine of Preaching,' and '*Ecclesiastes, sive de ratione concionandi*,' in *Essays on the Works of Erasmus*, ed. R.L. DeMolen; Charles Béné, *Erasme et Saint Augustin*, 372–425; Jacques Chomarat, *Grammaire et rhétorique chez Erasme*, 2: 1053–155; André Godin, *Erasme, lecteur d'Origène*, 302–47; John W. O'Malley, 'Erasmus and the History of Sacred Rhetoric.'

40 ASD V–4: 36.

41 O'Malley, 'Erasmus and the History of Sacred Rhetoric,' 13.

42 Holborn, 193.

43 Godin, *Erasme, lecteur d'Origène*, 303. On the *Ratio*, see Georges Chantraine, '*Mystère' et 'Philosophie du Christ' selon Erasme*, 155–362; Manfred Hoffmann, *Erkenntnis und Verwirklichung der wahren Theolo-*

gie; Godin, *Erasme, lecteur d'Origène,* 256–302; Peter Walter, *Theologie aus dem Geist der Rhetorik,* 212–26.

44 For a thorough treatment of Erasmus' criticism of the preaching of his contemporaries, see Chomarat, *Grammaire et rhétorique,* 2: 1071–92.

45 *Funus* (1526), *Familiaria Colloquia,* ASD I–3: 540.

46 ASD V–1: 123.

47 Holborn, 214; ASD V–4: 118.

48 Holborn, 297.

49 Telle, *Erasme de Rotterdam et le septième sacrement,* 159.

50 CWE 34: 276, 277.

51 Friedhelm Krüger, *Humanistische Evangelienauslegung,* 134–40.

52 Jane E. Phillips, 'The Gospel, the Clergy, and the Laity in Erasmus' *Paraphrase on the Gospel of John,*' 99.

53 CWE 7: 5, Ep. 995, lines 19–20.

54 Craig R. Thompson, 'Erasmus and Tudor England,' 53, 54.

55 Krüger, *Humanistische Evangelienauslegung,* 28.

56 Cornelis Augustijn, *Erasmus: His Life, Works, and Influence,* 102.

57 ASD V–4: 68.

58 PL 77: 49C–D.

59 ASD V–4: 144.

60 Holborn, 196, cf. 285; Manfred Hoffmann, *Rhetoric and Theology,* 106.

61 ASD V–4: 67.

62 Holborn, 222.

63 Ibid, 254.

64 ASD V–4: 174, 235–6.

65 Otto Schottenloher, 'Erasmus, Johann Poppenruyter und die Entstehung des *Enchiridion militis christiani.*'

66 CWE 66: xli.

67 CWE 66: 75, 123–6.

68 CWE 9: 414, Ep. 1347, lines 55–60.

69 Allen 6: 59, Ep. 1563, lines 26–8.

70 ASD V–4: 40.

71 William James, *The Varieties of Religious Experience,* 464.

72 Friedrich Heiler, *Das Gebet: Eine religionsgeschichtliche und religionspsychologische Untersuchung,* 5th ed., 494, 491.

73 Ibid, 1, 2.

74 Eamon Duffy, *The Stripping of the Altars,* 298.

75 Halkin, 'La piété d'Erasme,' 702.

76 ASD V–1: 127.

77 For a brief summary of the role of rhetoric in prayer according to the *Modus orandi Deum,* see Chomarat, *Grammaire et rhétorique,* 2: 1153–5.

78 ASD V–1: 128.

79 Halkin, 'La piété d'Erasme,' 706.

80 *Modus orandi Deum,* ASD V–1: 121.
81 *Paraphrase on Acts* (8: 35), LB VII: 701D–2A.
82 ASD V–4: 202.

CHAPTER ONE

1 R.J. Schoeck, 'Erasmus as Latin Secretary to the Bishop of Cambrai,' in *Erasmus of Rotterdam: The Man and the Scholar,* 12–13.
2 Roland Bainton, *Erasmus of Christendom,* 26.
3 CWE 29: 9.
4 CWE 29: 13. It is not clear what Erasmus means by 'warlike little prayers.' See Léon-E. Halkin, 'La piété d'Érasme,' 677.
5 LB V: 1227E.
6 LB V: 1236B, 1238E, 1236E.
7 *Paean,* LB V: 1228E, 1230F, 1231A–D, 1233A; *Obsecratio,* LB V: 1233E, 1235C–F. For a collection of medieval hymns to Mary, see *Lateinische Hymnen des Mittelalters,* ed. Franz Joseph Mone, vol. 2: *Marienlieder.*
8 LB V: 1230A, 1236B.
9 CWE 9: 322, Ep. 1314A, lines 742–5.
10 CWE 66: 61.
11 *Obsecratio,* LB V: 1233E, 1235F.
12 *Apologia adversus monachos quosdam hispanos* (1528), LB IX: 1087E.
13 LB V: 1239 A.
14 LB V: 1210E–11A.
15 LB V: 1210E.
16 LB V: 1211F, 1212D, E.
17 LB V: 1213C, 1214D–E.
18 LB V: 1214E–F.
19 LB V: 1213C, 1214E.
20 *Paean,* LB V: 1234 C; *Obsecratio,* LB V: 1240 A.
21 LB V: 1211D–F; 1212D.
22 LB V: 1212A–D.
23 LB V: 1212D.
24 LB V: 1215A–16A.
25 LB V: 1216A.
26 Paul Althaus, *Forschungen zur evangelischen Gebetsliteratur,* 25 and n. 1.
27 CWE 66: 30.
28 CWE 66: 30–1.
29 CWE 66: 36.
30 CWE 66: 31.
31 ASD V–1: 173–4.
32 CWE 66: 31, 35, 53, 76, 78, 80, 82.
33 CWE 66: 31.

34 CWE 66: 79.
35 Ibid.
36 CWE 66: 31.
37 CWE 66: 81.
38 *Paraphrase on 1 Timothy* (2: 8) [1519], LB VII: 1042A.
39 *Modus orandi Deum*, ASD V–1: 121.
40 Allen 6: 59, Ep. 1563, lines 15–17.
41 *Divi Iohannis Chrysostomi de orando deum.* Erasmus' Latin translation
    may also be found in LB VIII: 127–36. For the Greek text, see PG 50:
    775–86.
42 *Exomologesis*, LB V: 157C.
43 LB V: 657C–D.
44 *Vidua christiana*, CWE 66: 206.
45 Allen 6: 58, Ep. 1563, lines 5–6.
46 Halkin, 'La piété d'Erasme,' 697.
47 Allen 6: 28, Ep. 1550, lines 84–5.
48 Allen 6: 58, Ep. 1563, lines 7–8.
49 ASD V–1: 119.
50 ASD V–1: 113.
51 ASD V–1: 121.
52 Claude Backvis, 'La fortune d'Erasme en Pologne,' 195. For Erasmus'
    influence in Poland, see also Jean-Claude Margolin, *Erasme, précep-
    teur de l'Europe*, 192–218.
53 CCSL 1: 257–74.
54 ASD V–1: 117.
55 André Godin, *Erasme, lecteur d'Origène*, 597, 626.
56 PG 11: 415–562; *Origen: An Exhortation to Martyrdom, Prayer, First
    Principles*, trans. Rowan A. Greer, 81–170.
57 PL 33: 493–507.
58 *Summa Theologiae*, 2a2ae: 83, 9; 12; 13; 14; 14 ad 1.
59 CWE 66: xxxvi.
60 For Becon, see Derrick Sherwin Bailey, *Thomas Becon and the Reforma-
    tion of the Church in England.*
61 *The Early Works of Thomas Becon*, 128.
62 Edward Surtz, *The Works and Days of John Fisher*, 7–8. For the Latin
    text, see John Fisher, *Ioannis Fischerii Roffensis in Anglia Episcopi
    Opera*, 1708–33.
63 Lee Daniel Snyder, 'Erasmus on Prayer,' 22.
64 ASD V–1: 127.
65 Jean-Pierre Massaut, *Josse Clichtove: L'humanisme et la réforme du
    clergé*, 2: 321. See also Anton L. Mayer, 'Renaissance, Humanismus
    und Liturgie,' 48–96.
66 See Massaut, *Josse Clichtove*, 2: 285–335.
67 *Enchiridion*, CWE 66: 71.

68 See Erasmus' *Virginis matris apud Lauretum cultae liturgia* in ASD V–1: 97–109.

69 LB VII, **3v. For a discussion of this ceremony, see John B. Payne, *Erasmus: His Theology of the Sacraments*, 172.

70 ASD V–1: 167.

71 ASD V–1: 122. For Erasmus' views on music, see Jean-Claude Margolin, *Erasme et la musique*; Margolin's essay of the same title in his *Recherches Erasmiennes*, 85–97; and Clement A. Miller, 'Erasmus on Music.'

72 ASD V–1: 168.

73 Ibid.

74 Holborn, 142.

75 LB VII: 903B–E.

76 ASD V–1: 163.

77 ASD V–1: 166.

78 ASD V–1: 122.

79 Ibid.

80 ASD V–1: 124–5.

81 ASD V–1: 126.

82 *De fide orthodoxa*, 3, 24; PG 94: 1089.

83 Holborn, 29.

84 *Novum Instrumentum omne*, pt. 2, 524.

85 Ibid, pt. 2, 1.

86 *Erasmus' Annotations on the New Testament: Acts – Romans – I and II Corinthians*, 343.

87 *Paraphrase on Matthew* (6: 1) [1522], LB VII: 35B; *Paraphrase on 1 Thessalonians* (1: 2) [1520], LB VII: 1017D–E.

88 ASD V–1: 143, 171.

89 LB VIII: 127C, 128A; PG 50: 775. The real Chrysostom also understood prayer as conversation with God. In his *Homilies on Genesis*, he writes: 'Prayer is a conversation (*dialexis*) with God.' See PG 53: 280.

90 *The Spiritual Exercises of St Ignatius*, 56.

91 *The Early Works of Thomas Becon*, 128.

92 Allen 11: 191, Ep. 3036, lines 40–8.

93 ASD V–1: 126.

94 ASD V–1: 125.

95 ASD V–1: 175.

96 ASD V–1: 134–7.

97 ASD V–1: 128–9.

98 ASD V–1: 131.

99 ASD V–1: 132.

100 ASD V–1: 121.

101 ASD V–1: 128.

102 Ibid.

103 LB VII: 135D, 136A. See Matthew 26: 38, 44.

104 *Paraphrase on Acts* (1524), LB VII: 707D; *Paraphrase on Colossians*
     (1520), LB VII: 1006B; *Paraphrase on 1 Thessalonians*, LB VII: 1026A.

105 Holborn, 40.

106 LB V: 168C.

107 CWE 66: 219.

108 ASD V–1: 344.

109 ASD V–4: 76, 146, 128.

110 LB VII: 43E–4A. See Matthew 7: 8–11.

111 CWE 66: 238.

112 CWE 49: 65. See Mark 4: 40.

113 *Paraphrase on Mark* (1: 34), CWE 49: 26.

114 LB VII: 1002A. Erasmus is paraphrasing Philippians 4: 6.

115 *Paraphrase on Luke* (3: 21) [1523], LB VII: 315C–D.

116 ASD V–1: 129.

117 *Paraphrase on Luke*, LB VII: 338F–9B.

118 CWE 49: 83. Mark 6: 31 is the basis for Erasmus' comment.

119 ASD V–1: 138.

120 ASD V–3: 294.

121 ASD V–1: 165.

122 *Paraphrase on Matthew* (6: 8), LB VII: 36D.

123 *Paraphrase on Mark* (12: 34), CWE 49: 148; *Cyclops* (1529), in *Familiaria
     Colloquia*, ASD I–3: 607; and *Abbatis et Eruditae* (1524), in ibid, ASD I–
     3: 404; note on Matthew 6: 7, *Erasmus' Annotations on the New Testa-
     ment: The Gospels*, 33.

124 *Paraphrase on Matthew* (6: 7), LB VII: 36B.

125 ASD V–1: 138.

126 ASD V–1: 140.

127 PL 33: 501–2. Augustine's approach lies at the heart of Aquinas'
     answer to the question 'utrum oratio debeat esse diuturna.' See
     Summa Theologiae, 2a2ae: 83, 14.

128 The device of *quanto magis* is a species of *amplificatio*, much used in
     Renaissance preaching, to which John O'Malley refers in his *Praise
     and Blame in Renaissance Rome*, 57.

129 ASD V–1: 141–2.

130 CWE 66: 29–30.

131 Ernst-Wilhelm Kohls, *Die Theologie des Erasmus*, 1: 96.

132 *Enchiridion*, CWE 66: 91.

133 CWE 66: 118.

134 CWE 29: 57, 70.

135 ASD V–2: 38.

136 *Paraphrase on Romans*, CWE 42, 68; *Paraphrase on James* (1520), LB VII:
     1122A.

137 *Paraphrase on 1 Corinthians* (16: 23) [1519], LB VII: 914A; *Paraphrase on*

Galatians (6: 18) [1519], LB VII: 968A; *Paraphrase on Ephesians* (6: 24)
[1520], LB VII: 990E; *Paraphrase on Philippians* (4: 23), LB VII: 1004C;
Paraphrase on 1 Thessalonians (5: 27), LB VII: 1026D.

138 *Paraphrase on 2 Corinthians* (1519), LB VII: 942B–C.
139 *Paraphrase on Romans* (3: 24), CWE 42: 25; (4: 24) CWE 42: 32.
140 CWE 42: 33. The basis for Erasmus' comment is Romans 5: 6.
141 CWE 49: 14. Erasmus is extrapolating from Mark 1: 1.
142 LB V: 578B.
143 LB V: 568D, 570F–1C. Quote from LB V: 571C.
144 LB V: 561C–D.
145 LB V: 563E–4C.
146 LB V: 560C–D.
147 LB V: 150F–1A.
148 ASD V–1: 127, 128.
149 ASD V–1: 173.
150 ASD V–1: 125.
151 ASD V–1: 142.
152 Jean Delumeau, *Sin and Fear*, 291, 293, 401–21. Part 3 of Delumeau's
book is entitled 'An Evangelism of Fear in the Catholic World' (327).
Cf. Delumeau's earlier study, *La peur en occident (XIVe-XVIIIe siècles)*.
153 *Paraphrase on James* (1: 5), LB VII: 1119D.
154 LB V: 1113D: 'Homunculus accedis ad solium Dei. Deo nihil cogitari
potest sublimius: hoimne vero quid abjectius, qui etiam si pius sit, et
innocens spud homines, tamen omnium hominum puritas, impuritas est, si ad divinam puritatem coferatur.' The passage in ASD V–1:
142 is flawed: 'Homunculus accedis ad solium Dei. Deo nihil cogitari potest sublimius; homo [sic] quid abiectius, qui etiam si pius sit
et innocens spud homines, tamen ominum [sic] hominum puritas
impuritas est si ad diuinam puritatem conferatur.'
155 CWE 66: 118.
156 Holborn, 145.
157 ASD V–1: 171.
158 ASD V–2: 314. On the *De puritate*, see Charles Béné, 'Le *De Puritate
Tabernaculi*: Testament spirituel d'Erasme?'
159 ASD V–1: 142.
160 See *The Early Works of Thomas Becon*, 160.
161 ASD V–1: 142.
162 ASD V–3: 340, 342.
163 ASD V–1: 143.
164 Ibid.
165 ASD V–1: 144.
166 *Modus orandi Deum*, ASD V–1: 127.
167 ASD V–1: 139.
168 LB VII: 1002A.

169 *Paraphrase on Matthew*, LB VII: 51C.
170 CWE 49: 141. Erasmus is paraphrasing Mark 11: 22.
171 *Paraphrase on 2 Corinthians* (12: 9), LB VII: 938D.
172 LB VII: 1119 E–F. Erasmus is paraphrasing James 1: 6–7. For the importance of trusting in God, see also *Paraphrase on John* (16: 23–4) [1523], CWE 46: 189–90; *Paraphrase on John* (17: 1), CWE 46: 192; *Paraphrase on Romans* (12: 12), CWE 42: 72; *Paraphrase on James* (5: 13), LB VII: 1139D–E.
173 *Paraphrase on Mark* (11: 25–6), CWE 49: 141. While Erasmus essentially relates what the original text says, he leans on the idea that God forgives us our sins on condition that we forgive our neighbours.
174 *Paraphrase on Luke* (23: 4), LB VII: 462A–B. Cf. *Paraphrase on 1 Timothy* (2: 2), LB VII: 1040A–B: 'Vos contra, Christi vestigiis inhaeretis, qui quum sublatus in crucem audiret virulenta probra, vel ipso crucis supplicio graviora, non regessit convitia, non imprecatus est diras, sed ingenti clamore Patrem interpellavit, ut illis ignosceret.'
175 ASD V–1: 143.
176 *Concionalis interpretatio in Psalmum LXXXV*, ASD V–3: 346.
177 LB VII: 1159C.
178 CWE 66: 124.
179 *Paraphrase on Matthew* (5: 9), LB VII: 25F–6A.
180 LB VII: 101A–C.
181 LB VII: 663E–4A. Erasmus is paraphrasing Acts 1: 14.
182 LB VII: 1114A. The basis for Erasmus' comment is Jude 21.
183 LB VII: 683A.
184 CWE 27: 303.
185 CWE 8: 202, Ep. 1202, lines 7–11.
186 CWE 9: 252, Ep. 1334, line 232.
187 James D. Tracy, *Erasmus: The Growth of a Mind*, 219.
188 *In Psalmum XXII enarratio triplex* (1530), ASD V–2: 344.
189 Willi Hentze, *Kirche und kirchliche Einheit*, 35.
190 ASD V–1: 130.
191 Ibid: 'Nam perpetue pie viuendi studium iugis est deprecatio.'
192 See *The Early Works of Thomas Becon*, 170.
193 ASD V–4: 52, 68.
194 *Paraphrase on Acts* (10: 2), LB VII: 707C; (10: 4) LB VII: 707D.
195 CWE 9: 425, Ep. 1347, lines 404–14.
196 ASD V–1: 174.
197 Ibid.
198 LB VIII: 136C; PG 50: 786.
199 LB VIII: 129E–F; PG 50: 777.
200 Snyder, 'Erasmus on Prayer,' 25–6.
201 ASD V–1: 174.

202 M.A. Screech, *Ecstasy and the Praise of Folly*, 50, 196, 110. For a response to Screech, see Clarence H. Miller, 'Styles and Mixed Genres in Erasmus' *Praise of Folly*.'

203 Screech, *Ecstasy and the Praise of Folly*, 75, 86–7, 99.

204 ASD V–1: 125.

205 ASD V–1: 122.

206 ASD V–1: 121.

207 *The Praise of Folly*, trans. Clarence H. Miller, 137. The emphasis is mine.

208 ASD V–1: 157.

209 ASD V–1: 161. Cf. Augustine, PL 33: 499; Aquinas, *Summa Theologiae*, 2a2ae: 83, 1, ad 1.

210 ASD V–1: 157.

211 *Paraphrase on Matthew*, LB VII: 17D.

212 *Paraphrase on Mark*, CWE 49: 86.

213 *Paraphrase on Luke*, LB VII: 448D.

214 *Paraphrase on Luke* (1: 10, 13), LB VII: 285E, 286A–B.

215 *Paraphrase on Mark* (10: 48, 51), CWE 49: 134.

216 CWE 66: 64.

217 ASD V–1: 158.

218 ASD V–1: 157.

219 *Paraphrase on Acts* (21: 14), LB VII: 750C.

220 *Paraphrase on Mark* (14: 36), CWE 49: 162.

221 ASD V–1: 156, 159.

222 PL 33: 502–3.

223 ASD V–1: 160.

224 ASD V–1: 162.

225 For a discussion of the function, form, and content of the collect, see Joseph A. Jungmann, *The Mass of the Roman Rite*, 1: 359–90.

226 ASD V–1: 162–3.

227 ASD V–1: 164.

228 ASD V–1: 165–6.

229 ASD V–1: 166, 167–8. Cf. Augustine's letter to Proba, PL 33: 501.

230 ASD V–1: 172.

231 ASD V–1: 366.

232 ASD V–1: 170.

233 ASD V–1: 173.

234 LB VII: 1041F–2A. Erasmus is extrapolating from 1 Timothy 2: 8.

235 ASD V–1: 173.

236 ASD V–1: 168.

237 ASD V–1: 168–70. Seven months earlier Erasmus had already criticized the saying of the divine office by princes. God would not mind if duty called them away from their prayers. It must always be the case that whatever has been established by human authority, i.e. the

recitation of psalms, should give way to 'the more perfect office of charity.' See *Exomologesis*, LB V: 163E.
238 ASD V–1: 175.
239 ASD V–1: 164.

CHAPTER TWO

1 Allen 9: 162, Ep. 2443, lines 212–13. For Sadoleto, see CEBR 3: 183–7, especially 186.
2 For the relevant texts from the Augsburg Confession and from the Apology, see *Die Bekenntnisschriften der evangelisch-lutherischen Kirche*, 3d ed., 83b–c, 316–28. The Catholic case may be found in *Die Confutatio der Confessio Augustana*, 125–31.
3 Lee Palmer Wandel, *Voracious Idols and Violent Hands*, 193, 196.
4 Martin Brecht, *Martin Luther*, 2: *Ordnung und Abgrenzung der Reformation*, 47; quote from Ronald J. Sider, *Andreas Bodenstein von Karlstadt*, 168.
5 Carlos M.N. Eire, *War against the Idols*, 80–2, 108–13.
6 Ibid, 116–18; Roland Bainton, *Erasmus of Christendom*, 219–23.
7 *The Apostolic Fathers*, trans. J.B. Lightfoot and J.R. Harmer, 142.
8 *Theologische Realenzyklopädie*, s.v. 'Heilige/Heiligenverehrung': 'III. Anfänge der christlichen Heiligenverehrung,' 14: 650.
9 Peter Brown, *The Cult of the Saints*, 12–22.
10 Eamon Duffy, *The Stripping of the Altars*, 2, 292.
11 Brown, *The Cult of the Saints*, 36–7, 60–1; *Histoire de l'Eglise depuis les origines jusqu'à nos jours*, vol. 14: *L'Eglise au temps du Grand Schisme et de la crise conciliaire*, by E. Delaruelle et al, 857–8; D. Catherine Brown, *Pastor and Laity in the Theology of Jean Gerson*, 233–4.
12 *A Dialogue Concerning Heresies*, in *Complete Works of St Thomas More*, 6/1: 54.
13 Duffy, *The Stripping of the Altars*, 167, 156 (quote).
14 Donald Weinstein and Rudolph M. Bell, *Saints and Society: The Two Worlds of Western Christendom*, 108–9.
15 CWE 66: 65.
16 CWE 66: 55.
17 CWE 66: 84.
18 CWE 66: 86.
19 CWE 66: 104.
20 ASD V–1: 163.
21 *Ratio*, Holborn, 202.
22 Ibid; letter to Volz, CWE 66: 15.
23 CWE 66: 15.
24 CWE 66: 104.

25 Léon-E. Halkin, *Erasme parmi nous*, 39.
26 Ibid, 34.
27 CWE 1: 105–6, Ep. 50, lines 4–16.
28 CWE 1: 250, Ep. 124, lines 14–17.
29 For a discussion of Erasmus' 'conversion,' see Erika Rummel, *Erasmus' Annotations on the New Testament*, 3–18.
30 CWE 1: 51, Ep. 28, lines 9–11.
31 For a brief discussion of the poems on Saint Gregory the Great, Saint Anne, and the angels, see Clarence H. Miller, 'The Liturgical Context of Erasmus's Hymns,' 482–5.
32 CWE 86: 639.
33 CWE 85: 271–3.
34 CWE 86: 511.
35 CWE 9: 295–6, Ep. 1341A, lines 82–4, 88–91.
36 CWE 85: 113.
37 CWE 85: 117.
38 CWE 85: 121.
39 CWE 2: 17, Ep. 145, lines 157–9.
40 Beda Kleinschmidt, 'Zur Verehrung der heiligen Mutter Anna,' 'Die Blütezeit des Annakultes,' 'Das Trinubium (Dreiheirat) der hl. Anna in Legende, Liturgie und Geschichte,' especially 339–40.
41 CWE 86: 410; CWE 2: 13, Ep. 145, lines 14–15.
42 CWE 86: 410.
43 CWE 85: 9, 11, 13.
44 CWE 86: 696, note on line 5 of CWE 85: 338, no. 118. The 'Erasmi precatio Salve regina' was first published by Alaard of Amsterdam in *De vitando pernitioso libidinosoque aspectu carmen bucolicum* (Leiden: P. Balen, 1538). See CWE 86: 695.
45 Harry Vredeveld, 'Some "Lost" Poems of Erasmus from the Year 1499,' 334–5.
46 CWE 85: 279.
47 CWE 85: 299.
48 CWE 66: 61.
49 CWE 66: 62–3.
50 CWE 66: 63–4; quote from 64.
51 *The Praise of Folly* (1511), trans. Clarence H. Miller, 66.
52 CWE 3: 125, Ep. 337, lines 464–5.
53 CWE 3: 115, Ep. 337, lines 98–101.
54 *Enchiridion*, CWE 66: 64; *Praise of Folly*, 63.
55 CWE 66: 64.
56 CWE 66: 71–2.
57 CWE 66: 205.
58 CWE 66: 199, 213–14, 235.

59 CWE 66: 72.

60 CWE 3: 9, Ep. 301, lines 6–12, 20–2, 34.

61 Bainton, *Erasmus of Christendom*, 141, quips: 'One suspects that if Paul had known what Erasmus would do with the Epistle to the Romans he would have made him walk. The doctrine of predestination was emasculated.'

62 ASD V–1: 152.

63 ASD V–1: 100.

64 Eire, *War against the Idols*, 39.

65 *Modus orandi Deum*, ASD V–1: 161.

66 Walter Gordon, *Humanist Play and Belief*, 99.

67 Franz Bierlaire, *Les Colloques d'Erasme: Réforme des études, réforme des moeurs et réforme de l'Eglise au XVIe siècle*, 199. The fourth chapter of Bierlaire's book is entitled 'Les *Colloques*, guide de la vie chrétienne.'

68 See the prefatory letter to Erasmus Froben first printed in the March 1522 edition of the *Colloquies*, ASD I–3: 123.

69 ASD I–3: 156–7.

70 ASD I–3: 394.

71 ASD I–3: 425–9.

72 ASD I–3: 535.

73 ASD I–3: 535–6.

74 ASD I–3: 691. Duffy, *The Stripping of the Altars*, 185, notes the late medieval belief that a saint 'might punish or at least complain if slighted or if a client's devotion faltered.'

75 Quotes from Léon-E. Halkin, 'Erasme pèlerin,' in *Scrinium Erasmianum*, 2: 244, 245.

76 ASD I–3: 327–8.

77 ASD I–3: 328–9.

78 ASD I–3: 471.

79 ASD I–3: 489.

80 ASD I–3: 487–8.

81 ASD I–3: 477–8.

82 ASD I–3: 471.

83 ASD I–3: 471–4.

84 ASD I–3: 750.

85 ASD I–3: 172–4.

86 ASD I–3: 271–2; quote from 272.

87 ASD I–3: 273.

88 CWE 8: 243–4, Ep. 1211, lines 676, 686–92.

89 Walter Delius, *Geschichte der Marienverehrung*, 127–90, 'Schutzmantel-madonna': 190; and Georg Söll, 'Maria in der Geschichte von Theologie und Frömmigkeit,' 93–192.

90 *Exomologesis*, LB V: 159D–E.

91 ASD V–1: 172.

92 Quote from *Histoire de l'Eglise depuis les origines jusqu'à nos jours,* vol. 14, 853; Brown, *Pastor and Laity in the Theology of Jean Gerson,* 25.

93 ASD I–3: 535.

94 *De immensa Dei misericordia concio,* LB V: 557B–C.

95 Léon-E. Halkin, 'La Mariologie d'Erasme,' 42.

96 *Supputatio errorum in censuris Beddae* (1527), LB IX: 569F–70A, 570B. For the conflict between Erasmus and Béda see Erika Rummel, *Erasmus and His Catholic Critics,* 2: 29–59.

97 LB IX: 569D: 'Propositio XVIII: *Christus solus omnium nulla peccati labe contactus fuit.*'

98 LB IX: 569E.

99 *Praise of Folly,* 75.

100 LB IX: 569E.

101 Halkin, 'Mariologie,' 54.

102 *Praise of Folly,* 65.

103 ASD I–3: 535.

104 ASD I–3: 654.

105 Joaquín María Alonso, 'Erasmo, hombre-puente en la historia de la devoción mariana,' quote from 263. Cf. Hilda Graef, *Mary: A History of Doctrine and Devotion,* 2: 2–6; and Hans Düfel, 'Die Stellung des Erasmus von Rotterdam zur Marienverehrung,' 5: 431–51, especially 450–1.

106 CWE 2: 230, Ep. 262, lines 6–9.

107 CWE 86: 520.

108 CWE 85: 123.

109 ASD I–3: 478–9. In translating '... proficiamus et nos ad felicem illam infantiam columbinae simplicitatis' instead of '... proficiamus et nos ad felicem illam infantiam rationabliem' I am following Erasmus' revision of 1531 rather than the original 1526 edition.

110 ASD I–3: 480.

111 *New Catholic Encyclopedia,* s.v. 'Loreto,' by H.M. Gillet, vol. 8, 993.

112 Allen 5: 341, introduction to Ep. 1391; ASD V–1: 107–9; quote from 109.

113 ASD V–1: 100.

114 ASD V–1: 98. For an analysis of the sequence, see Miller, 'The Liturgical Context of Erasmus's Hymns,' 485–90.

115 ASD V–1: 107. For an explanation of the secret, see *The Oxford Dictionary of the Christian Church,* 1255; and Joseph A. Jungmann, *The Mass of the Roman Rite,* 2: 90–7.

116 ASD V–1: 97.

117 Halkin, *Erasme parmi nous,* 306. For Erasmus' controversy with Alberto Pio, see Rummel, *Erasmus and His Catholic Critics,* 2: 115–23 and the studies mentioned in ibid, 2: 184 n. 28.

118 *Apologia brevis ad viginti quatuor libros Alberti Pii quondam Carporum comitis* (1531), LB IX: 1163E. Pio had already been dead for several months when Erasmus published his apology.

119 Allen 5: 564, Ep. 1506, lines 1–2; Allen 6: 37, Ep. 1554, lines 25–9; Allen 6: 55, Ep. 1559, lines 119–22: 'Mittimus nunc libellum De libero arbitrio, quem scripsimus aduersus dogma Luteri; missuri libellum De modo orandi Deum, in quo aduersus eundem asserimus inuocationem Sanctorum, si senserimus hoc studium nostrum esse gratum.' Erasmus' use of the verb *asserere* is rather curious here, for in the *De libero arbitrio* he professes to Luther and to the rest of Christendom his great dislike of *assertiones* (LB IX: 1215D–E).

120 *Contra Faustum Manichaeum* (ca. 400), PL 42: 384–5.

121 *Contra Vigilantium* (406), PL 23: 344B.

122 *Summa Theologiae*, 2a2ae: 83, 4.

123 For a theological and historical summary of the controversy over the cult of the saints, see Gerhard Ludwig Müller, *Gemeinschaft und Verehrung der Heiligen*, 28–78.

124 Georg Kretschmar and René Laurentin, 'Der Artikel vom Dienst der Heiligen in der Confessio Augustana,' 256.

125 Robert Kolb, *For All the Saints*, 87.

126 *Sendbrief vom Dolmetschen*, WA 30/2: 644. See also Lennart Pinomaa, 'Luthers Weg zur Verwerfung des Heiligendienstes,' 35.

127 Peter Manns, 'Luther und die Heiligen,' in *Reformatio Ecclesiae*, 536–40.

128 Lennart Pinomaa, *Die Heiligen bei Luther*, 64–5. See WA 2: 696; WA 7: 575.

129 Pinomaa, *Die Heiligen bei Luther*, 55–62, 65, 79–88.

130 WABr. 2: 547–8, Ep. 501, lines 8–14, 19–21.

131 WA 10/2: 166.

132 Sider, *Karlstadt*, 160; von Karlstadt, *Von gelubden unterrichtung*, A2–C1.

133 Brecht, *Martin Luther*, vol. 2: *Ordnung und Abgrenzung der Reformation*, 127–32; quote from 127.

134 WA 12: 61: 'Ego velim, quod Mariae dinst werde gar aus gerot solum propter abusum.' Quoted in Reintraud Schimmelpfennig, *Die Geschichte der Marienverehrung im deutschen Protestantismus*, 11.

135 Brecht, *Martin Luther*, vol. 2: *Ordnung und Abgrenzung der Reformation*, 93–4.

136 WA 15: 183, 196.

137 WA 15: 192. A principal theme of Pinomaa's book is his argument: '... die "Heiligen im Himmel" verschwanden aus seinem [sc. Luthers] Blickfeld, und an ihre Stelle traten die Heiligen auf der Erde.' See Pinomaa, *Die Heiligen bei Luther*, especially 117–58; quote from 117.

138 WA 15: 197.

139 See, e.g., *Vom Abendmahl Christi Bekenntnis* (1528), WA 26: 508; *Sendbrief vom Dolmetschen* (1530), WA 30/2: 643–4.

140 WA 50: 210. Given Luther's categorical rejection of the cult of the saints, it is hard to agree with Manns, who argues that Luther, despite his later criticism of the invocation of the saints, never repudiated his original positive attitude towards this practice. This attitude, Manns claims, retains its validity and may still be maintained in Luther's name. See Manns, 'Luther und die Heiligen,' 563–80. Cf. Müller, *Gemeinschaft und Verehrung der Heiligen*, 38–48.

141 Manns, 'Luther und die Heiligen,' 553; Krethschmar and Laurentin, 'Der Artikel vom Dienst der Heiligen in der Confessio Augustana,' 266; Delius, *Geschichte der Marienverehrung*, 205, 220–2, 234, 230. For recent treatments of Zwingli's and Calvin's rejection of the invocation of the saints, see Pamela Biel, 'Personal Conviction and Pastoral Care'; Heribert Schützeichel, 'Calvins Einspruch gegen die Heiligenverehrung'; and Müller, *Gemeinschaft und Verehrung der Heiligen*, 56–60.

142 Müller, *Gemeinschaft und Verehrung der Heiligen*, 62–3, lists a series of Catholic writers who published *apologiae* for the invocation of the saints.

143 Josse Clichtove, *De veneratione sanctorum, opusculum: duos libros complectens.*

144 Jacob von Hoogstraten, *Dialogus de veneratione & invocatione sanctorum contra perfidiam Lutheranam.*

145 Johannes Eck, *Enchiridion locorum communium adversus Lutherum et alios hostes ecclesiae*, 173–90.

146 Johannes Cochlaeus, *De sanctorum invocatione et intercessione.*

147 A critical edition of Canisius' *Summa* in the Latin original and in German translation may be found in Peter Canisius, *S. Petri Canisii Doctoris Ecclesiae Catechismi Latini et Germanici*, 2 vols. For the relevant passage from the pre-Tridentine *Summa*, see 1: 15–16; for the post-Tridentine *Summa* see 1: 100–1. For the Roman Catechism, see *Catechismus ex decreto Concilii Tridentini ad parochos*, folio *editio princeps*, 227–9, and also 300–1.

148 Guiseppe Alberigo et al., ed., *Conciliorum Oecumenicorum Decreta*, 3d ed. 774–6; quote from 774.

149 See Austin P. Flannery, ed., *Documents of Vatican II*, new rev. ed., 1: 407–23.

150 ASD V–1: 146.

151 Ibid.

152 Clichtove, *De veneratione sanctorum*, 5v.; Eck, *Enchiridion*, 173; *Die Confutatio der Confessio Augustana*, 127.

153 Eck, *Enchiridion*, 188: 'Explicite non est praecepta sanctorum invoca-

tio in sacris literis.' This quotation appears in the final edition of the *Enchiridion* (1543). In the editions between 1525 and 1529, Eck provides a more elaborate treatment of the relationship of Scripture to the invocation of the saints. Here he states that Scripture neither enjoins nor forbids the invocation of the saints: 'Tametsi expresse non habeatur in scripturis, quod sancti sint invocandi, nihil tamen – nec iota quidem unum, aut apex – invenitur in scripturis contra sanctorum invocationem.' See Eck, *Enchiridion*, 188, note to the passage beginning 'Explicite non est ...'

154   ASD V–1: 146–7.

155   Schimmelpfennig, *Die Geschichte der Marienverehrung*, 13–14, 19–20, 22–4; and 'Die Marienverehrung der Reformatoren,' 64–5.

156   Brecht, *Martin Luther*, vol. 2: *Ordnung und Abgrenzung der Reformation*, 116; WA 11: 314.

157   WA 11: 319–20

158   ASD V–1: 147–8.

159   ASD V–1: 148.

160   ASD V–1: 146, 147, 148. For a thorough treatment of Erasmus' idea of the consensus, see James K. McConica, 'Erasmus and the Grammar of Consent.' See also Georg Gebhardt, *Die Stellung des Erasmus von Rotterdam zur römischen Kirche*, 52–72; Willi Hentze, *Kirche und kirchliche Einheit bei Desiderius Erasmus von Rotterdam*, 127–32; and Hilmar M. Pabel, 'The Peaceful People of Christ,' 77–81.

161   Allen 6: 372, Ep. 1729, line 27; Allen 7: 216, Ep. 1893, lines 59–60.

162   *Exomologesis*, LB V: 145B.

163   *De libero arbitrio*, LB IX: 1218E–F.

164   Allen 6: 206, Ep. 1636, lines 3–5.

165   Allen 6: 211, Ep. 1637, lines 94–5.

166   *Ad fratres Inferioris Germaniae* (1530), ASD IX–1: 362.

167   ASD V–1: 148.

168   Clichtove, *De veneratione sanctorum*, 8v.

169   Eck, *Enchiridion*, 183; *Die Confutatio der Confessio Augustana*, 125.

170   Alberigo, *Conciliorum Oecumenicorum Decreta*, 774.

171   ASD V–1: 148–9.

172   Eck, *Enchiridion*, 186–7; *Die Confutatio der Confessio Augustana*, 129; Cochlaeus, *De sanctorum invocatione et intercessione*, H4.

173   ASD V–1: 149.

174   ASD V–1: 149–50.

175   ASD V–1: 150.

176   Ibid.

177   Ibid.

178   Ibid.

179   *Paraphrase on Luke*, LB VII: 285E. A little further on Erasmus has Gabriel say to Zechariah: '... nunc in hoc peculiariter a Deo designa-

tus, ut in hoc negotio, quo non aliud unquam actum est majus aut mirabilius, inter Deum & homines internuntium agam' (LB VII: 287E).

180 ASD V–1: 150, 139.
181 ASD V–1: 151.
182 Ibid.
183 ASD V–1: 153.
184 ASD V–1: 151–2.
185 ASD V–1: 152.
186 ASD V–1: 149.
187 ASD V–1: 153.
188 Ibid.
189 ASD V–1: 149.
190 ASD V–3: 334.
191 ASD V–1: 154.
192 *Spongia adversus aspergines Hutteni*, ASD IX–1: 174.
193 *Modus orandi Deum*, ASD V–1: 154.
194 Clichtove, *De veneratione sanctorum*, 86.
195 Ibid, 88.
196 ASD V–1: 154.
197 ASD V–1: 154–6. The quote is from 154.
198 ASD V–3: 305.
199 ASD V–1: 154.
200 ASD V–1: 122.
201 Allen 7: 467, 461, Ep. 2037, lines 313–15, 56–8.
202 Clarence H. Miller, 'Erasmus's Poem to St Genevieve,' 483.
203 CWE 85: 169, 175.
204 Miller, 'Erasmus's Poem to St Genevieve,' 483.
205 Jean-Claude Margolin, 'Paris through a Gothic Window at the End of the Fifteenth Century,' 209.
206 *Praise of Folly*, 65.
207 CWE 85: 169, 171.
208 CWE 85: 175.
209 Miller, 'Erasmus's Poem to St Genevieve,' 485.
210 ASD V–1: 154.
211 Halkin, 'Erasme pèlerin,' 251. The emphasis is Halkin's.
212 Eire, *War against the Idols*, 52.
213 Alberigo, *Conciliorum Oecumenicorum Decreta*, 775–6.

CHAPTER THREE

1 Jean-Paul Audet, *La Didache: Instruction des apôtres*, 72.
2 Joachim Jeremias, *The Prayers of Jesus*, 88.
3 Six lengthy columns in the *Dictionnaire de Spiritualité* provide a com-

prehensive, but by no means an exhaustive, list of expositions of the Lord's Prayer from the Greek and Latin church fathers through the Middle Ages up to and including the sixteenth century. See *Dictionnaire de Spiritualité*, s.v. 'Pater Noster,' by Aimé Solignac, vol. 12/1, 389–95.

4 *Modus orandi Deum*, ASD V–1: 161, 156.

5 ASD V–1: 320.

6 CWE 7: 29, 28, Ep. 1000, lines 117, 87–90. For a comparison of Cyprian's and Erasmus' interpretation of the Lord's Prayer, see Hilmar M. Pabel, 'Erasmus' Esteem for Cyprian.'

7 *Explanatio symboli*, ASD V–1: 318.

8 Halkin, 'La piété d'Erasme,' 694–5.

9 *Paraphrase on Luke*, LB VII: 380B.

10 *Novum Instrumentum*, pt. 1, 11.

11 *Erasmus' Annotations on the New Testament: The Gospels*, 34: 'Sic fiat, quod tu uis in terris, hoc est, in tuo populo coelesti, quemadmodum fit in coelo, ubi nemo repugnat uoluntati tuae.' In 1527, Erasmus modified 'tuus populus coelestis' by inserting 'qui adhuc corpore uersatur in terris' between 'coelesti' and 'quemadmodum.'

12 The original Greek describes the bread for which we pray as 'epiousios,' a word almost utterly unique to Matthew 6: 11, since its use has been documented in no other place except for a list of expenses in a single papyrus. See *Theological Dictionary of the New Testament*, 2: 590–1. (I wish to thank Roy Hammerling for pointing out this reference to me.) In rendering the Greek word 'epiousios' as 'quotidianus,' which the Vulgate translates as 'supersubtantialis,' Erasmus opts for the way that the Latin Fathers, such as Tertullian and Cyprian, who preceded Jerome, as well as Jerome's contemporary, Augustine, understood the bread of the petition. In his *Commentary on Matthew*, Jerome suggests two ways of translating 'epiousios.' The first derives from dividing the word into two: the prefix, 'epi,' which means 'above,' and the noun, 'ousia,' which means 'substance.' This analysis yields 'supersubstantial.' The supersubstantial bread is above every substance; its ontological status exceeds that of every creature. Jerome bases the second way of translating 'epiousios' on the apocryphal Gospel according to the Hebrews, where, instead of the word for 'supersubtantial,' he found the Hebrew word 'mahar,' which means of or pertaining to tomorrow, or in Latin 'crastinus.' According to this translation, we pray: 'Give us today the bread for the morrow.' See Jean Carmignac, *Recherches sur le 'Notre Père,'* 121–43, especially 127, 129; and Jerome, *Commentariorum in Matheum libri IV*, 1 (Matthew 6: 11), CCSL 77: 37. Erasmus prefers the second translation, 'crastinus' (*Erasmus' Annotations on the New Testament: The Gospels*, 34–5).

13 Erika Rummel, *Erasmus and His Catholic Critics*, 1: 141; CWE 4: 265, Ep. 541, lines 92–9; CWE 6: 314, Ep. 948, lines 110–12, 117–19.

14 *Erasmus' Annotations on the New Testament: The Gospels*, 35. Relying on other scriptural passages and on the authority of Cyprian and Augustine, Erasmus adduces additional support for his case in the 1522 and 1535 editions of the *Annotations*.

15 *Erasmus' Annotations on the New Testament: The Gospels*, 37–8.

16 *Novum Instrumentum*, pt. 1, 152.

17 CWE 27: 309.

18 Richard L. DeMolen, ed., *Erasmus of Rotterdam*, 94.

19 Allen 5: 343, introduction to Ep. 1393. Allen incorrectly assigns the Spanish translation to 1549. For a brief discussion of the two Spanish translations published in 1528, see Marcel Bataillon, *Erasme et l'Espagne*, rev. ed., 1: 306–7. See also Augustin Redondo, 'La "Precatio Dominica" d'Erasme en Castillan.'

20 E.J. Devereux, *Renaissance English Translations of Erasmus*, 176–8. Margaret Roper's translation is reprinted in DeMolen, *Erasmus of Rotterdam*, 97–124. For studies of the translation, see Rita M. Verbrugge, 'Margaret More Roper's Personal Expression in the *Devout Treatise Upon the Pater Noster*,' in *Silent But for the Word*, 30–42; and Elizabeth McCutcheon, 'Margaret More Roper's Translation of Erasmus' *Precatio Dominica*.'

21 Augustin Renaudet, *Etudes Erasmiennes (1521–1529)*, 187.

22 CWE 9: 354, Ep. 1314A, line 1586.

23 Friedhelm Krüger, *Humanistische Evangelienauslegung*, 24–6.

24 Allen 5: 345, Ep. 1393, lines 34–6.

25 A date of impression is lacking, but the dedicatory epistle is dated October 1523.

26 *Precatio Dominica*, A3.

27 Ibid, B3.

28 ASD V–1: 320.

29 WA 10/2: 395–407; Vives, *Joannis Ludovici Vivis Valentini Opera Omnia*, 1: 132–65.

30 LB V: 1219A (first petition); 1222A, 1225F (second and fifth petitions); 1224F (fourth petition); 1223E, 1226D (third and sixth petitions).

31 *Erasmus' Annotations on the New Testament: The Gospels*, 34.

32 LB V: 1219B–C.

33 LB VII: 37C; LB V: 1198A.

34 LB V: 1219D.

35 *Precatio Dominica*, LB V: 1225B. See also the 'Precatio ad Patrem,' LB V: 1197C: 'Sed ante omnia, quoniam juxta tibi carissimum Paulum, praecipue Spirituum Pater es, pasce animos nostros alimonia spirituali ...' Although Erasmus here attributes the appellation 'Spirituum Pater' to Paul, he did not consider the Epistle to the Hebrews to have been written by Paul.

36 LB V: 1197A.
37 LB VII: 37B.
38 LB V: 1223E–F.
39 LB V: 1219A.
40 LB VII: 37E.
41 *Paraphrase on Matthew*, LB VII: 37E.
42 LB V: 1224F.
43 LB V: 1219A.
44 *Precatio Dominica*, LB V: 1219C.
45 LB V: 1220A–B, 1221D–E, 1221F; LB VII: 380D.
46 LB V: 1219C, 1220A.
47 LB V: 1222D, 1227C; 1224D.
48 *Precatio Dominica*, LB V: 1221E; 'Precatio ad Patrem,' LB V: 1197B; *Precatio Dominica*, LB V: 1223D.
49 LB V: 1222A–B.
50 *Precatio Dominica*, LB V: 1221E.
51 Ibid, LB V: 1221F, 1219C, 1220A.
52 Ibid, LB V: 1223A, 1224B, 1227B.
53 LB V: 1219D.
54 LB VII: 37E.
55 *Precatio Dominica*, LB V: 1225E, 1224E.
56 LB V: 1228A.
57 *Precatio Dominica*, LB V: 1219C.
58 LB V: 1219B.
59 ASD V–1: 319.
60 LB VII: 380B.
61 Jeremias, *The Prayers of Jesus*, 82–5.
62 *Paraphrase on Matthew*, LB VII: 37B; *Precatio Dominica*, LB V: 1219B.
63 LB V: 1219B.
64 *Precatio Dominica*, LB V: 1221B.
65 Ibid, LB V: 1222A.
66 Erasmus speaks of the 'tuo [sc. Patris] Spiritu renati' in the *Precatio Dominica*, LB V: 1219B, and of the 'per Christum renati' in the *Explanatio symboli*, ASD V–1: 319. That the baptized are reborn through Christ manifests itself again in the 'Precatio ad Patrem,' LB V: 1198A: 'Per verbum tuum [sc. Patris] nos genuisti quum nihil essemus, per idem ex Adam infeliciter natos denuo genuisti ...' In the *Paraphrase on Matthew*, LB VII: 37A–B, Erasmus indicates that the baptized are reborn for the life of heaven: 'Pater noster, qui nos semel infeliciter genitos ex Adam, rursum coelo genuisti ...'
67 'Precatio ad Patrem,' LB V: 1198B; *Precatio Dominica*, LB V: 1219B–C.
68 *Precatio Dominica*, LB V: 1219B. See also 'Precatio ad Patrem,' LB V: 1197A.
69 Renaudet, *Etudes Erasmiennes*, 176.

70 James K. McConica, *English Humanists and Reformation Politics*, 20.

71 CWE 66: 127.

72 See Erasmus' note on the meaning of 'Abba, pater' in Romans 8: 15, *Erasmus' Annotations on the New Testament: Acts – Romans – I and II Corinthians*, 384: 'Sed vocem Hebraeam reliquit, quo significaret peculiare quiddam esse in ipso uocabulo, quod & patres libenter audiunt, & pueri primum sonare discunt. Nam hoc statim implorant patris opem, cuiusmodi est apud Latinos pappus, uox infantibus peculiaris.'

73 LB V: 1222D; 1223B.

74 *Precatio Dominica*, LB V: 1219A.

75 Ibid, LB V: 1224B, 1224E.

76 *Enchiridion*, CWE 66: 26, 58.

77 LB VII: 36E.

78 LB VII: 36E, F.

79 *Explanatio symboli*, ASD V–1: 319.

80 LB V: 1219F–20A.

81 *Precatio Dominica*, LB V: 1219C, D; quote: LB V: 1219D.

82 *Explanatio symboli*, ASD V–1: 319.

83 LB V: 1219B, 1223C, 1223F–4A.

84 ASD V–1: 208, 319.

85 ASD V–1: 319.

86 LB V: 1220A. See also LB V: 1226B–C: 'Sic ille [i.e. Jesus] nos jussit orare, neque semel confirmavit nos exoraturos, quidquid abs te [i.e. Pater] in ipsius nomine peteremus.'

87 LB V: 1226D, F.

88 LB V: 1228C.

89 LB VII: 37A.

90 ASD V–1: 319.

91 *Precatio Dominica*, LB V: 1223F; 'Precatio ad Patrem,' LB V: 1197B. It was a medieval commonplace that the flesh, the world, and the devil were the main enemies of humankind. On this, see Siegfried Wenzel, 'The Three Enemies of Man.' I am indebted to Otfried Lieberknecht for this reference.

92 *Modus orandi Deum*, ASD V–1: 159.

93 LB V: 1224B.

94 Jeffrey Burton Russel, *Lucifer: The Devil in the Middle Ages*, 295; Roland Bainton, *Erasmus of Christendom*, 67.

95 'Precatio ad Patrem,' LB VII: 1198C.

96 *Paraphrase on Matthew*, LB VII: 37D.

97 *Paraphrase on Luke*, LB VII: 380F. For other references to the devil as tyrant see ibid, LB VII: 380D; *Precatio Dominica*, LB V: 1223B, C. For references to the devil's tyranny see *Paraphrase on Matthew*, LB VII: 37B, 38A; *Precatio Dominica*, LB V: 1222B, D; *Explanatio symboli*, ASD V–1: 319; 'Precatio ad Patrem,' LB V: 1198C.

98 LB V: 1197A.
99 *Paraphrase on Luke*, LB VII: 380C; 'Precatio ad Patrem,' LB V: 1197B, 1198B; *Precatio Dominica*, LB V: 1224C, 1225F, 1227C.
100 *Precatio Dominica*, LB V: 1222C.
101 LB V: 1219C.
102 LB V: 1219B, 1220D.
103 LB V: 1223E, 1224D.
104 LB V: 1223C, D; 1222E, 1227B.
105 LB V: 1219B–C, 1222B, 1222D, 1225A, 1226B.
106 LB V: 1224E–F.
107 LB V: 1221B.
108 LB V: 1221C.
109 LB V: 1223E.
110 ASD V–1: 159.
111 *Erasmus' Annotations on the New Testament: The Gospels*, 34.
112 *Precatio Dominica*, LB V: 1220B.
113 LB VII: 37E–F.
114 LB V: 1197A–B.
115 LB V: 1220A–B.
116 LB V: 1221E–F.
117 *Erasmus' Annotations on the New Testament: The Gospels*, 34.
118 LB V: 1220C.
119 LB V: 1220C–D.
120 ASD V–4: 146, 154. Erasmus' appeal for missionary preachers (ASD V–4: 146–56) has been noted and partially translated into German by Hans Trümpy, 'Ein Aufruf des Erasmus von Rotterdam zur Missionierung der Heiden.' See also Marcel Bataillon, 'Erasme et le Nouveau Monde,' in Bataillon, *Erasme et l'Espagne*, 3: 469–504.
121 Heiko A. Oberman, *The Roots of Anti-Semitism*, 40.
122 Hilmar M. Pabel, 'Erasmus of Rotterdam and Judaism.' Erasmus' attitude towards Judaism has been a subject of debate among scholars. Some believe that his hostile comments about Jews and Judaism should be taken metaphorically to refer to superstitious Christians who attribute too much importance to religious ceremonies: Gerhard B. Winkler, 'Erasmus und die Juden,' in *Festschrift Franz Loidl zum 65. Geburtstag*, ed. Viktor Flieder, 2 vols. (Vienna: Verlag Brüder Hollineck, 1970), 2: 381–92; Cornelis Augustijn, 'Erasmus und die Juden'; Shimon Markish, *Erasmus and the Jews*. Others argue that Erasmus should be taken at his word and that his comments point to an inveterate hatred of Jews and of their religion: Guido Kisch, *Erasmus' Stellung zu Juden und Judentum*; Heiko A. Oberman, *The Roots of Anti-Semitism*, 38–40; Pabel, 'Erasmus of Rotterdam and Judaism.'
123 LB V: 1220D–1A.

124 *Paraphrase on Matthew,* LB VII: 37B.
125 *Paraphrase on Luke,* LB VII: 380D.
126 *Precatio Dominica,* LB V: 1221B–C.
127 Ibid, LB V: 1221D.
128 *Paraphrase on Matthew,* LB VII: 37B; *Paraphrase on Luke,* LB VII: 380C; *Precatio Dominica,* LB V: 1222B–C.
129 LB V: 1222A–B.
130 LB V: 1222D, 1223D.
131 LB V: 1223B.
132 LB V: 1224F.
133 LB V: 1222C–D.
134 *Precatio Dominica,* LB V: 1222B; *Paraphrase on Matthew,* LB VII: 37B.
135 LB V: 1222F–3A.
136 *Paraphrase on Matthew,* LB VII: 37B; *Paraphrase on Luke,* LB VII: 380C; *Explanatio symboli,* ASD V–I: 319.
137 *Precatio Dominica,* LB V: 1222D.
138 Ibid, LB V: 1222E.
139 *Erasmus' Annotations on the New Testament: The Gospels,* 34.
140 *Precatio Dominica,* LB V: 1222D.
141 Ibid, LB V: 1222C.
142 Ibid, LB V: 1223C–E.
143 *De sermone Domini in monte,* 2, 6, 20, CCSL 35: 110.
144 See, for example, Luther's Large Catechism, WA 30/1: 199–201, and John Calvin, *Institutio christianae religionis* (1559) 3, 20, 42, OC 2: 667.
145 Karl Barth, *Prayer according to the Catechisms of the Reformation,* 46.
146 *Precatio Dominica,* LB V: 1224D–E.
147 'Precatio ad Patrem,' LB V: 1197B. See also *Paraphrase on Luke,* LB VII: 380E: 'Hactenus toto orbe regnavit Satanas per peccatum, cui servierunt homines illecti cupiditatibus impiis: tu [i.e. Pater] fac, ut sublatis peccatis & effuso tuo in eos Spiritu, tuae voluntati pareant omnes.'
148 *Erasmus' Annotations on the New Testament: The Gospels,* 34; *Precatio Dominica,* LB V: 1224E.
149 *Explanatio symboli,* ASD V–1: 319; 'Precatio ad Patrem,' LB V: 1197B.
150 *Paraphrase on Matthew,* LB VII: 37C.
151 *Explanatio symboli,* ASD V–1: 319.
152 *Paraphrase on Matthew,* LB VII: 37C; *Precatio Dominica,* LB V: 1223F.
153 *Precatio Dominica,* LB V: 1224A.
154 'Precatio ad Patrem,' LB V: 1197 C; *Precatio Dominica,* LB V: 1224A.
155 *Precatio Dominica,* LB V: 1224C–D.
156 Ibid, LB V: 1224A–B.
157 Ibid, LB V: 1224E; 'Precatio ad Patrem,' LB V: 1197C.
158 *Precatio Dominica,* LB V: 1224D–F.

159 Carmignac, *Recherches sur le 'Notre Père,'* 156–63. John Chrysostom is a notable exception to the general view of the Greek Fathers. He contents himself with a material explanation of the daily bread. See his *Homilies on the Gospel of Matthew,* 19, PG 57: 280.

160 *Expositio devotissima orationis dominicae videlicet Pater noster* in Aquinas, *Opuscula Omnia,* 4: 403–4.

161 Carmignac, *Recherches sur le 'Notre Père,'* 166–70.

162 WA 30/1: 304.

163 Carmignac, *Recherches sur le 'Notre Père,'* 170–7.

164 *Catechismus ex decreto Concilii Tridentini ad parochos,* folio *editio prin-ceps,* 331, 335.

165 ASD V–1: 159, 160.

166 ASD V–1: 319.

167 *Erasmus' Annotations on the New Testament: The Gospels,* 35 (quote), 34.

168 Martin Bucer, *Enarrationes perpetuae in evangelia* (1530), excerpted in John Calvin, *Institutes of the Christian Religion,* 1535 ed., trans. F.L. Battles, 354. Appendix II of Battles' translation is entitled 'Martin Bucer on the Lord's Prayer.'

169 For an assessment of Erasmus' influence on Bucer's theology, see Friedhelm Krüger, *Bucer und Erasmus: ... (bis zum Evangelien-Kommentar von 1530)* and 'Bucer und Erasmus,' in *Martin Bucer and Sixteenth Century Europe,* 2: 583–94.

170 Comment on Matthew 6: 11 in *Commentarius in harmoniam evangeli-cam* (1555), OC 45: 199.

171 LB VII: 37C, 380C.

172 LB V: 1224F.

173 LB V: 1225B.

174 LB V: 1225C.

175 LB V: 1225D.

176 *Precatio Dominica,* B5.

177 LB V: 1197C–8A.

178 *Precatio Dominica,* LB V: 1224F–5A. Cf. 'Precatio ad Patrem,' LB V: 1197C: 'Et quoniam juxta Filii tui doctrinam nequaquam de futuro solliciti, toti de largissimi Patris providentia pendemus ...'

179 LB V: 1225A.

180 *Paraphrase on Matthew,* LB VII: 37C.

181 *Precatio Dominica,* LB V: 1225D.

182 Ibid, LB V: 1224F. Cf. 'Precatio ad Patrem,' LB V: 1198A: 'Cibus vere vitam largiens est tui per sacras Scripturas cognitio tuique Spiritus gratia, per quam quotidianis virtutum accessibus juxta internum hominem grandescimus in te, donec adolescamus in virum, & in mensuram plenitudinis unigeniti tui Jesu Christi.'

183 'Precatio ad Patrem,' LB V: 1198A.

184 *Precatio Dominica*, LB V: 1225C.
185 Ibid, LB V: 1225C (quote), D–E.
186 *Explanatio symboli*, ASD V–1: 319.
187 'Precatio ad Patrem,' LB V: 1198B.
188 Cornelis Augustijn, *Erasmus: His Life, Works, and Influence*, 141. In the *Hyperaspistes II*, Erasmus writes (LB X: 1403C): 'Totum autem adscribitur divinae bonitati, non quod homo nihil agat, sed quod a Deo proficiscantur omnia, quibus aliquid possumus, volumus, agimus aut sumus. Nec est in homine malitiosa aversio a Deo, quemadmodum in Satana, sed infirmitas potius est, quam malitia: perversitas autem in nonnullis non tam est a natura, quam a consuetudine parta peccatis, graviora levioribus accumulando.'
189 CWE 49: 161, 168. Erasmus is paraphrasing Mark 14: 31, 72.
190 For Erasmus' references to human *imbecillitas* or *infirmitas*, see *Paraphrase on Matthew*, LB VII: 37C; *Paraphrase on Luke*, LB VII: 380C, 380 E; *Precatio Dominica*, LB V: 1221B, 1225D, 1225F, 1226A, 1226C, 1226 F, 1228C; 'Precatio ad Patrem,' LB V: 1197C, 1198B.
191 *Explanatio symboli*, ASD V–1: 319.
192 LB VII: 37C–D.
193 *De dominica oratione*, 8, 15, 23, CCSL 3A: 93, 99, 105.
194 ASD V–1: 159.
195 LB V: 1226C.
196 LB V: 1225F–6A.
197 *Erasmus' Annotations on the New Testament: The Gospels*, 35.
198 LB VII: 38 A–B. In his paraphrase of Matthew 5, Erasmus also urges a parallel between the way God treats his children and the way they should treat each other. Discussing Jesus' blessing upon peacemakers (v. 9), Erasmus teaches that the Father does not regard human beings as his children 'unless they treat their brothers in the same way as he treats all people' (LB VII: 25F–6A). At Matthew 5: 24, he writes: 'You will not experience God's favour unless your neighbour senses your favour towards himself' (LB VII: 30D). Erasmus sharpens Jesus' warning at Matthew 18: 35 that his Father will have no mercy on those who do not forgive their brother from their heart by asserting that the Father will not only not forgive those who do not forgive others but will also revoke his forgiveness of previous sins (LB VII: 102C–D).
199 The text in the RSV reads: 'For if you forgive men their trespasses, your heavenly Father also will forgive you; but if you do not forgive men their trespasses, neither will your Father forgive your trespasses.'
200 LB VII: 380E.
201 CWE 8: 126–7, Ep. 1171, lines 36–9.
202 *Explanatio symboli*, ASD V–1: 319.

203 LB V: 1226A.
204 LB V: 1226B.
205 LB V: 1226A–B.
206 LB V: 1198B.
207 LB V: 1226C, 1198B.
208 *De dominica oratione*, 23, CCSL 3A: 104.
209 *De sermone Domini in monte*, 2, 11, 39, CCSL 35: 130.
210 *Opuscula omnia*, 4: 406.
211 *Catechismus ex decreto Concilii Tridentini*, 341.
212 Carmignac, *Recherches sur le 'Notre Père,'* 234.
213 WA 30/1: 207.
214 *Institutio christianae religionis* (1559) 3, 20, 45, OC 2: 672.
215 Luther, WA 30/1: 207; Calvin, OC 2: 672.
216 LB V: 1223D–E.
217 Carmignac, *Recherches sur le 'Notre Père,'* 312–13.
218 Allen 5: 345, Ep. 1393, lines 36–40.
219 *Explanatio symboli*, ASD V–1: 319–20.
220 CWE 66: 24.
221 LB V: 1226E–F, 1227A.
222 *Enchiridion*, CWE 66: 108.
223 *Precatio Dominica*, LB V: 1226F.
224 *Paraphrase on Luke*, LB VII: 380D, F.
225 Carmignac, *Recherches sur le 'Notre Père,'* 245–8.
226 Ibid, 248; *De dominica oratione*, 25, CCSL 3A: 106.
227 Carmignac, *Recherches sur le 'Notre Père,'* 296–9.
228 Bucer, *Enarrationes perpetuae in evangelia*, in John Calvin, *Institutes of the Christian Religion*, 1535 ed., trans. F.L. Battles, 356.
229 *Commentarius in harmoniam evangelicam*, OC 45: 202; *Institutio christianae religionis* (1559) 3, 20, 46, OC 2: 674.
230 LB VII: 380F; LB V: 1226F; ASD V–1: 319.
231 LB VII: 37D; LB V: 1198C.
232 LB VII: 37D.
233 LB IX: 1245C.
234 *Paraphrase on James*, LB VII: 1121 B–C.
235 *Paraphrase on Matthew*, LB VII: 37 D; *Paraphrase on Luke*, LB VII: 380F; *Precatio Dominica*, LB V: 1226F–7A.
236 *Paraphrase on Luke*, LB VII: 380F; *Precatio Dominica*, LB V: 1227A.
237 *Precatio Dominica*, LB V: 1226F, 1227B.
238 *De dominica oratione*, 25, CCSL 3A: 106.
239 LB V: 1227B–C.
240 *Erasmus' Annotations on the New Testament: The Gospels*, 35.
241 LB V: 1227C–8A.
242 *Precatio Dominica*, LB V: 1228A–B.
243 *Explanatio symboli*, ASD V–1: 319.

244 *Precatio Dominica*, LB V: 1228A.

245 *Paraphrase on Matthew*, LB VII: 37D.

246 LB V: 1198C.

247 ASD V–1: 320.

248 Jacques Chomarat, *Grammaire et rhétorique chez Erasme*, 1: 663.

CHAPTER FOUR

1 Gerard Achten, ed., *Das christliche Gebetbuch im Mittelalter*, 15; quote from Helen C. White, *The Tudor Books of Private Devotion*, 32.

2 *De coenobiorum institutione*, 2, 5; referred to in Stephan Beissel, 'Zur Geschichte der Gebetbücher,' 28.

3 Joseph A. Jungmann, *Christian Prayer through the Centuries*, 77–8, quote from 67. The *De psalmorum usu* is printed in PL 101: 465–508.

4 For the *Officia per ferias*, see PL 101: 509–612.

5 Achten, *Das christliche Gebetbuch im Mittelalter*, 11.

6 Ibid, 9.

7 Joachim M. Plotzek, ed., *Andachtsbücher des Mittelalters aus Privatbesitz*, 9.

8 Beissel, 'Zur Geschichte der Gebetbücher,' 33, 35–40.

9 John Harthan, *Books of Hours and Their Owners*, 13.

10 Roger S. Wieck, ed., *Time Sanctified*, 27.

11 Harthan, *Books of Hours and Their Owners*, 16.

12 Ibid, 11. For a study of the French Books of Hours, see Virginia Reinburg, 'Popular Prayers in Late Medieval and Reformation France,' (Ph.D. dissertation, Princeton University, 1985), 25–172.

13 For examples of suffrages, see Wieck, *Time Sanctified*, 165–6; and Franz Unterkircher, *Das Stundenbuch des Mittelalters*, 177–215.

14 *Lexikon für Theologie und Kirche*, s.v. 'Hortulus animae (Seelengärtlein),' by F. Wulf, vol. 5: 498; Beissel, 'Zur Geschichte der Gebetbücher,' 175–6. For a summary of the contents of a Latin *Hortulus animae* published in Strassburg in 1503, see Franz Xaver Haimerl, *Mittelalterliche Frömmigkeit im Spiegel der Gebetbuchliteratur Süddeutschlands*, 123–34.

15 White, *The Tudor Books of Private Devotion*, 67–118, especially 71, 76–8, 90, 94–6, 109.

16 Ibid, 108, 113. For the pre-Reformation Primers, see Eamon Duffy, *The Stripping of the Altars*, 209–98.

17 WA 10/2: 340.

18 WA 10/2: 377–428.

19 Marc Lienhard, 'Prier au XVIe siècle,' 43 and n. 2. Brunfels' book also included an exhortation to prayer and advice on how to pray correctly: *Ermanung zu dem Gebett, und wie man recht betten sol*. Lienhard (47–54) sees many similarities between Brunfels' ideas about

prayer and those of Erasmus in the *Modus orandi Deum*, but he also indicates important differences. He writes: 'La proximité entre Erasme et Brunfels est indéniable, encore que ce dernier, à la suite notamment de Luther, soit allé plus loin qu'Erasme' (47).

20 Charles C. Butterworth, *The English Primers (1529–1545)*, 79, 237; White, *The Tudor Books of Private Devotion*, 134–9.

21 Paul Althaus, *Forschungen zur evangelischen Gebetsliteratur*, 59.

22 Ibid, 65.

23 J. Trapman, 'Erasmus's *Precationes*,' 775–7.

24 PG 58: 545.

25 Trapman, 773. See *Precationes aliquot novae*, 68–75.

26 *Precationes aliquot, quibus adolescentes assuescant cum Deo colloqui*, 179–84.

27 *Precationes aliquot, quibus adolescentes discant cum Deo colloqui*, 190–5. The Folger Shakespeare Library in Washington, DC possesses a copy of both the 1551 and 1563 editions.

28 *Simplex et succinctus orandi modus* (Cologne: Apud haeredes Arnoldi Birckmann, 1563), 199–287.

29 For the German text see WA 38: 358–75.

30 These two editions are listed in Irmgard Bezzel, *Erasmusdrucke des 16. Jahrhunderts in Bayerischen Bibliotheken*, 452, nos. 1640, 1642.

31 Allen 11: 130, Ep. 3016, lines 1–2.

32 Allen 10: 319, Ep. 2879, line 57.

33 CEBR 3: 60–1, quote from 60.

34 Allen 11: 70, Ep. 2994, lines 2–13.

35 WA 10/2: 471–2, 473–4, 475–6; *Prayers and Other Pieces of Thomas Becon*, 15–18, 75–6.

36 Allen 11: 70–1, Ep. 2995, lines 1–10.

37 For the prayers that Chrysostom lists in his *Homilies on Matthew*, see PG 58: 545.

38 See above, chapter 2, 85.

39 LB V: 1207D, 1209A.

40 LB V: 1208D.

41 LB V: 1208D, 1208E, 1209A, 1209B.

42 ASD V–1: 162. See above, chapter 1, 62.

43 LB V: 1202D. The Vulgate renders Phillipians 4: 13 a little differently: 'omnia possum in eo qui me confortat.' Erasmus writes: 'omnia possum in eo qui me corroborat.'

44 LB V: 1209D: 'Hic est Filius meus dilectus, in quo mihi complacitum est, ipsum audite.' This is Erasmus' translation of the Greek; cf. LB VI: 92A. The Vulgate reads: 'Hic est Filius meus dilectus, in quo mihi bene complacui; ipsum audite.'

45 Holborn, 147.

46 LB V: 1209D.

47 LB V: 1199D.

48 'Pro felici conjugio,' LB V: 1205C.

49 The quotation is a reference to Jacques Le Goff, *The Birth of Purgatory*. For a discussion of the memento of the dead in the canon of the Mass, see Joseph A. Jungmann, *The Mass of the Roman Rite*, 2: 237–48.

50 Frieder Schulz, 'Die evangelischen Begräbnisgebete des 16. und 17. Jahrhunderts,' 5, 18–21.

51 WA 10/3: 194–96, 409; *Vom Abendmahl Christi Bekentniss*, WA 26: 508.

52 *Institutio christianae religionis* (1559), 3, 5, 10, OC 2: 499–500 (praying for the dead); 3, 20, 21; 23; 27, OC 2: 647, 648–9, 653 (praying to the saints).

53 Vives, *Joannis Ludovici Vivis Valentini Opera Omnia*, 1: 98.

54 CWE 10: 425–6, Ep. 1518, lines 1–2.

55 Allen 10: 112, Ep. 2726, lines 45–7; Allen 10: 146–7, Ep. 2758, lines 80–2.

56 Allen 7: 462–3, Ep. 2037, lines 119–20.

57 CWE 9: 342, Ep. 1341A, lines 1188–9; Allen 9: 329, Ep. 2526, lines 20–1: 'Precor vt per Domini misericordiam bene sit illius manibus.'

58 Trapman, 774.

59 ASD V–3: 305.

60 For the Reformation's attitude to Mary, see Konrad Algermissen, 'Mariologie und Marienverehrung der Reformatoren'; Walter Delius, *Geschichte der Marienverehrung*, 195–234; and Reintraud Schimmelpfennig, *Die Geschichte der Marienverehrung im deutschen Protestantismus*, 9–51, and 'Die Marienverehrung der Reformatoren.' Walter Tappolet has edited a collection of texts in *Das Marienlob der Reformatoren*. See also Heiko A. Oberman, 'The Virgin Mary in Evangelical Perspective.'

61 Delius, *Geschichte der Marienverehrung*, 218–19; Schimmelpfennig, *Die Geschichte der Marienverehrung*, 34–47; 'Die Marienverehrung der Reformatoren,' 71–3.

62 *Three Primers Put forth in the Reign of Henry VIII*, 2d ed. 338–9, 341, 343, 347, 350, 352, 355, 360, 362, 368; quote from 339.

63 Ibid, 481.

64 Ibid, 66–8 (1535), 329 (1539), 459 (1545).

65 Thomas Esser, 'Geschichte des englischen Grußes,' 109–10, 112, 116.

66 WA 10/2: 407–9.

67 LB V: 1200B.

68 LB V: 1200C.

69 Vives, *Opera omnia*, 1: 127–8.

70 Ibid, 128.

71 Erika Rummel, *Erasmus' Annotations on the New Testament*, 167–8; quote from 168.

72 WA 10/2: 408.

73 *D. Martin Luthers Werke: Die deutsche Bibel*, 6: 210.

74 Hans Düfel, *Luthers Stellung zur Marienverehrung*, 49–57; quote from 51.
75 J.N.D. Kelly, *Early Christian Doctrines*, rev. ed., 493–4.
76 LB V: 1200A–B. On the contrast between Eve and Mary, see also the *Paraphrase on Luke*, LB VII: 317C.
77 Vives, *Opera omnia*, 1: 127.
78 Ibid.
79 Ibid.
80 *Erasmus' Annotations on the New Testament: The Gospels*, 169.
81 LB VII: 307D–E, 308B.
82 LB V: 1200C.
83 LB V: 1200C–D.
84 Althaus, *Forschungen zur evangelischen Gebetsliteratur*, 60.
85 LB V: 1199A.
86 LB V: 1204B.
87 LB V: 1206E; *Precationes aliquot novae* (1535), 55.
88 LB V: 1210A; 1210C.
89 'Consecratio mensae,' LB V: 1210B–C.
90 LB V: 1220E.
91 ASD V–1: 144.
92 ASD V–1: 145–6.
93 ASD V–1: 146.
94 See above, chapter 1, 66.
95 CWE 66: 24; ASD I–3: 752.
96 *Explanatio symboli*, ASD V–1: 271.
97 *Paraphrase on Romans* (1517), CWE 42: 49–50.
98 'Ad Filium,' LB V: 1199C; 'Sub noctem,' LB V: 1200F.
99 'Tempore veris,' LB V: 1201B–C; 'In autumno,' LB V: 1201E.
100 'Poenitentis,' LB V: 1204B.
101 'Pro gaudio spirituali,' LB V: 1206C.
102 'Pro custodia pudicitiae,' LB V: 1205A.
103 LB V: 1199F–1200A.
104 *Private Prayers Put forth by Authority during the Reign of Queen Elizabeth*, 457.
105 LB V: 1210C.
106 'Pro felici conjugio,' LB V: 1205B.
107 'Ad Filium,' LB V: 1198C; 'In autumno,' LB V: 1201E.
108 'Tempore veris,' LB V: 1201A–B.
109 For the Father: 'In hieme,' LB V: 1201F; the Son: 'In aestate,' LB V: 1201C; the Spirit: 'Ad Spiritum Sanctum,' LB V: 1200A.
110 See previous note and 'Pro docilitate,' LB V: 1202A; 'Euntis ad ludum litterarium,' LB V: 1209D.
111 'Precatio ad Patrem,' LB V: 1198A; 'In autumno,' LB V: 1201E; 'Pro felici conjugio,' LB V: 1205C; 'Sub nuptias,' LB V: 1205C.

112 'Poenitentis,' LB V: 1203D, F; 'Tempore pestilentiae,' LB V: 1205E, 1206A; 'Ad euangelium de nuptis in Cana,' LB V: 1209F; 'Pro custodia pudicitiae,' LB V: 1205A.

113 LB V: 1200F.

114 'In afflictione,' LB V: 1202F; 'Sub nuptias,' LB V: 1205D.

115 LB V: 1209F.

116 LB V: 1204B–C.

117 'Adversus tentationem,' LB V: 1202B.

118 'Iter ingressuri,' 'Navigaturi,' LB V: 1204D–F.

119 'Ad Filium,' LB V: 1199A; 'In aestate,' LB V: 1201C; 'Diluculo ad Christum,' LB V: 1200D; 'Mane a somno experrecti,' LB V: 1209C; 'Sub noctem,' LB V: 1200E.

120 LB V: 1198F–9A; 1199D–E.

121 LB V: 1201D.

122 'Sumturi Corpus Dominicum,' LB V: 1204C.

123 'Ad Filium,' LB V: 1199D.

124 'Precatio ad Patrem,' LB V: 1197A.

125 'Ad Filium,' LB V: 1199A; 'Tempore veris,' LB V: 1201B.

126 'Adversus tentationem,' LB V: 1202C; 'Pro victoria gratiarum actio,' LB V: 1202E.

127 'In afflictione,' LB V: 1202F–3A.

128 'Sub noctem,' LB V: 1200F.

129 'Poenitentis,' LB V: 1203F, 1204A.

130 Ibid, LB V: 1203E.

131 'In hieme,' LB V: 1201F–2A.

132 ASD V–1: 388.

133 Whereas in the Vulgate this passage begins: 'providebam Dominum in conspectu meo semper,' Erasmus writes: 'Providebo Dominum in conspectu meo semper.' See LB V: 1207B; *Precationes aliquot novae* (1535), 58.

134 LB V: 1207C; *Precationes aliquot novae* (1535), 58: 'Et si ambulavero in medio umbrae mortis, non timebo mihi, quoniam tu mecum es.' Either Erasmus misquotes this passage or the printer is guilty of a misprint. The Vulgate reads: 'non timebo mala.'

135 ASD V–1: 372, 380.

136 P.G. Bietenholz, 'Ludwig Baer, Erasmus and the Tradition of the "Ars bene moriendi,"' 164.

137 LB V: 1203B.

138 ASD V–1: 386.

139 LB V: 1203B.

140 LB V: 1203C.

141 ASD V–1: 346.

142 LB V: 1203C–D.

143 ASD V–1: 390.

144 Ross Dealy, 'The Dynamics of Erasmus' Thought on War,' 62. Many scholars have written about Erasmus' attitude towards war and peace. For a bibliography see Otto Herding's introduction to the *Querela pacis*, ASD IV–2: 22–4. See also J.A. Fernandez-Santamaria, 'Erasmus on the Just War'; Rudolf Padberg, 'Erasmus contra Augustinum,' 278–96; and Otto Herding, 'Erasmus – Frieden und Krieg.'
145 LB V: 1204F–5A.
146 Padberg, 'Erasmus contra Augustinum,' 281.
147 ASD V–1: 284.
148 John B. Payne, *Erasmus: His Theology of the Sacraments*, 118–19; quote from 119.
149 LB V: 706F–7A.
150 LB V: 676E.
151 LB V: 1205B.
152 LB V: 1205D–E.
153 LB V: 676D.
154 Emile Telle, *Erasme de Rotterdam et le septième sacrement*, 263–92. Payne, *Erasmus: His Theology of the Sacraments*, 116, disagrees with Telle.
155 LB VI: 855C, E.
156 LB V: 1205D.
157 ASD I–3: 372.
158 Willi Hentze, *Kirche und kirchliche Einheit bei Desiderius Erasmus von Rotterdam*, 100.
159 Otto Schottenloher, 'Erasmus und die Respublica Christiana,' 312; Hentze, *Kirche und kirchliche Einheit*, 100.
160 *In Psalmum XXII enarratio triplex* (1530), ASD V–2: 356.
161 ASD V–1: 125, 282. On *synaxis*, see Payne, *Erasmus: His Theology of the Sacraments*, 135–6; and M.A. Screech, *Ecstasy and the Praise of Folly*, 125–6.
162 'Sumturi Corpus Dominicum,' LB V: 1204C.
163 LB V: 1209F–10A.
164 Johan Huizinga, *Erasmus and the Age of Reformation*, 142.
165 Preserved Smith, *Erasmus*, 225; James D. Tracy, *Erasmus*, 181–3; Roland Bainton, *Erasmus of Christendom*, 155–6.
166 Margaret Mann Phillips, *Erasmus and the Northern Renaissance*, 181–2.
167 Tracy, *Erasmus*, 167; references to 'libertas,' 11, 169.
168 J.K. McConica, 'Erasmus and the Grammar of Consent,' in *Scrinium Erasmianum*, 2: 89.
169 CWE 8: 67, Ep. 1152, lines 19–20.
170 CWE 8: 167, Ep. 1192A, lines 18–20.
171 CWE 8: 212, Ep. 1203, lines 35–6.
172 CWE 8: 279, Ep. 1216, lines 343–4.
173 Allen 9: 9, Ep. 2361, lines 54–60.

174 Allen 8: 457, Ep. 2332, lines 31–5.
175 CEBR 3: 161–2.
176 Allen 9: 459, Ep. 2618, lines 1–6.
177 Allen 9: 463, Ep. 2623, lines 9–12; Allen 9: 482, Ep. 2634, lines 7–8.
178 ASD V–3: 300.
179 ASD V–3: 251.
180 LB V: 1215E–F.
181 LB V: 1216E, 1218D.
182 ASD V–3: 301.
183 ASD V–3: 303.
184 LB V: 1215F–16E.
185 LB V: 1216E.
186 LB V: 1217B.
187 LB V: 1218A.
188 LB V: 1215F.
189 LB V: 1216F.
190 LB V: 1217A.
191 LB V: 1217D.
192 LB V: 1217C.
193 LB V: 1218A.
194 ASD V–3: 303.
195 *De civitate Dei*, 19, 13, CCSL 48: 679.
196 LB V: 1218A–C.
197 LB V: 1218C–D.
198 'Gratiarum actio,' LB V: 1210 C–D.
199 'Tempore pestilentiae,' LB V: 1206A.
200 'Pro docilitate,' LB V: 1202B; 'Euntis ad ludum litterarium,' LB V: 1209D.
201 'Mane a somno experrecti,' LB V: 1209C.
202 LB V: 1210A.
203 Allen 11: 207, Ep. 3043, 18–20.
204 Allen 11: 215, Ep. 3048, lines 40–2. On Erasmus' physical ailments, see H. Brabant, 'Erasme, ses maladies et ses médecins,' and Jean-Pierre Vanden Branden, 'Le "corpusculum" d'Erasme.'
205 ASD V–1, 346.
206 Allen 11: 260, Ep. 3077, lines 8–9.
207 Allen 1: 53–4, Ep. III, lines 34–5. See C. Reedijk, 'Das Lebensende des Erasmus,' and N. van der Blom, 'Die letzten Worte des Erasmus.'
208 Richard Marius, *Thomas More*, 83.
209 LB V: 1199C–D.

CONCLUSION

1 *Catechismus ex decreto Concilii Tridentini ad parochos,* folio *editio princeps,* 292.

2 Marjorie O'Rourke Boyle, *Erasmus on Language and Method in Theology*, 69.

3 Manfred Hoffmann, *Rhetoric and Theology: The Hermeneutic of Erasmus*, 111.

4 Roland Bainton, *Erasmus of Christendom*, 32; Léon-E. Halkin, *Erasme parmi nous*, 407.

5 Paul F. Grendler, *Schooling in Renaissance Italy*, 333–62, quote from 335.

6 *Histoire du Christianisme des origines à nos jours*, vol. 7: *Le temps des confessions (1530–1620/30)*, 227–9; *History of the Church*, vol. 5: E. Iserloh et al, *Reformation and Counter Reformation*, 433–46.

7 John W. O'Malley, *The First Jesuits*.

8 *Histoire du Christianisme*, 7: 228 and n. 3.

9 *Acta Reformationis Catholicae*, 2: 160.

10 The text of the reform constitutions are in ibid, 2: 201–305; quotes from 246, 220.

11 Ibid, 2: 216, 254.

12 Ibid, 2: 255–71.

13 CWE 6: 278–9; Ep. 932, lines 9–11, 22–31, 36–9.

14 ASD V–4: 142.

15 Allen 6: 441, Ep. 1770, lines 10–12.

16 Lisa Jardine, *Erasmus, Man of Letters*.

17 Jacques Chomarat, *Grammaire et rhétorique chez Erasme*, 2: 1153.

18 See Jean Leclercq, François Vandenbroucke, and Louis Bouyer, *The Spirituality of the Middle Ages*, 373–406.

19 Albert Hyma, *The Youth of Erasmus*, 125; see also 34–5, 125–7, and Hyma, *The Christian Renaissance*; 226–35.

20 Richard DeMolen, 'The Interior Erasmus,' 46, 49, 52.

21 R.R. Post, *The Modern Devotion*, 670, 676.

22 John van Engen, introduction to *Devotio Moderna: Basic Writings*, 23, 49–52.

23 Ibid, 56. For the translated text see ibid, 245–315.

24 Myron P. Gilmore, 'Italian Reactions to Erasmian Humanism,' 93.

25 Andreas Flitner, *Erasmus im Urteil seiner Nachwelt*, 39.

26 Silvana Seidel Menchi, *Erasmo in Italia: 1520–1580*, 338.

27 Gerhard Bellinger, *Der Catechismus Romanus und die Reformation*, 21–2.

28 *Catechismus ex decreto Concilii Tridentini ad parochos*, 9.

29 Ibid, 234.

30 Ibid, 296.

31 Ibid, 307–8.

32 Ibid, 297.

33 Ibid, 309.

34 Allen 11: 350, Ep. 3139, line 100.

35 Paul Althaus, *Forschungen zur evangelischen Gebetsliteratur*, 73.
36 Ibid, 74, 82.
37 Ibid, 67.
38 Marcel Bataillon, *Erasme et l'Espagne*, rev. ed., 1: 614–21, 637–42.
39 *Excitationes animi in Deum* in Juan Luis Vives, *Joannis Ludovici Vivis Valentini Opera Omnia*, 1: 62. On Erasmus and Vives, see Alice Tobriner, 'The Private Prayers of Erasmus and Vives.'
40 Vives, *Opera Omnia*, 1: 72, 65, 75, 86.
41 Ibid, 1: 136–7.
42 Ibid, 1: 93, 94.
43 Charles Trinkaus, *In Our Image and Likeness*.
44 Althaus, *Forschungen zur evangelischen Gebetsliteratur*, 32, 116.
45 James K. McConica, *English Humanists and Reformation Politics under Henry VIII and Edward VI*, 150–99.
46 *Three Primers Put forth in the Reign of Henry VIII*, 2d. ed., 213–14.
47 Ibid, 500, 511–15, 515–16, 522–3.
48 *Prayers stirryng the mynd unto heavenlye meditacions*, E1v–E2v (= D1v–D2v).
49 Craig R. Thompson, 'Erasmus and Tudor England,' 57.
50 Compare the various prayers in the *Precationes aliquot novae* (LB V: 1197–1218) to the prayers, in the original Latin or in translation, in the prayer-books published in *Private Prayers Put forth by Authority during the Reign of Queen Elizabeth*, 18, 88, 95–6, 98–103, 109–10, 171, 183, 190, 192, 194, 202–3, 243, 367–71, 371–2, 376–7, 385–6, 390–4, 399, 441–2, 450–2, 453–7, 469–75, 483, 504, 518–19, 531–5, 536–7.
51 Bataillon, *Erasme et l'Espagne*, 1: 613.
52 Helen C. White, *The Tudor Books of Private Devotion*, 229.

Bibliography

PRIMARY SOURCES

Works by Erasmus

The 'Adages of Erasmus': A Study with Translations. Ed. and trans. Margaret Mann Phillips. Cambridge: Cambridge University Press, 1964.

Collected Works of Erasmus. Toronto and Buffalo: University of Toronto Press, 1974–.

Desiderii Erasmi Roterodami Opera Omnia. Ed. J. Leclerc. 10 vols. Leiden: 1703–6.

Desiderius Erasmus Roterodamus: Ausgewählte Werke. Ed. Hajo Holborn and Annemarie Holborn. Munich: C.H. Beck'sche Verlagsbuchhandlung, 1933.

Divi Iohannis Chrysostomi de orando deum, libri duo, Erasmo Rot. interprete. Adiunctus est iisdem modus orandi deum, autore Erasmo. [Cologne]: Eucharius Cervicornus, 1525.

Erasmus' Annotations on the New Testament: The Gospels. Ed. Anne Reeve. London: Duckworth, 1986.

Erasmus' Annotations on the New Testament: Acts – Romans – I and II Corinthians. Ed. Anne Reeve and M.A. Screech. Leiden: E.J. Brill, 1990.

Novum Instrumentum omne, diligenter ab Erasmo Roterodamo recognitum & emendatum ... una cum Annotationibus, quae lectorem doceant, quid qua ratione mutatum sit. Basel: Froben, 1516.

Opera Omnia Desiderii Erasmi Roterodami. Ed. C. Reedijk et al. Amsterdam: North-Holland Publishing Company, 1969–.

Opus epistolarum Des. Erasmi Roterodami. Ed. P.S. Allen, H.M. Allen, and H.W. Garrod. 12 vols. Oxford: Clarendon Press, 1906–68.

The Praise of Folly. Trans., intro., and commentary by Clarence H. Miller. New Haven and London: Yale University Press, 1979.

Precatio Dominica digesta in septem parteis [sic], *iuxta septem dies, per D. Erasmus Roterodamum.* Basel: Froben, (1523).

Precationes aliquot novae, ac rursus novis adauctae, quibus adolescentes assuescant cum Deo colloqui. Basel: Froben, 1535.

Precationes aliquot, quibus adolescentes assuescant cum Deo colloqui. Basel: Frobenius and Episcopius, 1551.

Precationes aliquot, quibus adolescentes discant cum Deo colloqui. Cologne: Apud haeredes Arnoldi Birckmann, 1563.

Other Primary Sources

Acta Reformationis Catholicae. Ed. Georg Pfeilschifter. 6 vols. Regensburg: Verlag Friedrich Pustet, 1959–74.

Alberigo, Guiseppe et al, eds. *Conciliorum Oecumenicorum Decreta.* 3d ed. Bologna: Istituto per le scienze religiose, 1973.

The Apostolic Fathers. 2d ed. Ed. Michael W. Holmes. Trans. J.B. Lightfoot and J.R. Harmer. Grand Rapids, MI: Baker Book House, 1989.

Becon, Thomas. *The Early Works of Thomas Becon.* Ed. John Ayre. Cambridge: The University Press, 1843.

– *Prayers and Other Pieces of Thomas Becon.* Ed. John Ayre. Cambridge: The University Press, 1844.

Die Bekenntnisschriften der evangelisch-lutherischen Kirche. 3d ed. Göttingen: Vandenhoeck and Ruprecht, 1956.

Calvin, John. *Corpus Reformatorum: Ioannis Calvini opera quae supersunt omnia.* Ed. Wilhelm Baum, Eduard Cunitz, and Eduard Reuss. 57 vols. Braunschweig: C.A. Schwetschke et Filium (M. Bruhn), 1863–97

– *Institutes of the Christian Religion* (1535). Rev. ed. Trans. Ford Lewis Battles. Grand Rapids, MI: Eerdmans, 1986.

Canisius, Peter. *S. Petri Canisii Doctoris Ecclesiae Catechismi Latini et Germanici.* Ed. Friedrich Streicher. 2 vols. Rome: Pontificia Universitas Gregoriana; Munich: Bavariae Officina Salesiana, 1933–6.

Catechismus ex decreto Concilii Tridentini ad parochos. Folio editio princeps. Rome: Paolo Manuzio, 1566.

Clichtove, Josse. *De veneratione sanctorum, opusculum: duos libros complectens.* Paris: Simone de Colines, 1523.

Cochlaeus, Johannes. *De sanctorum invocatione et intercessione.* Ingolstadt: Alexander Weissenhorn, 1544.

Corpus Christianorum: Series Latina. Turnhout: Brepols, 1954–.

Die Confutatio der Confessio Augustana vom 3. August 1530. Ed. Herbert Immenkötter. Corpus Catholicorum: Werke katholischer Schriftsteller im Zeitalter der Glaubensspaltung. Vol. 33. Münster: Aschendorffsche Verlagsbuchhandlung, 1979.

Devotio Moderna: Basic Writings. Trans. and intro. John van Engen. New York: Paulist Press, 1988.

Eck, Johannes. *Enchiridion locorum communium adversus Lutherum et alios hostes ecclesiae.* Ed. Pierre Fraenkel. Corpus Catholicorum: vol. 34. Münster: Aschendorfsche Verlagsbuchhandlung, 1979.

Fisher, John. *Ioannis Fischerii Roffensis in Anglia Episcopi Opera, quae hactenus inueniri potuerant omnia.* Würzburg: Georg Fleischmann, 1597.

Flannery, Austin P., ed. *Documents of Vatican II*, new rev. ed., vol. 1. Grand Rapids, Michigan: William B. Eerdmans, 1984.

von Hoogstraten, Jacob. *Dialogus de veneratione & invocatione sanctorum contra perfidiam Lutheranam.* Cologne: Peter Quentell, 1524.

Ignatius of Loyola. *The Spiritual Exercises of St. Ignatius.* Translated by Anthony Mottola. Garden City, New York: Image Books, 1964.

von Karlstadt, Andreas Bodenstein. *Von gelubden unterrichtung.* Wittenberg, 1521.

Luther, Martin. *D. Martin Luthers Werke: Briefwechsel.* 15 vols. Weimar: Hermann Böhlaus Nachfolger, 1930–78.

– *D. Martin Luthers Werke: Die deutsche Bibel.* Weimar: Hermann Böhlaus Nachfolger, 1906–61.

– *D. Martin Luthers Werke: Kritische Gesamtausgabe.* 61 vols. Weimar: Hermann Böhlaus Nachfolger, 1883–1983.

Mone, Franz Joseph, ed. *Lateinische Hymnen des Mittelalters.* 3 vols. Freiburg im Breisgau, 1853–55; rpt., Aalen: Scientia Verlag, 1964.

More, Thomas. *Complete Works of St Thomas More.* 15 vols. New Haven: Yale University Press, 1963–96.

Origen. *Origen: An Exhortation to Martyrdom, Prayer, First Principles: Book IV. Prologue to the Commentary on the Song of Songs, Homily XXVII on Numbers.* Trans. and intro. Rowan A. Greer. New York: Paulist Press, 1979.

Patrologiae cursus completus ... series graeca. Ed. J.-P. Migne. 161 vols. Paris: 1857–77.

Patrologiae cursus completus ... series latina. Ed. J.-P. Migne. 221 vols. Paris: 1878–90.

Prayers stirryng the mynd unto heavenlye meditacions collected oute of holy workes by the moste vertuous and gracious princesse Katerine queene of Englande, Fraunce, and Irelande. London: Thomas Berthelet, 1545.

Private Prayers Put forth by Authority during the Reign of Queen Elizabeth. Ed. William Keatinge Clay. Cambridge: The University Press, 1851.

Tappolet, Walter, ed. *Das Marienlob der Reformatoren.* Tübingen: Katzmann-Verlag, 1962.

Thomas Aquinas. *Opuscula Omnia.* Ed. Pierre Mandonnet. 5 vols. Paris: Lethielleux, 1927.

– *Summa Theologiae.* Blackfriars ed. 61 vols. London: Eyre and Spottiswoode, 1964–81.

Three Primers Put forth in the Reign of Henry VIII, 2d ed. Oxford: Oxford University Press, 1848.

Unterkircher, Franz, ed. and trans. *Das Stundenbuch des Mittelalters*. Graz: Akademische Druck- und Verlagsanstalt, 1985.

Vives, Juan Luis. *Joannis Ludovici Vivis Valentini Opera Omnia*. Ed. Gregorio Mayáns. 8 vols. Valencia: Benedict Monfort, 1782–90.

SECONDARY SOURCES

Achten, Gerard, ed. *Das christliche Gebetbuch im Mittelalter: Andachts- und Stundenbücher in Handschrift und Frühdruck*. Berlin: Staatsbibliothek Preußischer Kulturbesitz, 1980.

Algermissen, Konrad. 'Mariologie und Marienverehrung der Reformatoren.' *Theologie und Glaube* 49 (1959): 1–24.

Alonso, Joaquín María. 'Erasmo, hombre-puente en la historia de la devoción mariana.' *Estudios Marianos* 36 (1971): 235–64

Althaus, Paul. *Forschungen zur evangelischen Gebetsliteratur*. Gütersloh: C. Bertelsmann, 1927.

Audet, Jean-Paul. *La Didachè: Instruction des apôtres*. Paris: Librairie Lecoffre, 1958.

Auer, Alfons. *Die vollkommene Frömmigkeit des Christen: Nach dem Enchiridion militis Christiani des Erasmus von Rotterdam*. Düsseldorf: Patmos-Verlag, 1954.

Augustijn, Cornelis. 'The Ecclesiology of Erasmus.' In *Scrinium Erasmianum*. Ed. J. Coppens. Leiden: E.J. Brill, 1969. 2, 135–56.

– 'Erasmus und die Juden.' *Nederlands Archief voor Kerkgeschiedenis* 60 (1980): 22–38.

– *Erasmus: His Life, Works, and Influence*. Trans. J.C. Grayson. Toronto: University of Toronto Press, 1991.

Backvis, Claude. 'La fortune d'Erasme en Pologne.' In *Colloquium Erasmianum*. Mons: Centre universitaire de l'Etat, 1968. 173–202.

Bailey, Derrick Sherwin. *Thomas Becon and the Reformation of the Church in England*. Edinburgh: Oliver and Boyd, 1952.

Bainton, Roland. *Erasmus of Christendom*. New York: Scribner's, 1969.

Barth, Karl. *Prayer according to the Catechisms of the Reformation*. Trans. Sara F. Terrien. Philadelphia: Westminster Press, 1952.

Bataillon, Marcel. *Erasme et l'Espagne*, rev. ed. Ed. Daniel Devoto and Charles Amiel. 3 vols. Geneva: Droz, 1991.

Beissel, Stephan. 'Zur Geschichte der Gebetbücher.' *Stimmen aus Maria Laach* 77 (1909): 28–41, 169–85, 274–89, 397–411.

Bellinger, Gerhard. *Der Catechismus Romanus und die Reformation: Die katechetische Antwort des Trienter Konzils auf die Hauptkatechismen der Reformation*. Paderborn: Bonifacius-Druckerei, 1970.

Béné, Charles. 'Le *De Puritate Taburnaculi*: Testament spirituel d'Erasme?' In *Actes du colloque international Erasme*. Ed. Jacques

Chomarat, André Godin, and Jean-Claude Margolin. Geneva: Droz, 1990. 199–212.

– *Erasme et Saint Augustin.* Geneva: Droz, 1969.

Bezzel, Irmgard. *Erasmusdrucke des 16. Jahrhunderts in Bayerischen Bibliotheken.* Stuttgart: Anton Hiersemann Verlag, 1979.

Biel, Pamela. 'Personal Conviction and Pastoral Care: Zwingli and the Cult of the Saints, 1522–1530.' *Zwingliana* 16 (1985): 442–69.

Bierlaire, Franz. *Les Colloques d'Erasme: Réforme des études, réforme des moeurs et réforme de l'Eglise au XVIe siècle.* Paris: Société d'Edition 'Les Belles Lettres,' 1978.

Bietenholz, P.G. 'Ludwig Baer, Erasmus and the Tradition of the "Ars bene moriendi."' *Revue de littérature comparée* 52 (1978): 155–70.

Bietenholz, Peter G., and Thomas B. Deutscher, eds. *Contemporaries of Erasmus: A Biographical Register of the Renaissance and Reformation.* 3 vols. Toronto: University of Toronto Press, 1985–7.

Vanden Branden, Jean-Pierre. 'Le "corpusculum" d'Erasme.' In *Actes du colloque international Erasme.* Ed. Jacques Chomarat, André Godin, and Jean-Claude Margolin. Geneva: Droz, 1990. 215–31.

van der Blom, N. 'Die letzten Worte des Erasmus.' *Basler Zeitschrift für Geschichte und Altertumskunde* 65 (1965): 195–214.

Boyle, Marjorie O'Rourke. *Erasmus on Language and Method in Theology.* Toronto: University of Toronto Press, 1977.

Brabant, H. 'Erasme, ses maladies et ses médecins.' In *Colloquia Erasmiana Turonensia.* Ed. Jean-Claude Margolin. Toronto: University of Toronto Press, 1972. 1: 539–68.

Brecht, Martin. *Martin Luther.* Vol. 2: *Ordnung und Abgrenzung der Reformation, 1521–1532.* Stuttgart: Calwer Verlag, 1986.

Brown, D. Catherine. *Pastor and Laity in the Theology of Jean Gerson.* Cambridge: Cambridge University Press, 1987.

Brown, Peter. *The Cult of the Saints: Its Rise and Function in Latin Christianity.* Chicago: University of Chicago Press, 1982.

Butterworth, Charles C. *The English Primers (1529–1545): Their Publication and Connection with the English Bible and the Reformation in England.* Philadelphia: University of Pennsylvania Press, 1953.

Carmignac, Jean. *Recherches sur le 'Notre Père.'* Paris: Editions Letouzey et Ané, 1969.

Chantraine, Georges. *'Mystère' et 'Philosophie du Christ' selon Erasme.* Namur: Secrétariat des publications, Facultés universitaires, 1971; Gembloux: Editions J. Duculot, 1971.

– 'Théologie et vie spirituelle: Un aspect de la méthode théologique selon Erasme.' *Nouvelle Revue Théologique* 101 (1969): 809–33.

Chomarat, Jacques. *Grammaire et rhétorique chez Erasme.* 2 vols. Paris: Société d'Edition 'Les Belles Lettres,' 1981.

Dealy, Ross. 'The Dynamics of Erasmus' Thought on War.' *Erasmus of Rotterdam Society Yearbook* 4 (1984): 53–67.

Delius, Walter. *Geschichte der Marienverehrung*. Munich, Basel: Ernst Reinhardt Verlag, 1963.

Delumeau, Jean. *La peur en occident (XIVe–XVIIIe siècles): Une cité assiégée*. Paris: Fayard, 1978.

– *Sin and Fear: The Emergence of a Western Guilt Culture, 13th–18th Centuries*. Trans. Eric Nicholson. New York: St Martin's Press, 1990.

DeMolen, Richard L., ed. *Erasmus of Rotterdam: A Quincentennial Symposium*. New York: Twayne, 1971.

– 'The Interior Erasmus.' In DeMolen, R. *The Spirituality of Erasmus of Rotterdam*. Nieuwkoop: De Graaf, 1987. 35–67.

Devereux, E.J. *Renaissance English Translations of Erasmus: A Bibliography to 1700*. Toronto: University of Toronto Press, 1983.

Dictionnaire de Spiritualité. Paris: Beauchesne, 1969. S.v. 'Humanisme et spiritualité chez Erasme,' by Jean-Pierre Massaut. 7/1: 1006–28.

– Paris: Beauchesne, 1984. S.v. 'Pater Noster,' by Aimé Solignac. 12/1: 388–413.

Düfel, Hans. 'Die Stellung des Erasmus von Rotterdam zur Marienverehrung unter besdonderer Berücksichtigung der Frömmigkeitsgeschichte an der Wende vom Spätmittelalter zur Reformation.' In *De cultu Mariano saeculis XII–XV: Acta Congressus Mariologici-Mariani Internationalis Romae anno 1975 celebrati*. 6 vols. Rome: Pontificia Academia Mariana Internationalis, 1979–81. 5: 431–51.

– *Luthers Stellung zur Marienverehrung*. Göttingen: Vandenhoeck und Ruprecht, 1968.

Duffy, Eamon. *The Stripping of the Altars: Traditional Religion in England, 1400–1580*. New Haven: Yale University Press, 1992.

Eire, Carlos M.N. *War against the Idols: The Reformation of Worship from Erasmus to Calvin*. Cambridge: Cambridge University Press, 1986.

Esser, Thomas. 'Geschichte des englischen Grußes.' *Historisches Jahrbuch* 5 (1884): 88–116.

Fernandez-Santamaria, J.A. 'Erasmus on the Just War.' *Journal of the History of Ideas* 34 (1973): 209–26.

Flitner, Andreas. *Erasmus im Urteil seiner Nachwelt: Das literarische Erasmus-Bild von Beatus Rhenanus bis zu Jean Le Clerc*. Tübingen: Max Niemeyer Verlag, 1952.

Gebhardt, Georg. *Die Stellung des Erasmus von Rotterdam zur römischen Kirche*. Marburg an der Lahn: Oekumenischer Verlag Dr. R.F. Edel, 1966.

Gilmore, Myron P. 'Italian Reactions to Erasmian Humanism.' In *Itinerarium Italicum: The Profile of the Italian Renaissance in the Mirror of its European Transformations*, Ed. Heiko A. Oberman with Thomas A. Brady. Leiden: E.J. Brill, 1975. 61–115.

Godin, André. *Erasme, lecteur d'Origène*. Geneva: Droz, 1982.

Gordon, Walter M. *Humanist Play and Belief: The Seriocomic Art of Desiderius Erasmus*. Toronto: University of Toronto Press, 1990.

Graef, Hilda. *Mary: A History of Doctrine and Devotion*. 2 vols. New York: Sheed and Ward, 1963–5.

Grendler, Paul F. *Schooling in Renaissance Italy: Literacy and Learning, 1300–1600*. Baltimore: Johns Hopkins University Press, 1989.

Haimerl, Franz Xaver. *Mittelalterliche Frömmigkeit im Spiegel der Gebetbuchliteratur Süddeutschlands*. Munich: Karl Zink Verlag, 1952.

Halkin, Léon-E. 'Erasme contra la liturgie?' In *Miscellanea Moreana: Essays for Germain Marc'hadour*. Ed. Clare M. Murphy, Henri Gibaud, and Mario A. Di Cesare. Binghamton, NY: Medieval and Renaissance Texts and Studies, vol. 61, 1989, 421–5.

– 'Erasme et le célibat sacerdotal.' *Revue d'histoire et de philosophie religieuses* 57 (1977): 497–511.

– *Erasme et l'humanisme chrétien*. Paris: Editions Universitaires, 1969.

– *Erasme parmi nous*. Paris: Fayard, 1987.

– 'Erasme pèlerin.' In *Scrinium Erasmianum*. Ed. J. Coppens. Leiden: E.J. Brill, 1969. 2: 239–52.

– 'La Mariologie d'Erasme.' *Archiv für Reformationsgeschichte* 68 (1977): 32–54.

– 'La piété d'Erasme.' *Revue d'histoire ecclésiastique* 79 (1984): 671–708.

Harthan, John. *Books of Hours and Their Owners*. London: Thames and Hudson, 1977.

Heiler, Friedrich. *Das Gebet: eine religionsgeschichtliche und religionspsychologische Untersuchung*, 5th ed. Munich: Verlag von Ernst Reinhardt, 1923.

Hentze, Willi. *Kirche und kirchliche Einheit bei Desiderius Erasmus von Rotterdam*. Paderborn: Verlag Bonifacius-Druckerei, 1974.

Herding, Otto. 'Erasmus – Frieden und Krieg.' In *Erasmus und Europa*. Ed. August Buck. Wiesbaden: Otto Harrassowitz, 1988, 13–32.

Histoire de l'Eglise depuis les origines jusqu'à nos jours. 21 vols. Founded by Augustin Fliche and Victor Martin. Vol. 14: E. Delaruelle, E.-R. Labande, and Paul Ourliac. *L'Eglise au temps du Grand Schisme et de la crise conciliaire (1378–1449)*. Paris: Bloud et Gay, 1962–64.

Histoire du Christianisme des origines à nos jours. Ed. Jean-Marie Mayeur, Charles Pietri, André Vauchez, and Marc Venard. Vol. 7: *Le temps des confessions (1530–1620/30)*. Ed. Marc Venard. Paris: Desclée, 1992.

History of the Church. 10 vols. Ed. Hubert Jedin and John Dolan. Vol. 5: Erwin Iserloh, Joseph Glazik, and Hubert Jedin. *Reformation and Counter Reformation*. Trans. Anselm Biggs and Peter W. Becker. London: Burns and Oates, 1980.

Hoffmann, Manfred. 'Erasmus on Church and Ministry.' *Erasmus of Rotterdam Society Yearbook* 6 (1986): 1–30.

– *Erkenntnis und Verwirklichung der wahren Theologie nach Erasmus von Rotterdam.* Tübingen: J.C.B. Mohr (Paul Siebeck), 1972.
– *Rhetoric and Theology: The Hermeneutic of Erasmus.* Toronto: University of Toronto Press, 1994.
Huizinga, Johan. *Erasmus and the Age of Reformation.* Trans. F. Hopman. New York: Harper Torchbooks, 1957.
Hyma, Albert. *The Christian Renaissance: A History of the 'Devotio Moderna.'* New York: Century, 1925.
– *The Youth of Erasmus.* Ann Arbor: University of Michigan Press, 1930–1.
James, William. *The Varieties of Religious Experience: A Study in Human Nature.* New York: Longmans, Green, 1902.
Jardine, Lisa. *Erasmus, Man of Letters: The Construction of Charisma in Print.* Princeton: Princeton University Press, 1993.
Jeremias, Joachim. *The Prayers of Jesus.* Naperville, Il: Alec R. Allenson, 1967.
Jungmann, Joseph A. *Christian Prayer through the Centuries.* Trans. John Coyne. New York: Paulist Press, 1978.
– *The Mass of the Roman Rite: Its Origins and Development.* Trans. Francis A. Brunner. 2 vols. New York: Benziger Brothers, 1951–5.
Kelly, Faye L. *Prayer in Sixteenth-Century England.* Gainesville: University of Florida Press, 1966.
Kelly, J.N.D. *Early Christian Doctrines.* Rev. ed. San Francisco: Harper, 1978.
Kisch, Guido. *Erasmus' Stellung zu Juden und Judentum.* Tübingen: J.C.B. Mohr (Paul Siebeck), 1969.
Kleinhans, Robert G. '*Ecclesiastes sive de ratione concionandi.*' In *Essays on the Works of Erasmus.* Ed. Richard L. DeMolen. New Haven: Yale University Press, 1978. 253–67.
– 'Erasmus' Doctrine of Preaching: A Study of the *Ecclesiastes, sive de ratione concionandi.*' Th.D. diss., Princeton Theological Seminary, 1968.
Kleinschmidt, Beda. 'Die Blütezeit des Annakultes.' *Theologie und Glaube* 19 (1927): 488–512.
– 'Das Trinubium (Dreiheirat) der hl. Anna in Legende, Liturgie und Geschichte.' *Theologie und Glaube* 20 (1928): 32–44.
– 'Zur Verehrung der heiligen Mutter Anna.' *Theologie und Glaube* 18 (1926): 297–307.
Kohls, Ernst-Wilhelm. *Die Theologie des Erasmus.* 2 vols. Basel: Friedrich Reinhardt Verlag, 1966.
Kolb, Robert. *For All the Saints: Changing Perceptions of Martyrdom and Sainthood in the Lutheran Reformation.* Macon, GA: Mercer University Press, 1987.
Kretschmar, Georg, and René Laurentin. 'Der Artikel vom Dienst der Heiligen in der Confessio Augustana.' In *Confessio Augustana: Bekennt-*

nis des einen Glaubens. Ed. Harding Meyer and Heinz Schütte. Paderborn: Verlag Bonifacius-Druckerei; Frankfurt am Main: Verlag Otto Lembeck, 1980. 256–80.

Krüger, Friedhelm. *Bucer und Erasmus: eine Untersuchung zum Einfluss des Erasmus auf die Theologie Martin Bucers (bis zum Evangelien-Kommentar von 1530).* Wiesbaden: Franz Steiner Verlag, 1970.

– 'Bucer und Erasmus.' In *Martin Bucer and Sixteenth Century Europe.* Ed. Christian Krieger and Marc Lienhard. Leiden: E.J. Brill, 1993. 2: 583–94.

– *Humanistische Evangelienauslegung: Desiderius Erasmus von Rotterdam als Ausleger der Evangelien in seinen Paraphrasen.* Tübingen: J.C.B. Mohr (Paul Siebeck), 1986.

Le Goff, Jacques. *The Birth of Purgatory.* Trans. Arthur Goldhammer. Chicago: University of Chicago Press, 1984.

Leclercq, Jean, François Vandenbroucke, and Bouyer, Louis. *The Spirituality of the Middle Ages.* London: Burns and Oates, 1968.

Lexikon für Theologie und Kirche. Freiburg im Breisgau: Herder, 1960. S.v. 'Hortulus animae (Seelengartlein)' by F. Wulf. Vol. 5: 498.

Lienhard, Marc. 'Prier au XVIᵉ siècle: regards sur le Biblisch Bettbüchlein du Strasbourgeois Othon Brunfels.' *Revue d'histoire et de philosophie religieuses* 66 (1986): 43–55.

Lortz, Joseph. 'Erasmus – Kirchengeschichtlich.' In *Aus Theologie und Philosophie: Festschrift für Fritz Tillmann.* Ed. Theodor Steinbüchel and Theodor Müncker. Düsseldorf: Patmos-Verlag, 1950. 271–326.

Manns, Peter. 'Luther und die Heiligen.' In *Reformatio Ecclesiae: Beiträge zu kirchlichen Reformbemühungen von der Alten Kirche bis zur Neuzeit, Festgabe für Erwin Iserloh.* Ed. Remigius Bäumer. Paderborn: Ferdinand Schöningh, 1980. 535–80.

Mansfield, Bruce. *Interpretations of Erasmus, c. 1750–1920: Man on His Own.* Toronto: University of Toronto Press, 1992.

– *Phoenix of His Age: Interpretations of Erasmus, c. 1550–1750.* Toronto: University of Toronto Press, 1979.

Marc'hadour, Germain. 'Erasmus as Priest: Holy Orders in His Vision and Practice.' In *Erasmus' Vision of the Church.* Ed. Hilmar M. Pabel. Kirksville, MO: Sixteenth Century Publishers, 1995. 115–49.

Margolin, Jean-Claude. *Erasme et la musique.* Paris: Librairie Philosophique J. Vrin, 1965.

– 'Érasme et la musique.' In Margolin, J.-C. *Recherches Erasmiennes.* Geneva: Droz, 1969. 85–97.

– *Erasme, précepteur de l'Europe.* Paris: Editions Julliard, 1995.

– 'Paris through a Gothic Window at the End of the Fifteenth Century: A Poem of Erasmus in Honor of St Geneviève.' *Res Publica Litterarum* 1 (1978): 206–20.

Marius, Richard. *Thomas More: A Biography.* New York: Knopf, 1984.

Markish, Shimon. *Erasmus and the Jews.* Trans. Anthony Olcott. Chicago: University of Chicago Press, 1986.

Massaut, Jean-Pierre. *Josse Clichtove: L'humanisme et la réforme du clergé.* 2 vols. Paris: Société d'Edition 'Les Belles Lettres,' 1968.

– 'La position "oecuménique" d'Erasme sur la pénitence.' In *Réforme et Humanisme.* Ed. Jean Boisset. Montpellier: Presses de l'Imprimerie de Recherche – Université Paul Valéry, 1977. 241–81.

Mayer, Anton L. 'Renaissance, Humanismus und Liturgie.' *Jahrbuch für Liturgiewissenschaft* 14 (1938): 123–71. Reprinted in A.L. Mayer, *Die Liturgie in der europäischen Geistesgeschichte: gesammelte Aufsätze.* Edited by Emmanuel von Severus. Darmstadt: Wissenschaftliche Buchsgesellschaft, 1971. 48–96.

McConica, James K. 'Erasmus and the Grammar of Consent.' In *Scrinium Erasmianum.* Ed. J. Coppens. Leiden: E.J. Brill, 1969. 2: 77–99

– *English Humanists and Reformation Politics under Henry VIII and Edward VI.* Oxford: Clarendon Press, 1965.

– *Erasmus.* Oxford: Oxford University Press, 1991.

McCutcheon, Elizabeth. 'Margaret More Roper's Translation of Erasmus' *Precatio Dominica.*' In *Acta Conventus Neo-Latini Guelpherbytani.* Ed. Stella P. Revard, Fidel Rädle, and Mario A. Di Cesare. Binghamton, NY: Medieval and Renaissance Texts and Studies, vol. 53: 1988, 659–66.

Miller, Clarence H. 'Erasmus's Poem to St. Genevieve: Text, Translation, and Commentary.' In *Miscellanea Moreana: Essays for Germain Marc'hadour.* Ed. Clare M. Murphy, Henri Gibaud, and Mario A. Di Cesare. Binghamton, NY: Medieval and Renaissance Texts and Studies, vol. 61: 1989, 481–515.

– 'The Liturgical Context of Erasmus's Hymns.' In *Acta Conventus Neo-Latini Torontonensis.* Ed. Alexander Dalzell, Charles Fantazzi, and Richard J. Schoeck. Binghamton, NY: Medieval and Renaissance Texts and Studies, vol. 86: 1991, 481–90.

– 'Styles and Mixed Genres in Erasmus' *Praise of Folly.*' In *Acta Conventus Neo-Latini Guelpherbytani.* Ed. Stella P. Revard, Fidel Rädle, and Mario A. Di Cesare. Binghamton, NY: Medieval and Renaissance Texts and Studies, vol. 53: 1988, 277–87.

Miller, Clement A. 'Erasmus on Music.' *Musical Quarterly* 52 (1966): 332–49.

Müller, Gerhard Ludwig. *Gemeinschaft und Verehrung der Heiligen: Geschichtlich-systematische Grundlegung der Hagiologie.* Freiburg im Breisgau: Herder, 1986

New Catholic Encyclopedia. S. v. 'Loreto,' by H.M. Gillet. Vol. 8: 993–4. New York: McGraw-Hill, 1967.

Oberman, Heiko A. *The Roots of Anti-Semitism in the Age of Renaissance and Reformation.* Trans. James I. Porter. Philadelphia: Fortress Press, 1984.

– 'The Virgin Mary in Evangelical Perspective.' *Journal of Ecumenical Studies* 1 (1964): 271–98.

O'Malley, John W. 'Erasmus and the History of Sacred Rhetoric: The *Ecclesiastes* of 1535.' *Erasmus of Rotterdam Society Yearbook* 5 (1985): 1–29.

– *The First Jesuits.* Cambridge, MA: Harvard University Press, 1993.

– 'Grammar and Rhetoric in the *Pietas* of Erasmus.' *Journal of Medieval and Renaissance Studies* 18 (1988): 81–98.

– Introduction to *Collected Works of Erasmus,* Vol. 66. Toronto: University of Toronto Press, 1988.

– *Praise and Blame in Renaissance Rome: Rhetoric, Doctrine, and Reform in the Sacred Orators of the Papal Court, c. 1450–1521.* Durham, NC: Duke University Press, 1979.

Oxford Dictionary of the Christian Church, 2d ed. Ed. F.L. Cross and E.A. Livingstone. Oxford: Oxford University Press, 1974/1983.

Pabel, Hilmar M. 'Erasmus' Esteem for Cyprian: Parallels in Their Expositions of the Lord's Prayer.' Forthcoming in *Erasmus of Rotterdam Society Yearbook* 17 (1997).

– 'Erasmus of Rotterdam and Judaism: A Reexamination in Light of New Evidence.' *Archiv für Reformationsgeschichte* 87 (1996): 9–37.

– 'The Peaceful People of Christ: The Irenic Ecclesiology of Erasmus of Rotterdam.' In *Erasmus' Vision of the Church.* Ed. Hilmar M. Pabel. Kirksville, MO. Sixteenth Century Publishers, 1995. 57–93.

– 'Promoting the Business of the Gospel: Erasmus' Contribution to Pastoral Ministry.' *Erasmus of Rotterdam Society Yearbook* 15 (1995): 53–70.

Padberg, Rudolf. *Erasmus als Katechet.* Freiburg im Breisgau: Herder, 1956.

– 'Erasmus contra Augustinum: Das Problem des bellum justum in der erasmischen Friedensethik.' In *Colloque Erasmien de Liège.* Ed. Jean-Pierre Massaut. Paris: Société d'Edition 'Les Belles Lettres,' 1987. 279–96.

– 'Personale Seelsorge bei Erasmus von Rotterdam.' *Theologie und Glaube* 53 (1963): 207–16.

Payne, John B. *Erasmus: His Theology of the Sacraments.* [Richmond, VA: John Knox Press,] 1970.

Phillips, Jane E. 'The Gospel, the Clergy, and the Laity in Erasmus' *Paraphrase on the Gospel of John.*' *Erasmus of Rotterdam Society Yearbook* 10 (1990): 85–99.

Phillips, Margaret Mann. *Erasmus and the Northern Renaissance.* London: English University Press, 1949.

Pinomaa, Lennart. *Die Heiligen bei Luther.* Helsinki: Schriften der Luther-Agricola-Gesellschaft, 1977.

- 'Luthers Weg zur Verwerfung des Heiligendienstes.' *Luther-Jahrbuch* 29 (1962): 35–43.
Plotzek, Joachim M., ed. *Andachtsbücher des Mittelalters aus Privatbesitz.* Cologne: Locher, 1987.
Post, R.R. *The Modern Devotion: Confrontation with Reformation and Humanism.* Leiden: E.J. Brill, 1968.
Redondo, Augustin. 'La "Precatio Dominica" d'Erasme en Castillan: la première version et son auteur.' *Revue de littérature comparée* 52 (1978): 223–32.
Reedijk, C. 'Das Lebensende des Erasmus.' *Basler Zeitschrift für Geschichte und Altertumskunde* 57 (1958): 23–66.
Reinburg, Virginia. 'Popular Prayers in Late Medieval and Reformation France.' Ph.D. diss. Princeton University, 1985.
Renaudet, Augustin. *Etudes Erasmiennes (1521–1529).* Paris: Droz, 1939.
Rummel, Erika. *Erasmus and His Catholic Critics.* 2 vols. Nieuwkoop: De Graaf, 1989.
- *Erasmus' Annotations on the New Testament: From Philologist to Theologian.* Toronto: University of Toronto Press, 1986.
Russel, Jeffrey Burton. *Lucifer: The Devil in the Middle Ages.* Ithaca, NY: Cornell University Press, 1984.
Schimmelpfennig, Reintraud. *Die Geschichte der Marienverehrung im deutschen Protestantismus.* Paderborn: Ferdinand Schöningh, 1952.
- 'Die Marienverehrung der Reformatoren.' In *Maria in der Lehre von der Kirche.* Ed. Hans-Joachim Mund. Paderborn: Ferdinand Schöningh, 1979. 60–75.
Schoeck, R.J. 'Erasmus as Latin Secretary to the Bishop of Cambrai: Erasmus' Introduction to the Burgundian Court.' In *Erasmus of Rotterdam: The Man and the Scholar.* Ed. J. Sperna Weiland and W. Th. M. Frijhoff. Leiden: E.J. Brill, 1988. 7–14.
Schottenloher, Otto. 'Erasmus und die Republica Christiana.' *Historische Zeitschrift* 210 (1970): 295–323.
- 'Erasmus, Johann Poppenruyter und die Entstehung des *Enchiridion militis christiani.*' *Archiv für Reformationsgeschichte* 45 (1954).
Schulz, Frieder. 'Die evangelischen Begräbnisgebete des 16. und 17. Jahrhunderts.' *Jahrbuch für Liturgik und Hymnologie* 11 (1966): 1–44.
Schützeichel, Heribert. 'Calvins Einspruch gegen die Heiligenverehrung.' *Catholica: Vierteljahresschrift für ökumenische Theologie* 35 (1981): 93–116.
Screech, M.A. *Ecstasy and the Praise of Folly.* London: Duckworth, 1980.
Seidel Menchi, Silvana. *Erasmo in Italia: 1520–1580.* Turin: Bollati Boringhieri, 1987.
Sider, Ronald J. *Andreas Bodenstein von Karlstadt: The Development of his Thought, 1517–1525.* Leiden: E.J. Brill, 1974.

Smith, Preserved. *Erasmus: A Study of His Life, Ideals and Place in History.* New York, London: Harper, 1923.

Snyder, Lee Daniel. 'Erasmus on Prayer: A Renaissance Reinterpretation.' *Renaissance and Reformation* 12 (1976): 21–6.

Söll, Georg. 'Maria in der Geschichte von Theologie und Frömmigkeit.' In *Handbuch der Marienkunde.* Ed. Wolfgang Beinert and Heinrich Petri. Regensburg: Verlag Friedrich Pustet, 1984. 93–231.

Surtz, Edward. *The Works and Days of John Fisher.* Cambridge, MA: Harvard University Press, 1967.

Telle, Emile V. *Erasme de Rotterdam et le septième sacrement.* Geneva: Droz, 1954.

Theological Dictionary of the New Testament. Ed. Gerhard Kittel and Gerhard Friedrich. Trans. and ed. Geoffrey W. Bromley. 10 vols. Grand Rapids, MI: Eerdmans, 1964–1976. S.v. 'επιουσιος,' by Werner Foerster. 2: 590–9.

Theologische Realenzyklopädie. Berlin: Walter de Gruyter, 1985. S.v. 'Heilige/Heiligenverehrung,' by Günter Lanczkowski, Göran Larsson, Karl Hausberger, Christian Hannick, and Frieder Schulz. 14: 641–72.

Thompson, Craig R. 'Erasmus and Tudor England.' In *Actes du Congrès Erasme.* Ed. C. Reedijk. Amsterdam: North-Holland Publishing Company, 1971. 29–68.

Tobriner, Alice. 'The Private Prayers of Erasmus and Vives: A View of Lay Piety in the Northern Renaissance.' *Erasmus of Rotterdam Society Yearbook* 11 (1991): 27–45.

Tracy, James D. *Erasmus: The Growth of a Mind.* Geneva: Droz, 1972.

Trapman, J. 'Erasmus's *Precationes.*' In *Acta Conventus Neo-Latini Torontonensis.* Ed. Alexander Dalzell, Charles Fantazzi, and Richard J. Schoeck. Binghamton, NY: Medieval and Renaissance Texts and Studies, vol. 86, 1991, 769–79.

Trinkaus, Charles. *In Our Image and Likeness: Humanity and Divinity in Italian Humanist Thought.* 2 vols. Chicago: University of Chicago Press, 1970.

Trümpy, Hans. 'Ein Aufruf des Erasmus von Rotterdam zur Missionierung der Heiden.' *Basler Zeitschrift für Geschichte und Altertumskunde* 82 (1982): 189–93.

Vauchez, André. *La sainteté en occident aux derniers siècles du moyen âge.* Rome: Ecole Française de Rome, 1981.

Verbrugge, Rita M. 'Margaret More Roper's Personal Expression in the *Devout Treatise Upon the Pater Noster.*' In *Silent But for the Word: Tudor Women as Patrons, Translators, and Writers of Religious Works.* Ed. Margaret Patterson Hannay. Kent, OH: Kent State University Press, 1985. 30–42.

Vredeveld, Harry. 'Some "Lost" Poems of Erasmus from the Year 1499.' In *Fide et Amore: A Festschrift for Hugo Bekker on his Sixty-Fifth Birthday*. Ed. William C. McDonald and Winder McConnell. Göppingen: Kümmerle Verlag, 1990. 329–39.

- 'Towards a Definitive Edition of Erasmus' Poetry.' *Humanistica Lovaniensia* 37 (1988): 115–74.

Walter, Peter. *Theologie aus dem Geist der Rhetorik: Zur Schriftauslegung des Erasmus von Rotterdam*. Mainz: Matthias-Grünewald-Verlag, 1991.

Wandel, Lee Palmer. *Voracious Idols and Violent Hands: Iconoclasm in Reformation Zurich, Strasbourg, and Basel*. Cambridge: Cambridge University Press, 1995.

Weinstein, Donald, and Rudolph M. Bell. *Saints and Society: The Two Worlds of Western Christendom, 1000–1700*. Chicago: University of Chicago Press, 1982.

Weiss, James Michael. '*Ecclesiastes* and Erasmus: The Mirror and the Image.' *Archiv für Reformationsgeschichte* 65 (1974): 83–107.

Wenzel, Siegfried. 'The Three Enemies of Man.' *Mediaeval Studies* 29 (1967): 47–66.

White, Helen C. *The Tudor Books of Private Devotion*. Madison: University of Wisconsin Press, 1951.

Wieck, Roger S., ed. *Time Sanctified: The Book of Hours in Medieval Art and Life*. New York: George Braziller, 1988.

Winkler, Gerhard B. 'Erasmus und die Juden.' In *Festschrift Franz Loidl zum 65. Geburtstag*. Ed. Viktor Flieder. 2 vols. Vienna: Verlag Brüder Hollineck, 1970. 2: 381–92.

Index

accommodation, as pastoral principle 13–15, 17, 66, 73–4, 153–4, 190, 191, 194
Agricola, Rudolf 76
Albergati, Nicolò 192
Albert of Brandenburg 183
Albert the Great 150
Alcuin 155–6
Althaus, Paul 24, 158, 170
Ambrose 27, 71, 148, 156
Ammonio, Andrea 88
Anna van Veere, Lady 21–2, 66, 76
Aristotle 65
Auer, Alfons 4
Augsburg Confession 69, 94
Augustijn, Cornelis 5, 12, 143
Augustine, Saint 18, 27, 29, 42, 61, 64, 71, 90–1, 129, 135, 139, 147, 148, 156, 161, 187, 210 n.127, 222 n.12, 223 n.14

Baechem, Nicolaas 110
Baer, Ludwig 183
Bainton, Roland 4, 216 n.61
Barth, Karl 136
Bataillon, Marcel 200, 201
Batt, Jacob 21, 75
Becker, Jan 193, 194
Becon, Thomas 30, 36, 48, 53, 160
Béda, Noël 76, 87

Belgic Confession 94
Bernardino of Siena 166
Bierlaire, Franz 81
Bietenholz, Peter 178
Biétry, Thiébaut 89
Borckensis, Timmanus 199
Boyle, Marjorie O'Rourke 191
Brecht, Martin 93
Brown, Peter 70–1, 72, 107
Brunfels, Otto 158, 161, 231 n.19
Bucer, Martin 138, 139–40, 148, 150

Calvin, John 18, 138, 140, 147, 148, 150, 164, 166
Canisius, Peter 94
Capito, Wolfgang 201
Carmignac, Jean 147
Cervicornus, Eucharius 28
Charles V, Holy Roman Emperor 32, 90
Chomarat, Jacques 5, 195
Chrysostom, John 27, 94, 148, 152, 159, 161, 201, 209 n.89, 228 n.159
Cicero 65
Cisneros, Francisco Ximenes de 192
Cles, Bernhard von 184
Clichtove, Josse 31, 94, 95, 98, 103
Cochlaeus, Johannes 94

Colet, John 13, 15, 85, 103
Confutation of the Augsburg Confession 69, 95, 98
Council of Ephesus 86
Council of Trent 94–5, 98, 107, 198, 199
Craeys, Sebastiaan 110
Crocus, Cornelius 24–5
Cromwell, Thomas 157, 201
Cyprian of Carthage 15, 18, 85, 109–10, 143–4, 146–7, 148, 150, 151, 222 n.12, 223 n.14
Cyril of Jerusalem 109

David of Burgundy 7, 8, 21
Daye, Richard 173
Dealy, Ross 179
Delumeau, Jean 46
DeMolen, Richard 112, 197
Devotio Moderna 197–8
Didache 109
Dietz, Josse Ludwig 29, 112
Dorp, Maarten van 79
Düffel, Hans 167, 169
Duffy, Eamon 16, 71

Eck, Johannes 94, 95, 98, 219–20 n.153
Eire, Carlos 107
Episcopius, Nicolaus 159
Erasmus: as forerunner of the Second Vatican Council 5; and preaching 8–13; his principal attributes for God: power: 17, 24, 43–4, 67, 118, 153, 173–4, wisdom: 17, 24, 118, 153, 173–4, goodness: 17, 24, 44–6, 67, 119, 153–4, 173–4, 195, 201; his ecclesiology 52–3, 73, 100–1, 196; and consensus of the church 52–3, 97–8, 151
Works:
– Adages: Sileni Alcibiadis 11; Dulce bellum inexpertis 65

– Annotations on the New Testament 8, 35, 110–11, 115–16, 129, 130, 139, 144, 145, 167, 168, 181
– Antibarbari 21
– Catalogus novus omnium lucubrationum Erasmi Roterodami 112
– Christiani hominis institutum 15
– Christiani matrimonii institutio 15, 28, 180, 181, 198
– Colloquies 36, 81–2, 84, 107, 159, 198; Alcumistica 82; Apotheosis Capnionis 85, 161; Concio sive Merdardus 88; Confessio militis 82; Convivium religiosum 159; Exequiae seraphicae 83; Funus 11; Ichthuophagia (A Meal of Fish) 82, 87; Inquisitio de fide 124, 181; Naufragium 83; Peregrinatio religionis ergo 83–4, 88–9, 170; Pietas puerilis 85; Ptochoplousioi (The Wealthy Beggars) 82
– Concio de puero Jesu 44
– Concionalis interpretatio in Psalmum LXXXV 48–9, 51, 102
– De libero arbitrio 27, 90, 133, 148, 151, 183
– De misericordia Domini concio 27, 45, 87
– De praeparatione ad mortem 15, 39, 64, 177–9, 189
– De puritate tabernaculi sive ecclesiae christianae 47
– De sarcienda ecclesiae concordia 41, 104, 165, 184–5, 186, 187
– De utilitate colloquiorum 84, 172
– Ecclesiastes sive de ratione concionandi 7, 9, 10, 11–12, 13, 15,

17, 18, 19, 26, 54, 55, 78, 192,
194, 197
– *Enarratio in primum psalmum*
44
– *Enchiridion militis christiani*
14–15, 22, 25–7, 29, 33, 35, 39,
43–4, 47, 51, 60, 72, 73, 74, 75,
78, 79–80, 84, 88, 89, 106, 107,
110, 121, 122, 125, 149, 172, 193,
196, 197, 199
– *Encomium matrimonii* 180
– *Exomologesis sive modus confitendi* 15, 27, 28, 39, 45
– *Explanatio symboli apostolorum
sive catechismus* 15, 109, 115,
119, 123, 124, 125, 139, 148, 150,
153, 180, 182
– *Institutio principis christiani* 65,
193
– *Lucubrationes* 88
– *Lucubratiunculae* 23, 159
– *Modus orandi Deum* 3, 11, 15,
17, 18, 26, 27, 28–30, 32, 33–4,
35, 37–8, 40, 41, 42–3, 45–6, 47,
48, 49, 50, 53, 54, 56, 57, 60–8,
73, 81, 86, 90, 95, 96, 97, 98, 100,
102, 103, 104, 106, 107, 109, 115,
128–9, 139, 144, 148, 162, 171–2,
182, 190, 194, 200
– *Novum Instrumentum* 110
– *Obsecratio ad Virginem Matrem
Mariam in rebus adversis* 22–3,
24
– *Oratio de virtute amplectenda* 22
– *Paean Virgini Matri dicendus*
22–3, 24, 77
– *Paraclesis* 33, 47, 163
– *Paraphrases on the New Testament*: 12, 27, 28, 30, 35, 39, 44,
58, 67, 131, 198; Matthew 31,
35, 39, 40, 51–2, 58–9, 111, 116,
117, 119, 122, 125, 129, 139, 140,
143, 145, 150, 151, 152; Mark
40, 41, 45, 50, 59, 61, 112, 143;

Luke 40–1, 50, 59, 100, 110,
111, 112, 118, 120, 139, 140,
145, 150, 169; John 12, 112;
Acts 52, 54, 61; Romans 45,
81; 1 Corinthians 33, 193; 2
Corinthians 44, 50, 193;
Philippians 40, 49; 1 Timothy
64–5; James 44, 46, 50, 145,
151; Jude 53; 1 John 51
– *Praise of Folly* 57–8, 78–9, 81,
198
– *Precatio ad Dominum Jesum pro
pace ecclesiae* 159, 182, 184–8,
190, 196
– *Precatio ad Virginis Filium
Jesum* 22, 23–5, 43, 118, 158
– *Precatio Dominica* 3, 15, 27, 28,
112–53 passim, 155, 159, 194,
195, 196
– *Precationes aliquot novae* 3, 15,
18, 115, 155, 158–65, 167–82,
185–90, 194–5, 196; *Eiaculationes* 158, 159, 161, 162, 163,
170, 171, 173, 174, 178, 182,
189; 'Accedentis ad sacram
synaxim' 174, 182; 'Ad Christum pro vera pietate' 170,
182; 'Ad Filium' 170, 175–6,
190; 'Ad Spiritum Sanctum'
173, 186; 'Adversus superbiam et luxum' 162; 'Ad Virginem Matrem' 167–70;
'Consecratio mensae' 188–9;
'Diluculo ad Christum' 170–1,
201; 'Euntis ad ludum litterarium' 159; 'In aestate' 175, 176;
'In gravi morbo' 178–9; 'Inituri praelium' 179–80, 201; 'In
mortis periculo' 178; 'Poenitentis' 172–3; 'Precatio ad
Patrem' 115, 116, 117, 118, 126,
129–30, 139, 140, 145, 146, 150,
152–3, 175, 199–200; 'Pro
consensu dogmatum' 186;

'Pro docilitate' 159; 'Pro felici conjugio' 180; 'Pro gaudio spirituali' 173; 'Pro innocentia et rectitudine vitae' 162; 'Pro parentibus' 159–60, 170; 'Pro statu ecclesiastico' 162; 'Pro victoria gratiarum actio' 163; 'Revalescentis' 162; 'Sub noctem' 174; 'Sub nuptias' 180–1; 'Sumturi Corpus Dominicum' 170, 174–5; 'Tempore pestilentiae' 189
- *Querela pacis* 53, 111
- *Ratio verae theologiae* 10, 11, 12, 13, 73, 193
- *Vidua christiana* 15, 28, 39, 40, 80
- *Virginis Matris apud Lauretum cultae liturgia* 9, 13, 18, 81, 89–90, 106, 107, 159, 170, 196
- poetry: *Carmen de casa natalia Jesu* 75; *Des. Erasmi Roterodami divae Genovefae praesidio a quartana febre liberati carmen votivum* 105–6, 107; *Epigrammata* 77; *Erasmi precatio 'Salve Regina'* 75; *Erasmi Roterodami carmen iambicum, ex voto dicatum virgini Vvalsingamicae apud Briannos* 88–9, 106, 170; *In laudem beatissimi Gregorii papae* 75; *In laudem Michaelis et angelorum omnium* 75–6; *Paean divae Mariae, atque de incarnatione verbi* 77–8; *Rhythmus iambicus in laudem Annae, aviae Iesu Christi* 76–7, 159
Eschen, Jan von der 123
Eusebius of Caesarea 155

Fisher, John 12, 30
Francis I, king of France 32

Frellon, Jean 159
Froben, Johann 27, 28, 113, 123, 155
Frobenius, Jerome 159

Gallican Confession 94
Gebhardt, Georg 5
Geneva Catechism 94
George of Saxony, duke 28
Gerson, Jean 71, 86
Giberti, Gian Matteo 90, 192
Gilmore, Myron 198
Godin, André 10
Goes, Damião de 189
Gordon, Walter 81
Grafton, Richard 158
Granada, Luis de 200
Gregory of Nyssa 148
Gregory the Great, pope 13, 75, 156
Gryphe, Sébastien 159

Halkin, Léon 5–6, 18–19, 28, 87, 107, 110, 205 n.23
Heiler, Friedrich 16
Hendrik of Bergen 21
Henry VIII, king of England 157, 201
Hentze, Willi 5, 181–2
Hilary of Poitiers 53
Hilsey, John 157, 201
Hoffmann, Manfred 13, 191
Hoogstraten, Jacob von 94
Hugh of Saint Victor 150
Huizinga, Johan 4, 183
Hutten, Ulrich von 102, 165
Hyma, Albert 197

iconoclasm 69–70
Ignatius of Loyola 36, 192
Irenaeus 168

James, William 16

Jerome 27, 91, 98, 222 n.12
John Damascene 35
Jonas, Justus 53, 85
Jungmann, Joseph 4, 213 n.225
Justin Martyr 168

Karlstadt, Andreas Bodensee von
    70, 92–3
Kohls, Ernst-Wilhelm 44
Kolb, Robert 91
Konrad von Thüngen 184
Kretschmar, Georg 91
Krüger, Friedhelm 12
Krzycko (Cricius), Andreas 29

Lalemand, Jean 90
Lang, Johann 92
Laski, Hieronim 29
Latomus, Bartholomaeus 189
Laurentin, René 91
Lefèvre d'Etaples, Jacques 76
Leonico Tomeo, Nicolò 165
Longland, John 165
Lord's Prayer 3, 15, 18, 24, 27, 29,
    34, 61, 62, 83, 99, 156, 196; analy-
    sis of, by petition 129–53
Lorraine, Jean, cardinal of 90
Lortz, Joseph 4
Luther, Martin 3, 18, 70, 72, 90,
    91–4, 96, 97, 103, 113, 138, 147,
    157, 159, 164, 166, 167, 170, 182,
    183, 201

Manns, Peter 91, 219 n.140
Mantuanus, Baptista 76
Margolin, Jean-Claude 105,
    208
Marius, Richard 4–5
Mary, Blessed Virgin, cult of:
    77–8, 80, 81, 82, 84, 86–90, 92,
    96, 156–7; Ave Maria 87, 158,
    166–70; Salve Regina 23, 82, 83;
    Magnificat 88, 92; Erasmus' criti-
    cism of Marian piety 86–8; his

prayers to Mary 22–3, 88–9,
    167–70
Massaut, Jean-Pierre 5, 6, 31
McConica, James 5, 201
Melanchthon, Philip 69, 138
Miller, Clarence 105, 106
More, Thomas 71, 112, 194
Mountjoy, William Blount, lord 3,
    80
music, liturgical 32, 193

Nausea, Friedrich 199

Oecolompadius, Johannes 97
O'Malley, John 6, 10, 29
Origen 29, 138, 167
Osiander, Andreas 138

Padberg, Rudolf 6, 180
Parr, Katherine 201
Paul IV, pope 159, 198
Paul, Saint 13, 25, 33, 35, 38, 42, 61,
    71, 80–1, 85, 99, 101, 106, 121,
    172, 181, 193
Paumgartner, David 160, 161
Paumgartner, Johann 160
Payne, John 180
Pellican, Conrad 97
Pflug, Julius 160
Philip of Burgundy, admiral of
    Flanders and governor of
    Artois 31
Philip of Burgundy, bishop of
    Utrecht 8
Phillips, Jane 12
Pio, Alberto 90
Pius V, pope 166
Plato 65, 72
Polycarp of Smyrna 70
Poppenruyter, Johann 18–19
popular religion 70–1, 72, 73–4,
    106–7
Porras, Antonio de 200
Post, R.R. 197

prayer: liturgical 31–4; Erasmus
favours vernacular liturgy 33–4;
divine office 26, 31, 65, 115, 166,
197, 213 n.237; Erasmus not
interested in mystical 16–17,
57–8; as conversation with God
16, 17, 26, 35–7, 56, 66, 67, 105,
160, 200; God as recipient of 17,
43–7, 115–19; those who engage
in 17, 47–53, 119–28, 195, spiritual dispositions necessary for
17, 48–53, 67, humility 17, 47–9,
54, 67, 177, 188, 195, faith 17,
49–50, 124–5, 177–9, mercy 50–1,
145–8, concord 17, 51–3, 54,
122–4, 136, 143–5, 179–88; and
importance of spiritual transformation 17–18, 53–6, 67–8, 80, 88,
107, 121, 125, 134, 142, 176, 190,
195–6; reasons for 37–8; should
not be verbose 26, 42; should be
assiduous 38–40; spiritual *scopus* or object of 17–18, 58–61,
88–9, 153, 188–9, 195–6; wording
of 61–3, 115, 162; silent or vocal
64; time for 64; ejaculatory 64;
of princes and those who hold
public office 65; unanswered
65–6; for the dead 164–5
prayer-books: history of 155–8;
Books of Hours 16, 86, 155,
156–7, 162; *Book of Common
Prayer* 164
Pseudo-Chrysostom 36, 55–6
purgatory 164

Quintilian 13

Rabe, Ludwig 201
Redman, Robert 158
Renaudet, Augustin 4, 5, 31, 112,
120
Reuchlin, Johannes 85, 161
Rinck, Johann 184

Roman Catechism 18, 94, 138–9,
140, 147, 191, 192, 197, 199
Roper, Margaret 112
Rummel, Erika 167

sacraments: baptism 120–2, 196;
Eucharist 5, 19, 34, 91, 92, 97,
138, 139, 140, 142, 170, 174–5,
182, 196; marriage 180–1, 196
Sadoleto, Jacopo 69
saints, cult of: popularity in the
Middle Ages 71–2; Erasmus'
participation in 74–8, 80–1, 88,
105–6; Erasmus' criticism of
superstitions 78–9, 81–4; should
include imitation of the saints
74, 80, 84, 89, 107, 198; Erasmus'
defence of the invocation of
saints 95–103, 107; Protestant
rejection of 69–70, 91–4; Catholic apologists for 94–5, 98, 103;
individual saints: Agnes 85;
Anne 76–7; Anthony 82, 83;
Apollonia 78; Barbara 78, 82;
Benedict 104; Benno of Meissen 93; Christopher 78, 82, 83;
Dominic 104; Elizabeth of Hungary 80; Francis 80, 83, 104;
Geneviève 74–5, 80, 105–6;
George 78, 82; Gervasius and
Protasius 71; Gregory the Great
75, 157; Hiero 78; James 71, 83,
84; Jerome 85; Joseph 71; Mar-
tin 81; Michael 75–6; Peter 75,
84; Polycarp of Smyrna 70;
Raphael 75–6; Roch 78; Stephen
71; Thomas Becket 84, 103. *See
also* Augustine, Saint; Mary,
Blessed Virgin, cult of; Paul,
Saint
Schottenloher, Otto 182, 206
Schwenkfeld, Kaspar von 25
Screech, M.A. 57
Second Vatican Council 5, 95

Seidel Menchi, Silvana 198
Sigismund I, king of Poland 29,
    112
Spalatin, George 183
Stadion, Christoph von 184

Telle, Emile 11, 181
Tertullian 15, 29, 148, 168, 222 n.12
Theatines 192
Theophylact 37
Thomas Aquinas 18, 29, 91, 138,
    147, 210 n.127
Thompson, Craig 201
Tracy, James 53
Trapman, J. 159, 165
Trinkaus, Charles 201
Trithemius, Johannes 76

Vergy, Antoine de 89
Vigilantius 91, 98
Vitrier, Jehan 85

Vives, Juan Luis 113, 164, 167, 168,
    169, 200, 201
Volz, Paul 27, 164
Vos, Hendrik 123
Vredeveld, Harry 75, 77
Vroye, Joost 54
Vulgate Bible 35, 44, 110, 162, 167,
    181, 222 n.12, 232 nn.43, 44, 235
    nn.133, 134

Warham, William 7, 12, 164-5,
    193-4
White, Helen 202
Wieck, Roger 156
Wied, Hermann von 192
Wild, Johann 199
Witzel, Georg 199
Wyclif, John 97

Zerbolt, Gerhart 197
Zwingli, Huldreych 84, 166

Erasmus Studies

A series of studies concerned with Erasmus and related subjects

1 *Under Pretext of Praise: Satiric Mode in Erasmus' Fiction*
Sister Geraldine Thompson

2 *Erasmus on Language and Method in Theology*
Marjorie O'Rourke Boyle

3 *The Politics of Erasmus: A Pacifist Intellectual and His Political Milieu*
James D. Tracy

4 *Phoenix of His Age: Interpretations of Erasmus, c. 1550–1750*
Bruce Mansfield

5 *Christening Pagan Mysteries: Erasmus in Pursuit of Wisdom*
Marjorie O'Rourke Boyle

6 *Renaissance English Translations of Erasmus: A Bibliography to 1700*
E.J. Devereux

7 *Erasmus as a Translator of the Classics*
Erika Rummel

8 *Erasmus' Annotations on the New Testament: From Philologist to Theologian*
Erika Rummel

9 *Humanist Play and Belief: The Seriocomic Art of Desiderius Erasmus*
Walter M. Gordon

10 *Erasmus: His Life, Works, and Influence*
Cornelis Augustijn

11 *Interpretations of Erasmus, c 1750–1920: Man on His Own*
Bruce Mansfield

12 *Rhetoric and Theology: The Hermeneutic of Erasmus*
Manfred Hoffmann

13 *Conversing with God: Erasmus' Pastoral Writings*
Hilmar M. Pabel